Accounting Classics Series

Publication of this Classic was made possible
by a grant from Price Waterhouse Foundation

Suggestions of titles to be included
in the Series are solicited and should
be addressed to the Editor.

ACCOUNTING PUBLICATIONS OF
SCHOLARS BOOK CO.
Editor, Robert R. Sterling

ACCOUNTING PRACTICE AND PROCEDURE

by
ARTHUR LOWES DICKINSON

M. A. Cantab, Certified Public Accountant, Fellow of
the Institute of Chartered Accountants, Fellow
of the Institute of Actuaries, Member of
the Firm of Price, Waterhouse & Co.

Scholars Book Co.
4431 Mt. Vernon
Houston, Texas 77006

Library of Congress Card Catalog Number: 75-13487
ISBN: 0-914348-17-5
Manufactured in the United States of America

Foreword to the Reissue

Arthur Lowes Dickinson was born in London in 1859. Much of what is known of his ancestry comes from the biography of his brother Goldsworthy Lowes Dickinson, the noted poet and writer.

Educated at Cambridge, Arthur Lowes Dickinson graduated with highest honors in mathematics in 1882 and received an M.A. degree in 1888. He began practice as a chartered accountant in 1887, and was awarded first prize in the professional examinations in 1886.

In 1900 the London partners of Price Waterhouse & Co. were seeking a replacement for the managing partner of their American practice which was operating primarily under the name of Jones, Caesar & Co. Edwin Waterhouse began to search for a man with broad educational and professional background as well as a person who was familiar with American business conditions. In this search he recalled his association with Dickinson when the two had met and worked on the board of the Riverside Trust Co., an agricultural venture capitalized by British investors to irrigate several thousand acres of Southern California desert.

Waterhouse contacted Dickinson and an arrangement was made for the larger firm to become responsible for the practice of Lovelock, Whiffin and Dickinson and for Dickinson to be placed in charge of the American practice as of July 1, 1901. From this date, until he left the American practice to return in England in 1913, Dickinson's impact on the profession of accountancy in the United States was profound.

During the years he resided in America, Dickinson embraced the country as his own, and obtained citizenship in 1906. He established his professional credentials as a CPA in Illinois (1903) and New York (1913).

Among the most significant contributions made by Dickinson as a statesman among members of the early profession was his sponsorship of the Federation of Societies of Public Accountants in America, including a term as President in 1904. In that year the Federation undertook the sponsorship of the Congress of Accountants, the first attempt at a national and international meeting of North Atlantic accountants. Dickinson was instrumental in assuring the meeting's success and delivered the significant paper, "Profits of a Corporation."

During 1905 Dickinson served as secretary of the American Association of Public Accountants which later absorbed the Federation. One of his first contributions as an American practitioner was to devise a suitable format for the consolidated financial report of the recently formed United States Steel Corporation, thus providing a vehicle for the publicity of complex corporate financial statements.

Several leading practitioners of this era benefited from their association with Dickinson. In 1905 for example, Robert H. Montgomery wrote an American edition of L. P. Dicksee's *Auditing, A Practice Manual for Auditors*. This was made possible through the influence of Dickinson in securing from Dicksee permission for an American version of this work. And, George O. May, who succeeded Dickinson as senior partner of Price Waterhouse & Co. in America noted in his own memoirs that there was an immediate change in his professional and intellectual well being as a result of the inspiring personality of Dickinson.

The strain of developing a national practice and the efforts put forth in behalf of the profession during his decade of leadership and participation in the American profession led Dickinson to resign the senior partnership in New York and return to England in 1913, shortly before the outbreak of World War I. In England he continued to work in behalf of the public interest and the profession, and received knighthood from King George in recognition of his services to that country during the war.

While he lived in England, Dickinson's presence continued to be felt in America. *Accounting Practice and Procedure,* (first published in 1914) constitutes his primary postscript to the many contributions made in behalf of the advancement of accounting in this country. It is a synthesis of his major contributions to accounting literature and covers the broad range of topics, including asset valuation, profit determination, consolidated accounts, cost accounting theory and the role of the accounting professional. It was written from the unique view of one whose training and experience represented a portion of both of two great branches of the English speaking accounting profession. The immediate significance of the volume was reflected in the remarks of Henry Rand Hatfield in a review of the initial printing. Hatfield referred to Dickinson as a "high authority" and concluded that: "The book is searching in analysis, rich with material gained in a long professional career, clever in exposition, one which neither student nor practitioner can affort to omit from his library."

Such a laudatory comment by a contemporary suggests that it is appropriate to review the high points of the work now that it is being republished nearly a half century later.

Several matters warrant examination in attempting to place Dickinson's writings in historical perspective. It is well to remember that the profession was practicing in an environment much different than that of today—yet in relative terms, considering the potential and state of its development, accountancy then as now faced significant and unprecedented challenges.

The import of Dickinson's contribution is that it represents (in the sense of normative and positive statements) theoretical beliefs and practical experiences which are blended into a readable form by one of the most gifted and distinguished practitioners of the age. The influence of these writings up to this day is evidenced by the fact that the generic format of the modern income statement can be traced back to the works of Dickinson (see p. 64). This format, later revised and issued in the *Uniform Accounts* pronouncement of 1917 and then updated in the *Verification of Financial Statements* (1929) has evolved into the dominant model for income statements, even though rival approaches have been available. It seems that Dickinson's form, which he first publicly presented at the St. Louis Congress in 1904, was not only most suited to the needs that existed but it was also adaptable in light of the subsequent emphasis on income reporting and measurement which arose in response to the national income tax laws in the next decade.

Among the other significant notions discussed in *Accounting Practice and Procedure* is the matter of the cost of interest as a production charge. Dickinson argues for the exclusion of both rent and interest from the cost accounts. He notes that, in theory, interest and rent (so far as the latter represents a payment for the use of land and buildings and does not include any charge for other services) could only be considered a division of profit.

Dickinson's writings on the duties and responsibilities of the public accountant evidenced both his concern for and belief in the nature of the profession and stressed ability, tact, honesty and impartiality. It is indeed interesting to find that over a half century ago accountants were also struggling with the issue of their responsibility with regard to estimates of future earnings (pp. 224-227) and the proper disclosure of extraordinary profits and losses (p. 217).

After the publication of *Accounting Practice and Procedure* and until his death in 1935 Dickinson continued to contribute to professional literature on a wide range of subjects. The essence of his theory of accounting, to which the roots of many of today's practices can be traced, is found here in the writings which reflect Dickinson's experience while in practice in the early years of this century in America.

Professor Sterling and the Price Waterhouse Foundation who sponsored this republication are to be commended for restoring to view this vital link in the transformation of modern accounting thought.

Gary John Previts, President
The Academy of Accounting Historians
December 1, 1974

PREFACE

The profession of accountancy is at a great disadvantage in comparison with that of law, by reason of the fact that the decisions reached on the important questions which arise from day to day are not publicly rendered and available as authorities for the rest of the profession, but are made privately and as a rule are accessible only to a few.

In issuing this volume, therefore, it is my hope that the record it contains of some of the problems encountered in the course of twenty-five years of practice on both sides of the Atlantic may be of value to my fellow accountants and may in some measure serve to discharge some part of the debt I owe to the profession to which I belong.

The first eight chapters deal with problems relating to the income account and balance sheet. These are followed by one on some problems involved in cost accounting; while the last chapter deals with the accountant's responsibility to the public—a subject that is becoming more important every day.

It has been my endeavor to avoid technicalities and so to render the book useful to the student entering the profession and also to lawyers, bankers and professional men generally, who are vitally interested in accounting but have not had the accountant's training.

In my practice it has been my good fortune to be in close touch, in partnership and otherwise, with many leading practitioners both in the United States and England, and in association with them to deal with many of the problems herein discussed, so that, while the responsibility for the views expressed is solely mine, the value they may possess is drawn from wider sources.

A. LOWES DICKINSON.

October 10, 1913.

CONTENTS

Chapter III. The Profit and Loss Account and the General Principles Governing Its Preparation

Chapter IV. Balance Sheet Assets

I. CAPITAL ASSETS

(1) FIXED PROPERTY
Land and Improvements
Buildings and Structures
Plant, Machinery and Fixed Tools
Movable Equipment
Furniture and Fixtures
Patterns, Drawings, Dies, etc.
Patents, Goodwill and Franchises
Changes in Value of Capital Assets

(2) PERMANENT INVESTMENTS
Investments for Purposes of Control
Investments Controlling Facilities or Output
Minor Investments
Non-Income Producing Investments
Advances

(3) INVESTMENT OF RESERVES

II. WORKING ASSETS

(1) STORES AND SUPPLIES

(2) ADVANCES TO AGENTS

(3) EXPENSES INCURRED IN ADVANCE OF ACCRUAL

Chapter V. Balance Sheet Assets (Continued)

III. CURRENT ASSETS

(1) STOCKS ON HAND
Essentials for Ascertaining Correct Profits
Taking the Inventory
Cost Accounting
Distribution of Expense Burden
Allocation of Expenses
Selling Expenses as Part of Manufacturing Cost
Status of Interest
Increasing Value of Seasoning Material
Treatment of Carrying Charges
Profits on Work in Progress
Reserves for Contingencies

Chapter VI. Balance Sheet Liabilities

Chapter IX.   Some Theories and Problems in Cost Accounting

Chapter X.   The Duties and Responsibilities of the Public Accountant

Canadian Audit Practice
Accountant's Responsibility for Audit Certificates
Qualified Certificates
Accountant's Moral and Legal Responsibility

(3) IN RESPECT OF LIQUIDATION AND RECONSTRUCTION
Responsibility of Accountant in Case of Business Failure
Causes or Conditions Leading Up to Insolvency
Reorganization

Appendix

ACCOUNTING
Practice and Procedure

CHAPTER I

BOOKKEEPING

Bookkeeping is the essential foundation of accounting, and a thorough knowledge of its elementary principles and general methods is necessary to the proper understanding of accounting principles. While, therefore, it is not within the scope of the present book to put forth an exhaustive treatise on bookkeeping, it will serve a useful purpose to devote some space to a consideration of the principles involved and to modern methods of carrying these principles into effect.

Double-Entry Bookkeeping

The term "bookkeeping" is commonly and loosely used to describe any method of entering accounts of transactions in money, but the only scientific system which is worth notice here is that known as "double-entry bookkeeping," which is based on the fact that every transaction involves a transfer of property or its equivalent from one person to another, the terms "property" and "person" being used in the widest possible sense. This operation of receiving and giving is expressed in bookkeeping by the use of the terms "debit" and "credit" which may be thus defined:

A person is debited with whatever is received from another.

A person is credited with whatever is transferred to another.

Every debit necessarily involves a corresponding credit, and after any number of transactions have been thus entered it follows that the sum of all the debits will exactly equal the sum of all the credits.

Impersonal Accounts

It is customary in treatises on bookkeeping to draw a somewhat sharp line of distinction between a personal and an impersonal account, meaning by the first an account kept with some definite person or group of persons whether corporate or otherwise, and by an impersonal account one which expresses merely a condition. In effect, however, all impersonal accounts are merely subdivisions of the personal account of the person or group of persons by or for whom the accounts are kept, who may briefly be termed the "principal." These accounts are devised, according to modern ideas, not so much for the purpose of determining the financial relation of the principal to those with whom he deals (although of course this is important) as to show his own incomings and outgoings, possessions and obligations, in such full detail as will enable him best to control his affairs and to determine his own financial position.

Function of Impersonal Accounts

The demands of bookkeeping would be satisfied if A, carrying on a business, debited himself with all he received and credited himself with all he parted with, correspondingly crediting and debiting those from whom he received and to whom he transferred. In such a case all his side of the transactions would be merged in one account only in his books; and a very detailed analysis of this account, and a complete inventory of all his property and assets, would be required 'o furnish information of his own position, either as to profits or capital.

In order to furnish continuously this detailed analysis, impersonal or nominal accounts so-called have been introduced, and the principle of debit and credit has been applied to them as if they were persons. Such accounts may, therefore, be considered as a continuous and daily analysis of the principal's own account; or, from another aspect, may be treated as a division of his personality into a number of pockets, each one of which represents some specific part of his activities, and the gathering together of all of which will represent his condition. It is in this gathering together of impersonal accounts that bookkeeping passes the imaginary dividing line that separates it from accounting. The balancing of the conditions surrounding each one of these accounts, and the determination of the exact bearing of each upon the position of the principal, is the duty of accounting. The problems involved in the determination of the value in money to be placed upon each, form the main subject of this volume.

Opening the Books

On the principles already outlined the principal first distributes all his property to various imaginary locations, crediting himself as the transferor, and debiting the localities, each of which has a suitable name, such as Land, Buildings, Investments, Cash, etc., with what each receives in this imaginary distribution. Similarly, he credits himself with amounts received by other individuals from him which at this stage represent debts owing to him, and debits himself with what he has received from other individuals which also represents debts owing by him to them. When this distribution is completed in his books the sum of all the debits, now representing various classes of property and debtors, must exactly equal the sum of all credits representing creditors and his own account, this latter showing his capital or worth in gross while all the remaining accounts, both debit and credit, show of what this worth is composed. This process, which is generally known as "opening the books," is followed by an exactly similar record of each subsequent transaction, each being debited and credited to the particular account concerned, whether Property, or Debtor, or Creditor. In the same way amounts due to others from himself for use of their facilities or due to him by others for their use of his facilities (such as rent, interest, wages, etc.) are debited or credited to accounts in his books representing his outgoings or incomings under their various headings, other than property, and credited or debited to the other parties to the transactions.

The Trial Balance

At any stage the same equation between the sums of all debits and all credits should exist if the entries have all been made with clerical accuracy, so far as the two sides, debit and credit, are concerned. Errors due to debits or credits being made to a wrong account cannot be detected by this means, but require a critical re-examination of each entry, a process which is essential at some time before a final balance is reached. This equation of debits and credits is known as a Trial Balance, and its main object is to prove the clerical accuracy of the work and to form a basis for the further critical examination required.

The methods by which, under modern conditions, this equation between debits and credits is reached are of considerable importance.

Early Bookkeeping Methods

The old-fashioned routine of bookkeeping was as follows:

Firstly, a record was made in a book known as a "Day Book" of each transaction as it occurred, e.g.—

"Bought 100 tons of pig iron from B at $15 per ton.

Accepted B's draft for $1,500."

and so on.

Secondly, the entries in the day book were converted into a form specifying the accounts which should be debited and credited in each particular case, known as "journalizing" the entry from the fact that this was entered in a book known as a "Journal," e.g.—

Pig Iron, Dr. $1,500
    To B., Cr. $1,500
        For 100 tons of pig iron
            at $15 per ton.
    _____

B., Dr. $1,500
    To Bills Payable, Cr. $1,500
        For B's draft accepted this day.

Thirdly, each side of each entry in this journal would be entered, or "posted," to a debit (left-hand) or credit (right-hand) page in a third book called a "Ledger," headed with the account name shown in the journal entry, so completing the record.

As business developed it was found that if this elementary process were applied to a business of any magnitude, the work involved would be enormous; and accordingly it became customary to group transactions of similar character so that in the ledger the totals only of a number of similar transactions might be dealt with.

The most important elementary examples of such grouping are found in the "Cash Book" and the "Sales Day Book," which contain characteristics of both the day book and the ledger of our first example. The cash book is in itself in its common form a ledger account for cash, which from the fact that it is easily counted and balanced in money values, a quality possessed by no other kind of property, came to be considered of some special importance. This ledger account of cash, therefore, instead of being written up or posted from the day book to the journal, and the journal to the ledger, came to be used as a book of original entry, in place of the day book, for all cash transactions, whether incoming or outgoing, the other half of the entry being obtained by posting each individual item directly from the cash book to the ledger, thus eliminating altogether the intermediate journal. In the case of the sales day book a similar method was adopted, all sales being entered in a separate day book, the items being posted directly to the accounts of the customers and the total to the credit of the sales account, thus again completing the double entry and entirely eliminating the journal.

The Subsidiary Ledger

As business increased in volume, so the opportunity for clerical error in carrying transactions through the various books and the consequent difficulty of obtaining an accurate trial balance also increased, and attempts were made at sectional balancing by which portions of the ledger might be proved and balanced without the necessity of dealing with the whole. This was applied firstly to the sales, which affected only a certain class of accounts. The ledger was divided into two portions, one of which contained only customers' accounts; the debits to these accounts came from the sales day book, and the credits were obtained by employing a separate cash book or a separate column in the general cash book for all amounts received from customers, the totals of which were carried into the general cash book or "general" column of the cash book at fixed intervals. By making separate summaries of the sales day book and sales column in the cash book, and by also keeping a separate list of all discounts allowed on customers' accounts, all the debits and credits which affected the sales ledger could be put together and balanced with the totals of that ledger independently of any other part of the books. Then it was found simpler, and more conducive to accuracy, to take the totals of all the individual entries and put them through the journal, which had fallen into disuse, these totals being posted to an account in the main part of the ledger or "General Ledger" with some such title as "Customers Account" or "Sales Ledger Account."

The process thus shortly described may be more clearly shown by an example:

(1) A customers' ledger contains accounts with 100 different individuals, showing on January 1st a number of balances, or debts, due, aggregating say $1,500.

(2) During the month of January sales are made to various customers, each of which is entered in the day book as made and subsequently posted to the debit of some account in the customers ledger (1). The day book at the end of January is added up and the total found to be $10,000.

(3) During the month of January collections are made from customers, and entered individually, as received, in a book, and posted to the credit of the corresponding account in the ledger (1). As these postings are made a note is made in the cash book, against the cash receipt, of the amount of discount allowed. At the end of the month the cash and discount items are separately added up and found to amount to $10,200 and $300 respectively.

(4) At January 31st the balances on the customers ledger (1) are again taken off and found to amount to $1,000, and it is desired to know whether or not this is the correct amount.

(5) The proof is as follows:

Balances at January 1st (1)		$ 1,500
Add—Sales for month (2)		10,000
	Total	$11,500
Deduct:		
Cash received (3)	$10,200	
Discount allowed (3)	300	10,500
Balance should be and is (4)		$ 1,000

The following would be specimen journal entries for such a group of transactions:

Customers Account, Dr. $10,000
   To Sales Account, $10,000

   For total of sales for the
   month as shown by
   sales day book, p.—

Discount allowed, Dr.   300
   To Customers Account,   300

   For discounts allowed to customers during the month as per discount day book (usually a separate memorandum column in sales cash book).

Cash Account, Dr.   10,200
   To Customers Account,   10,200

   For cash received from customers during the month.

Controlling Accounts

From the nature of these entries it will be seen that all debits and credits which have been posted individually to the accounts in the customers ledger have also been posted in total through the above entries to the Customers account in the general ledger, and that consequently the balance on the latter account must always equal the sum of all balances in the former ledger.

Accounts such as "Customers Account" above-mentioned are known as "controlling accounts," and their use is now common in all large concerns and is applied not merely to sales but to any group of accounts of sufficient magnitude to make such a course desirable. Their use necessitates a number of subsidiary books or subsidiary columns in principal books, each one representing some separate controlling account or even some subdivision of such an account. The elementary example just given, which involves nothing but simple arithmetic and common sense, is typical of all such controlling systems and no other principle is involved therein.

Loose-Leaf Records

Up to this point only bound books, in which all the necessary entries were made, have been considered. As the magnitude of business concerns increased, further subdivisions became necessary if the accounts were to be kept reasonably up to date. This was at first accomplished by dividing subsidiary books into two or more portions for use on alternate days as books of original entry; and in the intervening periods for posting and other bookkeeping purposes. This method served the purpose for a long period and is still considerably used. Progressive minds, however, advanced the idea of using loose sheets for original record, which after transfer of the information to the final books of account, *i.e.,* the ledgers, were bound up and filed away for reference purposes; and this process has been extended very largely to subsidiary ledgers and under suitable precautions even to principal ledgers. In the offices of banks and brokers and other similar institutions the original entry frequently consists of a rough memorandum on a small piece of paper. These, known as "tickets," have by the end of the day served all their bookkeeping purposes and are filed away in bundles for reference if need be. It would be thought that such methods must lead to a large increase in errors, but in practice this is not found to be the case, while the time saved is undoubtedly very great. The fact that by these methods the work is segregated and each class of entry grouped under the supervision of one clerk who is thoroughly familiar with it and has at short intervals to prove and balance his portion of the work, has conduced to greater care and accuracy; and the loss of any portion of a loose original record before at least one side of it has found a more permanent abiding place, is very rare.

Mechanical Aids in Bookkeeping

Various mechanical devices have gradually come into considerable use in bookkeeping, such as adding machines; combined typewriter and calculating machines; book typewriters, etc.; all of which have entirely revolutionized bookkeeping methods as they formerly existed, and while they do not call for a high order of intelligence on the part of those who are responsible for subsidiary records, they require something a good deal beyond a mere knowledge of bookkeeping on the part of those who control and interpret the final processes and results.

Modern Bookkeeping Methods—Pro Forma System

The following *pro forma* system illustrates modern bookkeeping methods now in common use, without giving effect to many further refinements, particularly in the use of more mechanical devices which already find a limited but ever-extending use in large accounting organizations.

(1) Sales and Customers Records

Invoices to customers for sales made are typewritten in multiple copies, of which one copy is sent to the customer and another forms the sales record. These are totalled periodically by means of an adding machine after they have been individually posted to the debit of the customers account in the usual loose leaf or card ledger. The totals of the adding machine slips form the basis of a journal entry prepared on a loose-leaf form entitled "journal voucher," and debiting "Customers Ledger Account" and crediting the "Sales Account." Generally there will be two or more customers ledgers arranged for different groups of initial letters, such as A to E; F to L; M to O; P to S; T to Z, the invoice forms in use for each being either printed on a different colored paper or bearing some distinctive reference mark. These invoice forms are sorted out by ledgers, separate totals made of each on an adding machine, and a separate controlling account kept for each ledger, either in the general ledger or in a separate subsidiary ledger which is itself controlled by one Customers Ledger account on the general ledger. In more refined systems the invoice and the entry on the debit of the customers account are made at one writing by means of a book-typewriter; and a tabulating machine attached gives the total of all invoices automatically.

Detailed analyses of sales, which are now required in most businesses, will frequently be made by means of an electric sorting and tabulating machine, based upon cards punched in such manner as to record thereon all the salient facts on the original invoice.

Credits to customers' accounts are handled in an exactly similar manner to the debits, the debits and credits being of course reversed.

Cash receipts for sales will be entered up, as they are received, on a loose sheet which contains separate columns for cash items and discount items corresponding to each customers ledger; or in a very large business the remittances will be first sorted by ledgers and those relating to each ledger entered on a separate sheet. The daily totals of these sheets will be handed to the chief cashier after the sheets are completed, and by him agreed with an adding machine slip of the remittances which he has received and paid to bank, and will then be entered in his general cash book in separate totals for each customers ledger. The cash sheets will be sent by the entering clerk to the ledger clerks, who post the items into the corresponding customers ledgers and at the same time enter on sheets and ledgers the corresponding discounts. The sheets are then sent to the treasurer for filing in permanent binders, where they are always available for reference. Frequently the postings of debits and credits to customers' accounts are taken off, totalled and balanced daily with the adding machine lists of sales, cash sheets and credit slips so as to insure a correct balance of the customers ledgers at the end of the month.

(2) Cash Records

The daily totals of cash received from customers as shown upon the subsidiary sheets are entered on the principal cash book together with all other general items. This book is sometimes provided with separate analysis columns under frequently recurring headings and with a column for each bank in which the daily payments into bank are entered. If the bank accounts are numerous only one column is kept in the principal cash book for payments into banks, and this is supported by a subsidiary book containing a separate column for each bank in which debits and credits are entered in totals each day from the additions, on a bank paying-in slip, of the receipts and, on stubs of cheque books, of the payments; the sum of the totals of all columns on this subsidiary book should always agree with the total bank balance as shown by the principal cash book. The best accounting practice provides for all receipts being paid into bank daily; any loose cash required being provided by a fixed sum in the hands of the cashier, which is replenished as often as may be necessary by cheques drawn for the total disbursements made thereout.

Liabilities are usually paid by what is known as a "voucher cheque" or by a voucher against which a cheque is drawn. A typical form of such a voucher contains space at the top for name and particulars of account; in the centre for details of bills supported by original invoices and the total payable; and at foot for signatures of the various officials whose duty it is to pass the same for payment. On the back will be found a "card" or list of accounts to one or more of which the items on the voucher are chargeable, this list forming a complete distribution of the voucher. Against the voucher when completed the cashier will issue a cheque; which very frequently forms an integral part of the voucher and the whole document then becomes a voucher cheque.

(3) Passing Bills for Payment

The most usual and approved routine through which these documents go before they are finally issued to the creditor is as follows: Bills or invoices are rendered by the shipper and are received by a designated official; upon receipt they are immediately despatched to the department which receives the goods or has incurred the expense, and are there certified as to the due receipt of the goods or services and as being correct as to quantity and quality. The invoice is then sent to the official by whom the order was given, who certifies that it is in accord with the order given and that the price is correct. It is then returned to the accounting department where all calculations are checked and it is filed under the supplier's name, attached to an "Invoice Card" on which the amount of the bill is also entered. Sometimes daily reports are made by the ordering and receiving departments to the accounting department of all goods ordered or received, and the verification of the invoice is made in the latter. At the end of the month, or perhaps at more frequent intervals, all the invoices for each supplier are entered on the voucher, proper discounts deducted and the voucher sent, with the original bills attached, to the head of the consuming department for a general certification. The whole docket then returns to the chief accountant, who enters it in his voucher record, certifies the voucher, and forwards it without the supporting bills to the cashier or treasurer for payment.

(4) Creditors or Purchase Records

The voucher record to which reference has already been made, is, as will be seen, ruled in columns and is a self-balancing book, the first cash column being the total amount due to the creditor and being followed by distribution columns arranged according to the accounts which may be required. This book is frequently very bulky and much time and labor is saved by having it in loose-leaf form and in several sections, the leaves as completed being filed in binders one for each section. The double entry is obtained in the general ledger by posting the total of the first column to the credit of an account entitled "Vouchers Payable" and the totals of each of the analysis columns to the debit of the respective accounts affected.

The detail items in the creditors column are sometimes again posted to the credit of accounts for each creditor in a subsidiary ledger, exactly as in the case of sales; and in such cases the payments are similarly dealt with, being entered up on separate sheets as the cheques are issued, the totals of these sheets carried daily into the general cash book and the discounts also entered in the special discount column on the sheets. More frequently, however, no ledgers are kept for creditors' accounts; but the voucher record is itself provided with a column in which the payments are entered, often even this being dispensed with and the date of payment only being noted. In this case the voucher record is itself the ledger, and the open items at the end of any month taken off on an adding machine will agree with the balance on the vouchers payable account in the general ledger. An index is provided for the voucher record by which any individual account can readily be found; and this index serves as a reference for all the supporting data which are numbered to correspond with the voucher.

(5) Expense and Cost Accounts

The vouchers are chargeable to either Property, Operating or Expense accounts, which are represented by corresponding columns in the voucher record.

The labor, material and factory expense items which enter into the cost of the product in a manufacturing business are often entered in a single column of the voucher record and posted to an account in the general ledger headed "Cost Ledger" or some similar designation. The detailed items will be carried into the cost accounts from the original data before they reach the voucher register. Any cost system worth the name arrives with a considerable degree of accuracy at the cost of goods sold, which may be described as the output of the cost ledgers. In the general ledger the account controlling these cost ledgers is accordingly credited with the cost of all goods sold during the month, an account styled "Cost of Sales" being debited. It follows that the Cost Ledger account not only forms a controlling account over the cost ledgers, but itself represents the amount sunk in goods, finished or partly finished, and in materials and supplies used in their manufacture. This account therefore forms what is known as a continuous or running book inventory, a term to which full reference will be made in a subsequent chapter. It is only necessary here to note that the accuracy of this book inventory depends upon that of the item "Cost of Sales" which forms the credit to the account, and this again is entirely dependent on the substantial accuracy of the system in force for ascertaining costs.

On account of the number of expense accounts required it is often customary to keep a separate subsidiary ledger, or analysis book as it is sometimes called, corresponding to one expense column only in the voucher record, this ledger being posted from the original data before they reach the voucher itself, as in the case of cost data. The corresponding expense account in the general ledger is a controlling account over this expense ledger or expense analysis book.

(6) Journal Entries

So far it will be seen that little use has been made of a journal, the totals for cash book and general ledger being posted monthly directly from subsidiary books. Such a plan is frequently adopted in practice; but in other cases each of these totals is made the subject of a journal entry in form similar to those given on pages 20, 21. The adoption of this plan is perhaps more theoretically correct but in practice it is not found to result in greater accuracy. A journal is, however, still necessary for special entries, correction entries, and other miscellaneous matters which do not fall within the scope of any of the books or forms described. For all such entries it is usual to prepare vouchers similar to the cash vouchers already mentioned, each being certified by the proper official. Frequently these journal vouchers are prepared in the form of journal entries and postings are made direct therefrom. It should be noted that while they have reference primarily to the general ledger, if the general ledger account affected is a controlling account, an additional posting is also necessary to some account in the controlled ledger, and this would usually be made direct from the voucher before the latter is entered in the journal itself. The omission of such double postings is a frequent source of error in balancing books.

(7) General Ledger Accounts

It will be seen that by the use of subsidiary records the accounts in the general ledger are reduced to comparatively few in number, each representing some general class of account, and undoubtedly the ideal form of general ledger, not perhaps very frequently found in practice, would contain only one account corresponding to each heading in the periodical balance sheet and to the main headings in the Income account. A trial balance taken off such a ledger would therefore provide, by the simple process of putting down totals, a balance sheet and summarized Income account. The use of such figures, however, without a periodical examination of all the subsidiary records and a proof that the latter are in agreement with the corresponding accounts in the principal ledger, is a course not to be recommended.

Progress of Bookkeeping

The rapid sketch of a modern bookkeeping system here given must not be considered as by any means exhaustive, and is in fact only intended to show in a general way the advance that has been made of late years in general methods. Progress in this direction is continuous and rapid, particularly in the direction of a greater use of mechanical devices which eliminate causes of error and minimize the skill and knowledge required by the human element. This is perhaps unfortunate in that it does not call for a higher but rather a lower order of intelligence on the part of the majority of the clerks employed, but it is in line with progress in other fields; and, as in those fields, it demands the exercise of higher faculties on the part of those directing the work and interpreting the results. It is to the latter that a clear conception of the fundamental principles involved in the most complicated system of bookkeeping is of vital importance; and experience shows again and again that the key lies in the short phrase "Every debit must have a credit."

CHAPTER II

THE BALANCE SHEET

The objective of a set of books kept on sound principles and with accuracy is to enable the actual financial condition to be ascertained at any time. This condition is evidenced by the values of both property owned and debts due, which are together generally described as assets; the actual or estimated value of all liabilities; the surplus of one over the other, which represents the net worth or value; and a summary of the operations by which this net worth has been either created, increased or diminished.

Balance Sheet An Approximation

It is generally claimed that a balance sheet must represent facts, but in the strict sense this is not altogether possible in any case that can be imagined.

If an individual possessing a certain definite amount of cash embarks this cash in various ventures which are all in due course liquidated, with the result that at the close of all his operations he finds himself with another definite amount of cash either greater or less than that with which he started, then he knows exactly what his profit or loss has been during the intervening period. But such a condition is an almost impossible one in practice except as applied to individual transactions.

A contractor may embark on a large piece of construction work, purchasing with cash all materials and supplies required; carry through his contract and at the close sell off all the residue for cash; he then knows exactly what his position is as regards this one contract. In practice, however, before one contract is completed, another is begun and plant and material used for the first are not sold but are transferred to the second, so that his activities form a continuous series of overlapping operations which may never come to an end or at any rate not for a long period of years. In the meantime he desires from time to time to ascertain as far as he can what his position is and how his contracts are working out, and he must for this purpose endeavor to put some value upon all his assets and probably estimate most of his liabilities.

Consequently, it follows that a balance sheet can only be an approximation to facts, the degree of approximation depending upon the skill and accuracy with which the estimates are made. The first necessary step to such an approximation is the summary of debits and credits taken from the books of account, generally known as a trial balance. The trial balance is the work of the bookkeeper, while the conversion of this trial balance into a substantially accurate financial estimate of position, or balance sheet, is the work of the accountant. Assuming that such balance sheets have been prepared at different periods, each showing as at the date on which it was prepared the net worth of the individual or group concerned, then a comparison of the difference between the total of the assets and the total of the liabilities at any two separate dates shows the progress made during the period either upwards or downwards. This figure, however, by itself does not tell the story of the intervening period but merely shows the relative conditions at its beginning and end.

Causes Affecting Net Worth

The change shown in the net worth may be due to any or all of the following causes:

(1) Appreciation or depreciation in the estimated values of the property or assets not in any way due to the activities or expenditures of the individual or group concerned, such as changes in value of land due to greater or less demand, or to discoveries of minerals; and in values of buildings, machinery or commodities due to a rise or fall in prices of labor and material since they were acquired.

(2) Capital brought into or drawn out of the business during the period.

(3) Gifts of property of any kind by or to the concern, not in any way connected with its business activities.

(4) Loss or gain arising from the excess or deficiency of ordinary expenditures made on trading or manufacturing as compared with the income from the sale of products.

(5) Loss or gain arising from excess or deficiency of ordinary expenditures on personal matters as compared with income from personal sources, such as interest on stocks or bonds, or rents.

In any complete system of bookkeeping the changes due to these various causes will be clearly shown by a careful examination of the accounts kept, the last two groups being those most difficult of ascertainment in full detail.

Balance Sheet Accounts

In a general ledger, such as has already been outlined, an account would be kept for each generic group of assets and liabilities, and a balance account generally known as the "Profit and Loss Account" or the "Surplus Account" would include all other items. This account would be supported by such subsidiary accounts as might be necessary, either kept in the same ledger and closed periodically into the Profit and Loss account, or kept in a subsidiary ledger or ledgers controlled by the Profit and Loss account.

Form of Balance Sheet

The following may be given as a specimen of a balance sheet designed to show the financial position in considerable detail and yet in a simple and understandable form:

ASSETS:*
 Fixed Property (after deduction of estimated depreciation due to use):
  Land and improvements thereon, including mineral rights and development thereof, but not structures of any kind.
  Buildings and structures.
  Plant, machinery, fixed tools, permanent way for railroad, etc.
  Movable equipment.
  Furniture and fixtures.
  Patterns, drawings, dies, etc.
  Patents, goodwill, franchises, etc.

 Permanent Investments in stocks, shares, bonds or obligations of any kind held to produce income or other increment, or for purposes connected with the business (if any) carried on, including advances made for similar purposes but excluding investment of reserves.

 Investment of Reserves.

 Working Assets:
  Stores and supplies for use in operations.
  Advances to agents for business expenses and purposes.
  Insurance, interest, taxes, royalties, etc., paid in advance of the period over which they accrue.

 Current Assets:
  Materials carried for sale or conversion and products partly or wholly manufactured intended for sale.
  Accounts and bills due from outside parties for goods supplied or short term advances made, and recoverable in cash, or its equivalent in some other class of current assets.
  Investments in securities of any kind held as a temporary employment of surplus cash.

---

*See Chapters IV and V for detailed discussion of balance sheet assets.

Cash at banks on deposit and current account, and cash on hand.

Suspense Debits:

Consisting of discount on bonds, expenses of organization or other extraordinary losses or expenses which it is desired to write off to Income account over a period of years.

LIABILITIES:*

On Capital Account:

Partners' capital (in a private business).

Capital stock (in a corporation).

Loans secured by mortgage or otherwise and running for terms of years, otherwise known as "Funded Debt."

On Unfunded Debt:

For capital, as distinct from current, purposes.

Current Liabilities:

On current bank loans and commercial paper:

Secured.

Unsecured.

On trade bills payable.

On trade accounts payable.

On miscellaneous accounts payable.

Accrued interest, taxes and other periodical payments.

Provision for losses actually incurred, the amount of which is not definitely ascertained.

Provision for contingencies likely to arise out of past operations.

Suspense Credits:

Consisting of items which will eventually become credits to Income or Surplus but cannot be at present adjusted.

Surplus:

Appropriated to meet future contingencies which have not yet arisen.

Appropriated for repayment of debt (by sinking fund or otherwise).

Appropriated for capital expenditures.

Appropriated to equalize dividends.

Profit and Loss account—being undistributed or unappropriated balance of profits (or losses).

*See Chapter VI for detailed discussion of balance sheet liabilities,

Order of Assets and Liabilities

Much discussion has taken place in the past as to whether a balance sheet should be drawn up with the assets on the debit side, as is the American practice, or on the credit side, as is the English practice. The balance of argument would seem to favor the latter on the theory that a balance sheet is intended to set forth the position of the owner of the property, who should therefore be credited with what he possesses and charged with what he owes.

For the clear understanding and recording of his affairs, the owner distributes himself into a number of different pockets and considers that into each pocket he places some particular class of his property. According to the rules of bookkeeping he therefore debits each pocket with the value placed upon the particular class, and credits himself as the one from whom it is received. These pockets represent the various property and expense accounts in his ledger, and the corresponding credit account is himself or, as it is generally styled, "Capital Account." In the balance sheet prepared from his books he is summarizing the distribution made by totalling the amount in each separate pocket. His balance sheet shows *his* position in relation to his books, and he is therefore credited with the items which he has placed into those pockets and charged with those items which he has received through other pockets from other people. In other words, the English method, which seems more correct theoretically, is "A in account with his books," while the American method, which is the reverse, is "His books in account with A." This brings out the only really important point in this whole discussion, viz.: that every kind of account stated must be considered from the point of view of the purpose for which it is prepared. If an account is headed "A in account with B," A should be credited with what he has given to B; while if the account is headed "B in account with A," it will be reversed. A familiar example is often found in a banker's pass book, in which the customer's deposits are usually entered on the credit side and his withdrawals on the debit; while in the depositor's own books the record is reversed—the pass book is "A in account with the bank," while the cash book is "The bank in account with A."

Apart from the theory involved the matter has perhaps little importance except as illustrating the modern tendency to ignore forms and get at results which after all are the most important. By convention American balance sheets are prepared with the assets on the debit, or left-hand, side of the account, just as by convention in England they are prepared in the reverse way. It is also usual to dispense with the signs "Dr." and "Cr." on each side of the balance sheet and instead use captions such as "Property and Assets" and "Capital and Liabilities"; and frequently also even the fiction of sides disappears, the assets appearing on the upper part of the sheet and the liabilities on the lower, or the reverse.

In such directions as these accounting diverges sharply from bookkeeping, striving always to adopt such forms and methods as will result in statements understandable by those uninitiated into the so-called "mysteries of bookkeeping." In the strenuous field of modern business clearness is almost as important as accuracy; for a statement that is strictly accurate so far as figures are concerned may fail of being understood by want of care in making it show clearly what is called for without a further compiling or unraveling of figures. The form of balance sheet already given will be found to lend itself to a clear statement of affairs, as the following explanatory remarks will show. It remains in subsequent chapters to consider to what extent it can achieve the much more difficult ideal of accuracy.

Analysis of Balance Sheet Assets

The first essential in clearness is that each caption should express the nature of the items included therein. The six main headings adopted are:

(1) Fixed Assets.
(2) Permanent Investments.
(3) Investment of Reserves.
(4) Working Assets.
(5) Current Assets.
(6) Suspense Debits.

(1) Fixed Assets

Fixed assets include all property which is directly possessed and used by the owner himself for his enjoyment or for his business purposes, and maintained in a fixed condition for long periods of time subject only to wear and tear and depreciation from use. The figures in the balance sheet should be supported by detail schedules showing the amount at the beginning of the year, the additions during the year, and the deductions for depreciation due to use in the business. The conditions under which account should be taken of other kinds of depreciation or of appreciation are discussed later.

(2) Permanent Investments

Under permanent investments is included partial or entire ownership in facilities of other persons or corporations or similar bodies the ownership or control of which is a compulsory or necessary one; either because it is a trust ownership for special purposes extending over long periods of time, or because it is so intimately connected with the owner's activities that a sale would diminish or otherwise interfere with the continuance of those activities. Under this heading should also appear advances made to such persons or corporations and employed by them, for the time being at any rate, in carrying on their business. These advances differ in many respects from ordinary accounts receivable for goods sold, for they are usually found upon inquiry to be so much locked up in fixed or working assets as to be not readily realizable and are not in fact intended to be repaid as long as the business for which the advances were made is carried on. In practice these advances are frequently and erroneously treated as accounts receivable under current assets, thereby often concealing a serious shrinkage in liquid assets which may endanger the solvency of the concern.

(3) Investment of Reserves

The caption "Investment of Reserves" serves to show what proportion of any reserves which appear on the liability side of the balance sheet is specifically earmarked and invested. There should not be included any part of the assets unless they are specifically segregated for the service of the reserves. Any difference between the total of the reserves and the amount of these investments represents the proportion of the reserves which is invested in the general assets and which can only be available by correspondingly reducing the latter.

(4) Working Assets

These assets form another class equally necessary with the first, consisting of those assets which, while they are not intended for sale, are necessarily consumed in the process of carrying on the owner's activities, whatever they may be, and are not directly represented anywhere in the results of those activities. While they are not permanent, because they are continually being consumed, their equivalent is permanent because they must be continually renewed and replaced. Thus the activities of a railroad consist in the transportation of persons and commodities from place to place; and in this process coal, oil, and other supplies are continually being consumed, leaving no trace behind, and as continually being replaced. In a manufacturing business the same kind of articles are being used in the same kind of way in carrying out operations on other materials, which latter, while they change their shape in the process, still remain in existence, are intended for sale and are therefore treated as current assets. Balances in hands of agents which do not as a rule exist wholly in the form of cash and are not available for the ordinary purposes of a cash balance, are perhaps on the border line between working and current assets, but conservative practice places them in the former group. The third group of items, representing payments made in advance to cover expenses of a subsequent period, and not therefore in the ordinary course of business recoverable, are also conservatively treated as a part of the working assets. This whole class is as to the value, but not as to the property, permanent capital, subject only to fluctuations due to conditions of trade; it differs from that of fixed assets in that both the value and the property included in the latter are of a permanent nature.

(5) Current Assets

Under current assets are included, firstly, the property which by the aid of the fixed and working assets is being continuously converted from one form into another, with the purpose of earning a profit by subsequent sale and conversion into cash; in this respect differing markedly from the two classes of fixed and working assets. Secondly are included the intermediary instruments, such as bills and accounts receivable, by means of which the conversion into cash is made; thirdly, the equivalent of cash in the shape of realizable and temporary investments held only until an outlet for the surplus cash is found either in divisions of profit or in extensions of the business activities; and fourth-ly, the cash itself.

(6) Suspense Debits

The term "Suspense Debits" is sufficiently defined in the subcaption. The items to be included consist entirely of those which represent no value and must sooner or later be written off entirely as losses or expenses; such for instance as debit balances on ventures or undertakings not yet completed and not represented by ascertainable assets; discounts on bonds outstanding, etc.

Analysis of Balance Sheet Liabilities

Among the liabilities the first item by convention is the fixed capital invested, although in theory the deduction to be first made from the total assets should be the liabilities to outside parties, the difference representing the net worth, which is made up partly of the fixed amount contributed as permanent capital and partly of the accretions thereto. The arrangement adopted is, however, convenient in that where the balance sheet is arranged on the debit and credit principle, the capital liabilities and unfunded debt for capital purposes appear opposite to the fixed and working assets in which they are invested, followed by the current liabilities which have to be provided for by the continuous liquidation of the current assets; the last item being the surplus (or it may be deficit, which would be a deduction or red figure) left after providing for capital and liabilities.

Capital Stock

It is desirable in the case of a corporation that the balance sheet should show not only the amount of capital which has actually been raised but also that which is still available if required in the future without any change in the charter. Such available capital may be either:

(a) Capital authorized by the charter but not yet created by any action of the corporation through its stockholders.

(b) Capital authorized by the charter, created by resolution of the stockholders but not yet issued by any action of the directors.

(c) Capital authorized by the charter, created by resolution of the stockholders, issued by authority of the directors but not yet sold to any parties for cash and consequently still remaining in the treasury of the corporation.

(d) Capital authorized by the charter, created by resolution of the stockholders, issued by authority of the directors and sold to outside parties; but upon which only a proportion of the par value has been paid, leaving the balance due in cash either immediately or when called for.

It is a common practice to treat stock issued but not sold as an asset and include it among either the fixed or current assets. This practice is entirely incorrect in theory and also inconvenient in practice. In theory, treasury stock or bonds are merely so many legalized pieces of paper entitling the holder either to a certain share in the assets or to a certain lien on those assets. In neither case can such pieces of paper be in any sense assets of the corporation creating and issuing them; for the assets themselves already appear and cannot be duplicated by resolutions of stockholders or directors. In practice difficult questions arise as to the valuation of such treasury stock and bonds; the value to the corporation is clearly the par value for which the corporation itself is liable; the market value for which they can be sold may be either more or less, and until they are sold, and the proceeds become available for the purposes of the corporation, it is impossible to say what their value is. The real fact is that they have no value in themselves and only differ from similar securities not yet authorized in that certain clerical formalities have been completed which render them more available either for sale when further capital is required or for pledging as security for loans. This latter fact is certainly one that should be made apparent in connection with the balance sheet, and this can be done correctly and without infringing any sound principles of finance by attaching to the balance sheet an exhibit in the following form:

Description of Stock or Bond	How Authorized	Amount Authorized	Amount Created	Amount Issued	Amount in Treasury		Amount Issued to Public
					Pledged	Unpledged	

Funded and Unfunded Debt

A distinction is made between permanent or long term loans or Funded Debt which, subject to their conditions and amount, are a source of strength as representing permanent capital, and other loans raised for capital purposes and payable on demand or at short dates, which are frequently termed "Unfunded Debt." For the former, except in case of default, no immediate provision requires to be made other than for the sinking fund payments providing for gradual redemption for which alone the current assets are obligated. The latter, on the other hand, are a source of weakness, evidencing the necessity of an increase in the permanent capital and in the meantime constituting a direct obligation against the current assets which might at any time lead to difficulties if not to disaster.

Current Liabilities

Under current liabilities appear, firstly, those to bankers and others for temporary loans raised for current purposes, such as to provide for seasonal or temporary expansion of business, which will be automatically retired as business again returns to the minimum or normal condition. The distinction between such loans and unfunded debt may easily be a fine one; for any permanent increase in current assets due to progressive growth of the business should undoubtedly be provided for, not by such temporary loans, but by an addition to the permanent capital. There is, however, a fairly clear line of demarcation between loans raised to meet additions to fixed capital and those raised for temporary additions to current or circulating capital, and it is this distinction for which the classification adopted is intended to provide. Ordinary liabilities on bills and accounts payable call for no explanation, but it should be noted that provision is made under the caption of current liabilities for losses actually incurred but not definitely ascertained, and for contingencies that may arise out of past and completed transactions, such as claims for defects when a term guarantee is given. Such items are direct liabilities which must be met in a short time out of current assets, as distinct from the provision made for contingencies at present unknown and unforeseen which may arise out of future operations. The latter are clearly a mere allocation of surplus made for reasons of prudence.

Depreciation

There is another class of provisions intermediate between these two, viz.: those for depreciation, or wear and tear, of fixed capital arising out of its use in the activities of the business; and for exhaustion of minerals and other subsoil products due to their actual removal from the land with a consequent reduction in the property represented in the fixed assets. If these provisions are included on the liability side of the balance sheet they will require a separate main heading, such as "Provisions for Depreciation," which should find its place between current liabilities and surplus. They are not a part of the surplus because they represent an estimate of losses actually incurred, nor are they current liabilities because they do not necessarily become a charge upon current assets; or, if they do, they act as a replacement of wasted property, *i. e.,* a transfer from current to fixed assets. Both in theory and practice such provisions should preferably be deducted from the fixed assets to which they relate, and the *pro forma* balance sheet here submitted is so drawn up. The argument for including provision for depreciation and exhaustion on the liability side of the balance sheet is largely one of expediency, in that in practice it has been found easier to bring home the importance of adequate provision when the amount so set aside from year to year is kept in evidence; and also because the amount is necessarily an estimate only and at some time in the future involves the actual expenditure of at any rate a large part of the accumulated provision.

Suspense Credits

Under Suspense Credits should be grouped items which in all probability will ultimately form credits to Income or Surplus; such for instance as credit balances on ventures or undertakings not yet completed; premiums on outstanding bonded debt, etc.; but not including payments received in advance of due dates which, until such dates arrive and the service for which they are received is performed, are a direct liability.

Surplus

Under the head "Surplus" should be included all those provisions which may be styled voluntary, although in practice this course is seldom followed. There can be no doubt that all such are in effect allocations of surplus, specially earmarked, for purposes which may never arise; and that merely to give different names to such allocations does not alter the facts. On the other hand, some of the contingencies provided against will, according to the law of averages, arise at some time; and inasmuch as accidents and such like contingencies, which only occur at considerable intervals of time, should perhaps be treated as accruing year by year, there is reason for building up a fund to meet them when they do arise, by annual contributions from surplus. It is submitted, however, that until the contingency does arise the sum provided is part of the surplus; and its probability is sufficiently and more accurately recognized by such an allocation as that suggested than by the more usual method of creating a separate group heading of "Provisions and Reserves" between current liabilities and surplus. This is particularly true of sinking fund appropriations which are usually mere accumulations of surplus to take the place in the permanent capital of bonded indebtedness retired. Unless these sinking fund provisions have been applied in lieu of depreciation or exhaustion, in which case they should be deducted from the asset account, they differ in no way from undistributed profits, which are also largely employed to provide permanent capital for the extension of business.

Appropriated Surplus

"Other Appropriations for Capital Purposes" would represent amounts specifically set aside out of profits for additions to and extensions of the fixed or working assets. A similar caption is found in the balance sheet prescribed by the

Interstate Commerce Commission for the use of transportation companies under the heading of "Appropriated Surplus," representing the appropriations made by such companies out of surplus earnings for capital purposes, which under former methods disappeared from the accounts altogether, being directly charged against the annual profits.

The allocation of profits for capital expenditures should be considered a temporary appropriation thereof only, as by raising further fixed capital to provide for these expenditures the profits so set aside become again available for distribution. The allocation may at any time be made permanent by converting it into capital stock by means of a stock dividend.

Profit and Loss

The item "Undistributed Balance of Profits (or Losses)" may be a debit instead of a credit if more than the profits earned have been distributed or there have been losses instead of profits; and technical bookkeeping would then require that this figure be placed on the asset instead of the liability side of the balance sheet. Where the other captions of the surplus account are together in excess of the debit on "Undistributed Balance of Profits (or Losses)," it will conduce to a clearer understanding of the true position if the latter item is retained in the same position and is especially noted as a debit, which in practice is done by entering the figures either (if typed or written) in red ink signifying a deduction, or (if printed) in italics, frequently with a star referring to a footnote reading "Deficit"; or by inserting the word "deduct" and changing the caption so as to read "Deduct—Deficit on Profit and Loss Account." By thus adhering to the form, whether there are profits or losses, uniformity is secured and the comparison of conditions and results is made easier, particularly to those who have to study the figures without any special bookkeeping knowledge.

English Requirements as to Balance Sheet

It will be useful to refer here to the requirements as to balance sheets in England contained in Section 26 of the Companies (Consolidation) Act 1908, which provides that every company must furnish once in each year and forward to the Registrar of Joint Stock Companies a summary of its affairs, including "a statement, made up to such date as may be specified in the statement, in the form of a balance sheet, audited by the company's auditors, and containing a summary of its capital, its liabilities, and its assets, giving such particulars as will disclose the general nature of those liabilities and assets, and how the values of the fixed assets have been arrived at, but the balance sheet need not include a statement of profit and loss."

Balance Sheet Forms

In the form of balance sheet most commonly adopted in England, each class of asset is separately extended in the balance sheet in an order corresponding to the ease of liquidation—that is to say, the more fixed assets are stated first, followed by those which are slightly more realizable, and ending with the most realizable of all, viz.: cash, but with no group classifications into fixed, working and current assets.

The difference between the two forms, both of which may with equal accuracy and clearness set forth the true financial position, makes it necessary to state that while the form given in this chapter may be ideal for a balance sheet, it does not follow that it is the only correct form and that an accountant in the exercise of his public duties ought not to certify to any other. The proprietors or directors who submit the accounts to their associates or stockholders have the right to decide upon the form in which those accounts shall be submitted, and to require the accountant to certify to them in that form, or to state in what respect he finds them incorrect or misleading. The latter will have his own ideas as to the best method of stating the accounts, and is fully entitled to put his views before his clients and endeavor, in so far as he can, to mould their ideas to his, but he must remember that the object of the accounts is to set forth the "true financial condition" and that there is no stereotyped way in which this should be done. There is a good deal to be said for uniformity in the matter of form of statements of similar concerns, but this is a matter of convenience more than of necessity, and no preconceived ideas as to the superiority of one form over another should be allowed to interfere with the rights of the proprietors or directors to state the accounts in any form they please and to call upon the accountant to certify them in such manner as he may think fit.

If a balance sheet is to be of any use to those into whose hands it may come, it is a first essential that in whatever form it may be drawn up, the different captions should clearly show what class of items they cover and should not be used to conceal items of an entirely different nature.

Misleading Statements in Balance Sheets

The following instances of misleading descriptions which are not unknown in practice will show clearly the danger involved to those who may rely on the balance sheet as a guide to the financial position.

Land, buildings, plant and machinery may be stated in one item without any reference to such items as franchises, patents, and goodwill, which may make up more than half the total. This would convey to a reader of the balance sheet that the concern owned a much more valuable plant than was actually the case; and while the inclusion in the caption of the terms omitted would not give him any very definite information it would lead to inquiry and so to a truer appreciation of the facts.

An item of cash and cash assets may be given which really includes (1) investments not readily saleable; (2) accounts and bills receivable many of which are irrecoverable; (3) material and supplies. This is an entire misdescription of important items and gives no idea whatever of the true position. In fact, this caption itself while occasionally used is so vague as to be without any value and it should never be employed.

Accounts receivable may be entered at their face value, while the reserves made for bad and doubtful accounts may be included in miscellaneous provisions made out of surplus. In this way the value of the asset is overstated and the facts concealed.

Investments or accounts receivable under the group of current assets may include investments in or advances to concerns which are vital to the continuance of the business and for that reason cannot be realized. In this way the current assets available to meet current liabilities may be seriously overstated.

Many other instances might be given but the above are sufficient to show the importance of an accurate classification and description, and the fuller discussion of the principles governing the correct valuation of different classes of assets and liabilities will throw further light on this subject.

Condensed Financial Statement

The following condensed form of statement is frequently employed and has the advantage of clearly showing the relation of property assets and liabilities to capital and surplus:

Fixed Property:
   Land and Buildings.................. $
   Plant and Machinery, Tools and Fix-
      tures ....
   Patterns, Drawings and Dies........
   Patents, Goodwill and Franchises.....
                             ——— $

Permanent Investments...............
Working Assets......................
Current Assets:
   Materials and Products of Manufac-
      ture .... $
   Accounts and Bills Receivable.......
   Investments ....
   Cash ....
                           $

Less—Current Liabilities............
           Net Assets............. $

    Represented by
      Share Capital............ $
      Loan Capital............
      Surplus ....$
      Suspense Balance..
                $

Such a form which can be incorporated in a general report with comments on each item is frequently of use in bringing the facts clearly before those who have no familiar knowledge of the technicalities of bookkeeping.

Statutory Forms of Balance Sheet

Reference may here be made to the following statutory forms of balance sheet:

Transportation companies in the United States are now required by the Interstate Commerce Commission to file balance sheets in certain forms, and those relating to two important classes of companies, viz.: steam railroads and steamships, are given in Appendix VI. The Interstate Commerce Commission also issues pamphlets giving full details of the manner in which items should be grouped.

These balance sheets give a very full statement of all the

assets and liabilities of the company, but that for railroad companies is defective in that it provides that all securities, whether stock or funded debt, of the company which are owned by the company should appear as assets under the head of "Securities" as well as on the liability side of the balance sheet under the heads of "Stock" and "Mortgage, Bonded and Secured Debt," thus in effect duplicating to that extent the property of the company and raising further difficulties which are dealt with more fully in Chapter VI.   In the steamship balance sheet, issued by the Interstate Commerce Commission at a later date than that for railways, this error has been corrected and the stocks and bonds of the company held in its own treasury are properly deducted from the liability thereon so as to show as a liability the net amount in the hands of the public.

The classifications of the balance sheets are open to objection, particularly in the captions of Working Assets and Deferred Debit Items.

"Working Assets" includes all the items which are usually styled Current Assets, and in addition "Agents' and Conductors' Baalnces," "Materials and Supplies" and "Other Working Assets" which in the form of balance sheet given on page 34 would be included as Working Assets. Moreover, the term "Other Working Assets" is objectionable in that it does not clearly show the nature of the items included thereunder.

"Deferred Debit Items" includes temporary advances to proprietary companies, *i. e.,* companies forming part of the permanent investments.   Such advances should preferably be treated as permanent investments unless they are recoverable in cash in the ordinary course of business, when they should be treated as current assets.   "Advances for Working Funds" and "Rents and Insurance Paid in Advance" are proper working assets, while "Cash and Securities in Sinking

Funds" should be placed in the caption of "Investment of Reserves." The subheading of "Other Deferred Debit Items" is objectionable in that it provides a place for concealing accounts without any proper classification of their nature; an inspection of railroad balance sheets shows that full advantage is taken of this caption, the items placed under which frequently amount to very large sums.

On the liability side of the balance sheet, Current Liabilities are styled Working Liabilities. In the next caption liabilities accrued but not due are separately stated. The caption of "Deferred Credit Items" includes some items which are really part of surplus and others which are really working, as distinct from current, liabilities.

National banks are called upon to file a very detailed form of statement (Appendix VII) which is frequently much shortened and simplified by collecting the assets and liabilities into groups for the purpose of the published balance sheet which circulates among the stockholders and depositors.

Life assurance companies are compelled to present their accounts in a form which in many respects is peculiar and cannot be recommended as a model of accurate accounts. These forms vary in the different states, but are all more or less similar, and that required in the State of New York (See Appendix VIII) will serve as an illustration. The statement is a very long one and, except for the fact that it shows the operations of the company in the greatest possible detail, has little to justify it. The balance sheet is not a separate statement as is usual, but is merged with the so-called account of "Income and Disbursements"; the latter is made up entirely on a cash receipts and cash disbursements basis taking no account of outstanding assets or liabilities. These assets and liabilities are, however, brought into the balance sheet portion of the account which is comprised under the headings "Ledger" and "Non-Ledger Assets," "Liabilities and Other Funds." Attempts have been made from time to time to amend this form in conformity with current accounting practice, and this could be done without in any way interfering with the detailed information contained in the present statement. So far, however, these efforts have proved unsuccessful and the form remains at the present time as a model of just what a balance sheet and statement of income account should not be.

Each of these statutory forms suffers no doubt from the want of agreement upon details and possibly also from a want of knowledge of accounting principles among the committees who advised upon their preparation. On the other hand, they have resulted in uniformity of statements in place of the diversity and chaos which previously existed. It is now easy to compare any two companies and there is no doubt that the possibility of such comparisons, even upon a basis that is defective in form, must go a long way to compensate for any defects that may exist.

CHAPTER III

THE PROFIT AND LOSS ACCOUNT
AND THE GENERAL PRINCIPLES GOVERNING
ITS PREPARATION

Loss and Gain Terminology

The item of "Undistributed Balance of Profits (or Losses)" in the balance sheet discussed in the last chapter will be supported by an account, made up from the books, to which various names are given in practice. The variety of terms used has resulted in the absence of any clear understanding as to the use or meaning of "Manufacturing Account," "Trading Account," "Profit and Loss Account," "Revenue Account," "Gross Revenue Account," "Net Revenue Account," "Income Account," "Gross Income Account," "Net Income Account," and there is urgent need for an agreement upon a proper terminology in this as in so many other matters relating to accounts. It is proposed here to attempt to introduce some order into this confusion by suggesting a use of the terms upon which agreement might be obtained.

Varying Purposes of Financial Statements

It should first be noted that just as the values of assets and liabilities set forth in a balance sheet are estimates of value only, so too the balance of undistributed profits and losses is an estimate revised up to date. It therefore is a cumulative account and must include all items of profit and loss which have not been brought into account previously, whether such items accrued in the period under immediate review or in a previous period. In this connection a distinction must be drawn between a statement of profits and losses made up annually or at some regular interval for the purpose of showing as nearly as possible the results for each consecutive period shortly after the close of that period; and a comparative statement of profits for a series of such periods, made up for the purpose of determining as accurately as possible the earning capacity of the business. In the latter case the review is made at a longer interval after the occurrence of the transactions and a more accurate statement is thus possible. Moreover, as the object of such a comparative statement is to reflect as nearly as possible the true conditions of the business, many adjustments and reserves made in annual accounts for the purpose of safety will not be required and in fact will often be incorrect when a measure of earning capacity is required. On the other hand, overlapping items belonging to previous periods, which in preparing statements of earning capacity would be relegated to the periods to which they belong, should not be excluded from an annual statement of profits and losses, for the reason that the latter is merely a revision up to date of all profits and losses incurred as far as the same are ascertainable. In other words, a statement of earning capacity necessarily and properly involves more facts and less estimates than a recurrent annual statement of profits and losses.

Classification of Activities

The account which analyzes the manner in which gains or losses have occurred may be divided into separate portions corresponding to distinct stages in the process of arriving at the final balance. For the purpose of defining these stages, activities may be grouped into the following classes:

(1) Manufacturing.
(2) Merchandising.
(3) Agency and Commission.
(4) Transportation.
(5) Banking.
(6) Professional.
(7) Private.

(1) Manufacturing

In a manufacturing business the activities consist in converting materials by means of labor and the use of fixed and working assets into a shape in which they are saleable. The sale price forms the gross earnings from sales and, after deductions of returns, allowances and discounts, gives the net earnings. The difference between the net earnings from sales and the cost of conversion is the gross profit derived from the activity; but in order to realize this gross profit, *i.e.,* to convert it into net profit, expenses must be incurred for selling the products and for general supervision. Deducting these expenses the net profit for the period is obtained which is applicable to provide for general reserves and for remuneration of the capital employed. Any surplus remaining after making these deductions would be added to the surplus of previous periods and be available to make good extraordinary losses not due to the activities carried on; or to extend the business; or for such other voluntary purposes as may be determined; and this final amount would also be subject to increase by accretions to property or assets arising from causes not connected with the activities.   Hence, we have the following main divisions of account:

(1) *Manufacturing account* (a term already in general use), to the credit of which would be placed the gross earnings from sales, which by deduction of allowances and trade discounts would show net earnings from sales; on the debit side would be shown the cost of manufacture up to the point where the products would be ready for sale; and the balance would be the gross profit from manufacture.

(2) *Income account,* which will take up the expenses of sale and supervision necessary to convert this gross profit into available or net profit.

(3) *Net Income account,* showing the disposition made of net profit and the surplus profit remaining, leading up to—

(4) *Profit and Loss account* (frequently styled "Surplus"), which is a cumulative account of all profits and losses whether arising from the activities dealt with in the earlier accounts or otherwise, the balance of which will form the item of undistributed profits and losses in the balance sheet.

Dividends on stocks may be charged either to Net Income account if it is desired that they be paid only out of the results of the period, or to Profit and Loss account if, as is generally proper, they are to be paid out of cumulative results.

(2) Merchandising

In a merchandising business the processes and accounts would be the same, except that in place of conversion the first operation is to buy and collect in bulk, divide into small packages and store in shape convenient for sale. The various costs entering into this operation are different in nature from, and very much simpler than, those which enter into the operation of manufacture, and the term "Trading Account" already in general use for the purpose may well be continued as the title of the first division in place of "Manufacturing Account." The other three accounts would remain the same.

(3) Agency and Commission

In an agency or commission business no merchandise or property of any kind is dealt in for the account of the owner of the business, but is merely handled for the account of the seller or purchaser, the owner of the business being remunerated by a commission which forms his gross profit, from which are deductible the expenses of supervision, losses on guarantees, etc., the balance being the net profit from his agency business. If, as is frequently the case, he takes shares in ventures with his customers he is in effect carrying on also a different business, coming under one of the other categories enumerated and subject to the same considerations. His accounts as an agency and commission merchant will thus consist only of the Income account, Net Income account and Profit and Loss account.

(4) Transportation

In a transportation business conditions are materially different. There is no manufacturing or merchandising involved in the main business of transportation, although such frequently exists as a side issue, and the results of these would be brought from their respective Manufacturing, Trading and Income accounts into the Net Income account. The main activity is the transportation of passengers, merchandise, etc., at fixed rates and the revenue from this source forms the gross earnings and after deduction of any allowances results in the net earnings. Before these net earnings are available, just as in the case of net earnings from sales, the service of transportation must be performed, and the balance remaining after performing this service is the gross profit. To follow out the analogy of manufacturing and jobbing activities there should be charged against this gross profit the expense of obtaining customers and of general supervision. Accounts of transportation companies are, however, governed by the rules of the Interstate Commerce Commission and of the various Public Service Commissions, which have ignored this distinction; and all these expenses are merged with the cost of transportation into one general term "operating expenses" so that the true "gross profit" is lost and the first balance reached is net profit. Hence, the main divisions of account are reduced to these, viz.:

(1) Income account, generally known as Operating account, which is credited with net earnings from operation and charged with operating expenses and taxes, resulting in the net profit or operating income.

(2) Net Income account, generally known as Income account.

(3) Profit and Loss account.

The use of the two last accounts is identical with that stated for manufacturing activities.

(5) Banking

In banking accounts net earnings are gross profit as there are usually no deductions representing cost of the specific service performed. In the case, however, of the activity generally known as "Promotion," the net earnings will generally be subject to many direct charges for purchases, expenses, etc., relating to the particular promotion, and an account similar to a trading account will be required; this term, with a prefix to indicate the particular promotion or other activity concerned, might well be retained.

The principal credits in the income account will be the gross profit from these separate trading accounts as well as interest received, brokerage on sales and purchases of securities for customers, etc., all of which latter are net earnings and income; and on the debit side interest paid to customers, general business expenses, etc., the balance being the net profit as before. It should be noted that, as bankers are dealers in money, interest paid to or received from customers in the ordinary course of business, which in other cases is a division of profit, becomes an expense; but this does not apply to interest paid to parties who share directly or indirectly in the business activities carried on, which would still be a division of profit and as such chargeable to Net Income account. In this case, therefore, there are also four accounts:

(1) Trading account (for each separate promotion or similar activity)

(2) Income account

(3) Net Income account

(4) Profit and Loss account

Where, as in a private firm, the entire profits are regularly divided at the end of each period there will be no profit and loss account.

(6) Professional Activities

In professional activities such as those of lawyers, accountants, engineers, doctors, etc., the net earnings, i. e., gross fees received less any out-of-pocket expenses incurred on any particular case and included in the bill rendered, are subject to deduction of the cost of the service rendered in each case, the balance being the gross profit against which general business expenses are charged, leaving as before the net profit for disposal. In these cases there will still be four divisions of account, but neither of the terms "Trading Account" or "Manufacturing Account" seems applicable. An analogous term "Business Account" is suggested and the four divisions will be:

(1) Business account

(2) Income account

(3) Net Income account

(4) Profit and Loss account

In the case of private firms there will usually be no profit and loss account.

(7) Private Accounts

Private accounts are intended to include only such as do not represent any activities. They are the next step to the Net Income account of activities, commencing only with the share of profits arising therefrom, and by common custom the term Income and Expenditure account has long been applied thereto and may conveniently be retained. One account only is required which is credited with the net income accruing and charged with all the personal expenditures and other dispositions, not being additions to capital, made thereto, the balance being carried to the personal capital account of the individual.

Suggested Terminology

In considering the foregoing accounts it is necessary to note that it is perhaps seldom that any of the five classes considered exists by itself, and to the extent to which the activities overlap so will the accounts suggested for one group appear also in the other; but the Net Income account will be the final gathering place of all the profits and losses for the period under review from the various income accounts representing different activities.

The terms suggested for use are thus confined to the following:

(1) Manufacturing account, **or**
   Trading account, or
   Business account

(2) Income account

(3) Net Income account

(4) Profit and Loss account (frequently called "Surplus")

The term "Surplus," which is in quite common use, is better confined to the surplus of assets over liabilities, made up, as shown in the *pro forma* balance sheet, of appropriations for various purposes as well as of the balance of undistributed profit and loss.

Of the remaining terms at present variously used, "revenue" and "net revenue," are synonymous with "income" and "net income," and are frequently so used, *e. g.,* in accounts of English railways and in Government accounts; it is suggested that they are not required and should be abandoned entirely. "Gross income" and "gross revenue" as names of accounts also should be abandoned as useless, the distinction between income and net income being quite sufficient.

Forms for Statements of Loss and Gain

The various accounts above defined would usually be prepared in debit and credit form. For the better understanding of those interested, summaries of these accounts are frequently prepared in the form of additions and deductions under the general heading of income and profit and loss account; and the following forms will be found suitable for each case, the further details required being given in exhibits.

The forms up to the point where net profits are ascertained will be as follows:

Manufacturing and Merchandising:
        Gross earnings from sales................ $........
            Less—Returns, allowances and discount   ....

        Net earnings from sales................ $........
            Deduct—Cost of production or service   ....

        Gross profit........................... $........
            Deduct—Cost of selling................ $........
                Expenses of management.....   ....
        Net profit from operations.............. $........

Agency and Commission:
        Commissions earned..................... $........
            Deduct—Expenses of management..... $........
                Cost of guarantees...........   ....
        Net profit from operations.............. $........

Transportation:
        Earnings from operations................ $........
            Deduct—Operating expenses........... $........
                Taxes ....
        Net profit from operations or operating
            income .... $........

Banking:
        Earnings from—
            Interest .... $........
            Commissions ....
            Other profits .... $........
            Deduct—Expenses of operation and
                management ....
        Net profit from operations.............. $........

Professional:
        Gross earnings from fees................ $........
            Less—Out-of-pocket expenses included
                therein ....
        Net earnings from fees................. $........
            Deduct—Expenses of operation and
                management ....
        Net profit from operations.............. $........

The form for the remainder of the statement will be the same in all cases, viz.:

```
Net profit from operations............... $........
Other income ...........................  ........ $........
                                                    _____
Deduct—Interest on bonds............. $........
        Other fixed charges...........  ........  ........
                                                    _____
Surplus for the year....................          $........
Extraordinary profits (detailed)..........         ........
Surplus brought forward from preceding
    year ...............................            ........
                                                    _____
                                                  $........
Deduct—Extraordinary charges........              ........
Total surplus available...................        $........
Dividends on stocks.....................           ........
Surplus carried forward.................          $........
```

Items Properly Chargeable to Profit and Loss

There is a tendency to omit from the account which shows the balance of the year and charge to the account of undivided profits items of a special character or even of an ordinary character which may belong properly to a previous period. As the practice of charging to Profit and Loss in preference to income is to be deprecated, unless in exceptional cases, it may be well to state generally what items may properly be so charged, with the inference that everything which does not come within this classification should go to either Income account or Net Income account. Proper charges or credits to Profit and Loss may be defined as follows:

(1) Extraordinary items of receipt or expense not applicable to any particular year, such as profits realized on sales of property, or losses on sales or dismantlement of property, or due to its reconstruction. The loss in this class of cases is closely related to the renewal or depreciation

charges on the same property, which should properly go to the operations of a particular year. Frequently a property is abandoned for purposes of reconstruction, which, if it had not been for such reconstruction, would have remained in service for a long period to come and have been maintained in a perfectly efficient condition at a small fraction only of the loss caused by its abandonment. In such cases it would seem that the proper distribution of the charges between the Income account and Profit and Loss account should be to charge to the Income account so much of the difference between the original cost and the value at the time of abandonment as has not already been provided for through charges to income for depreciation, and to charge the balance—namely, the difference between the depreciated value at the time of abandonment and the scrap value realized—to Profit and Loss account. This is a principle fairly easy of application, which might well be adopted universally.

(2) Discounts and premiums on bonds. Discounts and premiums on bonds are in effect an addition to or deduction from the interest rate paid on the bonds over their life, and as such should strictly be included with interest charges in the net income account by proper instalments each year. In practice, however, it is frequently desired to write off the whole of the discount at as early a date as possible, in preference to carrying it as a deferred and unrealizable asset for a long period of years; no objection can be raised in such a case to providing for the full amount out of the surplus earnings of previous years. It must, however, be remembered that such a course conceals the true rate of interest paid on borrowed money, the latter being a factor of great importance in forming an opinion on the financial condition.

On the other hand, ordinary earnings and expenses of previous years omitted therefrom either by mistake or because they were at that time incapable of ascertainment, should invariably be included in Income account and never in Profit and Loss account. To include them in the latter would preclude that account from disclosing over a period of years the true result of that period; and if in one year charges or credits have been understated it necessarily follows that in some other year they must have been correspondingly overstated.

Nature of Profits

Before turning to the consideration of the important accounting principles involved in the determination of the values of assets and the ascertainment of profits, which form the subject of following chapters, the nature of profits as set forth in the above statements and the legal and general principles involved in their accurate determination may be shortly considered.

In the widest possible view, profits may be stated as the realized increment in value of the whole amount invested in an undertaking; and, conversely, loss is the realized decrement in such value. Inasmuch, however, as the ultimate realization of the original investment is from the nature of things deferred for a long period of years, during which partial realizations are continually taking place, it becomes necessary to fall back on estimates of value at certain definite periods, and to consider as profit or loss the estimated increase or decrease between any two such periods.

Single-Entry Determination of Profits

This method would permit any business concern to revalue periodically the whole of its assets and liabilities, and to record the difference between its surplus so ascertained at the commencement and the end of the year as its profit or loss, respectively; and provided that this estimate were fairly and reasonably made, there would be no objection to such a course. In other words, every appreciation of assets is a profit, and every depreciation a loss; and in many private concerns this method, technically known as "single entry," of ascertaining profits has been regularly adopted for years without bad results.

Corporate Profits

A corporation being endowed by statute with special privileges is subject to special restrictions, among others that of a definite fixed capital stock upon which dividends are declared out of the profits of the undertaking. Hence, the consideration of profits as applied to a corporation involves the consideration also of the limitations placed, either by law or by sound principles of accounting, upon their distribution as dividends. It is in the legal interpretation of the term "profits of a corporation" (which has come to mean profits available for dividends), and in the distinction between the strictly legal and the conservative accounting view of the principles upon which they should be ascertained, that the difficulties of the subject chiefly lie.

Corporate Profits—English Rule

The law, represented mainly by case law, has considerably modified the definition given above; and as up to the present time a larger number of cases have been decided and more definite results arrived at by the English than by the United States courts, it will be useful here to consider briefly the present condition of the English law on the subject. The decisions given there have been based on the principles of common law rather than on statutes relating to corporations, and these decisions are freely quoted in American text books which, though in slightly different form, appear to arrive at substantially the same conclusions. The summaries which follow are given with some hesitation in view of the difficulty of extracting definite principles from a number of more or less conflicting decisions, but they will at any rate serve to illustrate the difficulties which have to be met.

The regulations of a corporation in England formerly provided that no dividends should be paid except out of *profits arising from the business of the corporation,* but in article 97 of the form of Articles of Association given in table A of the Companies (Consolidation) Act, 1908* (which schedule is permissible but not compulsory), the words "arising from the business of the company," which appeared in the original table A of the Companies Act, 1862, are omitted. This change of wording clearly expresses the present law that all profits, however arising, may be distributed as dividends, unless the regulations of the company impose any limitation thereon.

In order to carry on its business a corporation requires certain capital or fixed assets, which must be maintained in a reasonable state of efficiency as long as the business continues; while its profits or losses arise from the employment of its fixed assets in continuously changing the condition of its current or circulating assets from one form to another, and consist of the difference between the realizable values in the final and in the original condition, subject to deduction of the cost of the change and the expenses of realization.

Changes in the value of capital assets are not generally realizable during the continuance of the business, and hence in the determination of profits available for dividend under the above regulation no increment in the value of its capital assets can be considered; but it would seem to be legally permissible to divide among stockholders as dividend a realized profit on the sale of a fixed asset if there were no depreciation on other fixed assets to be made good. On the other hand, it is not necessary to charge trading profits with

*See Appendix II.

any decrement of value not due to causes arising directly out of the business; but any waste of fixed assets taking place in the operation of deriving profits out of the circulating assets must, generally speaking, be made good out of profits. There is, however, a possible exception to this rule when the constitution of the corporation contemplates the investment of its capital in certain specified wasting assets, such for instance as mines, and its regulations do not call for any provision out of profits to replace this waste by means of a sinking fund or otherwise; in such cases the English courts at one time held that there is no legal obligation to charge the waste against profits earned from the operations. The decisions referred to, viz.: Lee v. Neuchatel Asphalte Company and Verner v. General & Commercial Investment Trust, have in the later cases of Dovey v. Corey and Bond v. Barrow Haematite Company been discredited, and the tendency of the courts now appears to be that provision must be made for any assets lost or wasted in the process of earning profits whether they are fixed or circulating. In the last case mentioned the court specifically held that an amount expended in mines, blast furnaces and cottages which were afterwards abandoned must be regarded as circulating capital and made good before dividends could be paid.

In the case of circulating assets the position is clear. The enhancement in the value of these assets being the source of the profits of the business, it is necessary and the law requires that they shall be maintained intact, and that only the surplus realizable in excess of the amount invested is profit; or, conversely, that any deficit is a loss.

The exact distinction between capital and current assets depends necessarily on the nature of the business. What are capital assets for one business may be current assets for another, according as the business of the corporation is to make a profit by using them continuously in their existing shape or by converting them into some other shape. For instance, if a corporation owns investments for the purpose merely of collecting the dividends thereon, and dividing these among its stockholders, it is not legally bound to make good out of profits a fall in the value of the investments. But if its business were to traffic in investments, or if it were in fact trafficking in them, any fall in value would be a loss, and any rise in value a profit, chargeable or creditable to profit and loss.

Apart from the distinction between capital and current assets the following legal principles would seem to be fairly established.

The ascertainment of profit being necessarily a matter of estimate and opinion, all that is required is that the estimates be fairly and honestly made without any fraudulent intention or purpose of deceiving any one, and that they conform to the constitution of the corporation.

The payment of interest to stockholders before any profits have been realized is stated to be "ultra vires"; but interest paid on borrowed capital employed in the construction of works, and in the meantime unproductive, may be properly chargeable to capital account; and by a recent act of Parliament interest may under certain restrictions be paid to stockholders during the period of construction and considered as part of the cost of the property.*

It also seems probable that a corporation having made a loss on the operations of previous years, and commencing the year with a deficit in its circulating capital, may legally distribute dividends to its stockholders out of the current year's profit without making good such deficit. In one recent decision on this point a deficit of previous years is treated as a loss of capital assets, and it is stated that the capital having been lost, a distribution of subsequently earned profits can-

*See Appendix IV.

not be a payment of dividend out of capital that had been previously lost.

Corporate Profits—American Rule

The general law in the United States as laid down in the chief text books is based, to a considerable extent, on the decisions in the English courts.

Dividends can be paid only out of profits, *i .e.*, out of the net increase in the original investment after deducting from the assets all present debts and making provision for future or contingent claims reduced to their present value. But in arriving at this increase the permanent or fixed capital may be valued at the price actually paid for it, although at the time of estimating said increase it could only be sold at a loss. All that is required is that the whole capital originally contributed by the stockholders shall be put into the business and kept there, and that no part of it shall be taken out again directly or indirectly and given back to them. On the other hand, any depreciation due to wear and tear arising out of the use of the fixed assets must be made good out of earnings before the surplus can be applied to the payment of any dividend, unless perhaps these fixed assets are of a wasting nature, such as mines. There seems also to be a consensus of opinion that dividends can only be paid out of the surplus profits derived from the use of the capital of the company for those purposes for which the corporation was constituted.

The statute laws vary in every state, but the above principles seem to apply generally, with the exception of certain classes of business governed by special laws; such as banks, which may not pay dividends out of interest accrued but not received, however well secured, and insurance companies, which may not distribute unearned premiums; and in Connecticut it has been held that if at the time of declaration of a dividend the property is not actually worth the par value of the stock which was issued for it, the dividend is illegal.

Corporate Profits—General Rule

From an accounting standpoint, perhaps the only exception that can be taken to the law as at present interpreted is that there is some doubt as to whether the latter requires the maintenance of wasting fixed assets which are used up by slow degrees in the process of earning profits. On practical, if not on theoretical, grounds, the principle must be accepted that a decrease in value of fixed assets not of a wasting character, arising otherwise than in the process of earning profits, need not be provided for. It is true that in the long run all shrinkage of these assets is a loss, and that no profits can be earned unless the capital, both fixed and circulating, is maintained intact. But the changes in actual values of capital assets due to a lower range of prices, the introduction of improved processes of manufacture, etc., may be so great and at the same time so indefinite, and the actual realization thereof is as a rule deferred to such distant periods, that it becomes quite impracticable to provide for shrinkage in value due to such causes as a direct charge against profits; although it is a prudent course to accumulate a sufficiently large reserve or surplus, and to make such liberal provision for depreciation, as will insure the integrity of the investment and provide ample funds for keeping it continually in the highest state of efficiency.

The sound accounting principles for the determination of profits may be summed up as follows:

(1) All waste, both of fixed and circulating assets, incident to the process of earning profits by the conversion of circulating assets must be made good out of the profits earned.

(2) Profits realized on sales of fixed assets should be

first applied to make good estimated depreciation (if any) in other fixed assets not resulting from the ordinary conduct of the business. If there is no such depreciation, such profits may be distributed as dividends, but should be distinguished from the operating profits.

(3) A sufficient surplus should be accumulated (in addition to the provisions required to maintain wasting capital assets) for the purpose of making good losses due to shrinkage in values of fixed assets arising from causes other than the ordinary operations of the company. This provision must, however, be considered more a question of policy than a requirement of sound accounting.

These principles are best illustrated by a practical consideration of the different elements which enter into the determination of profits from the viewpoint of the maintenance of assets, and a discussion of the principles of valuation which should be adopted for the various assets and liabilities in the balance sheet, and of the effect which each would have on the profits. If the balance sheets at the beginning and end of a period are theoretically and practically accurate, and show the true financial position at those dates, the increase or decrease of the surplus, after allowing for distributions of profit during the interval, represents the true profit or loss for the period, subject always to the factor of "estimate" necessarily present in the valuation of assets and liabilities.

The detailed consideration on these lines of all the elements which must be taken into consideration in determining profits from an accounting standpoint will be taken up in the following chapters.

CHAPTER IV

BALANCE SHEET ASSETS

I. CAPITAL ASSETS

(1) Fixed Property

In the second chapter the following distribution was given of fixed assets, viz.:

Land and improvements thereon, including mineral rights and development thereof.

Buildings and structures.

Plant, machinery and fixed tools, permanent way of a railroad, etc.

Movable equipment.

Furniture and fixtures.

Patterns, drawings, dies, etc.

Patents, goodwill, franchises, etc.

These subheadings are sufficient to give a clear description of the nature of all expenditures upon fixed assets for the purposes of a balance sheet, although in the books of account themselves considerably more detail will be found necessary.

In the correct determination of the amounts to be carried under any of these headings, it is necessary to insure that the expenditures included are such as may be properly treated as additions to the assets; that none are included which should properly be deemed renewals or replacements of existing facilities, and that full provision has been made for all expenditures necessary to prevent or make good depreciation due to wear and tear, obsolescence or other causes.

In the first place it is desirable to consider with some care what are the various items of property comprised in each of these captions.

Land and Improvements

Land and its improvements represent either the ownership in fee or the enjoyment under lease of real estate. Here at once arises a distinction of vital importance, in that in the former case the valuable life of the expenditures is coterminous with the life of the improvement, while in the latter it is limited to a term of years either more or less than that life. Improvements will consist of all expenditures of any kind that add a long term or permanent value, such as levelling off for foundations for structures; filling in swamp, or shallow water lands to make them serviceable; stripping off surface, sinking shafts or driving tunnels to make minerals available; care and upkeep of growing trees; construction of embankments, cuttings, tunnels, etc., for the permanent way of a railroad; generally anything which alters the shape or condition of the land or effects a permanent change in it and adds value. With the exception of mining expenditures and those upon growing timber, these expenditures are not subject to depreciation by wear and tear, although they may be subject to provision for obsolescence or abandonment.

Expenditures upon development of mines and those upon the planting and care of timber must be considered specially with regard to the life of the property in respect of which they are incurred. Those upon mines must follow the rules laid down for the minerals dependent upon them which are discussed in Chapter VII; with the proviso that if their life is less than the term over which the exhaustion of minerals dependent thereon would extend, they must be written off in the shorter period. Expenditures upon growing timber are directly reflected in its increased size and consequent relative value, though owing to market conditions the actual value of the timber itself may be so reduced as to offset or even more than offset the expenditures. In such cases it would not be safe to continue adding the expenditures to capital account unless there is a fair certainty that the ultimate value when sold will at least cover the whole of the original cost, subsequent expenditures on care and upkeep and cost of marketing.

Both mines and timber are subject to special risks of considerable magnitude, such as fires and floods, which may in a short period result in partial or even entire destruction. Such catastrophes can hardly be foreseen, and when they arise must usually by force of circumstances be dealt with as losses of capital which can only be guarded against financially by the creation of substantial reserves out of profits previously earned.

Buildings and Structures

Buildings and structures will include the cost of buildings erected for the purpose of housing people, animals or property of any kind; such structures have a long but terminable life and are therefore subject to regular depreciation.

Plant, Machinery and Fixed Tools

Plant, machinery and fixed tools include all the permanent facilities required and directly used in any activity; which are fixed and immovable as long as they are in use and yet have to be continuously kept up and replaced from time to time. All this class of asset is subject to depreciation not only for wear and tear but for obsolescence.

Movable Equipment

Movable equipment consists of all the varying articles the position of which is not fixed but which are continuously moved from place to place according to demands for their use. From their nature they are subject to frequent replacement both for wear and tear and loss, while the factor of obsolescence hardly exists. In many cases, in lieu of providing for depreciation, they are treated as working assets, all expenditures, including the amount necessary to reduce the balance to an inventory value, being written off to cost of operations.

Furniture and Fixtures

The item of furniture and fixtures is almost self-explanatory, consisting of furniture in the ordinary sense, machines for clerical use, gas and electric light fittings and other items of a similar nature. The asset is worth comparatively little when its use is abandoned, and yet has a fairly long life while it is in use. It is usual to write this asset down to a breakup or nominal value, although a smaller provision is frequently made.

Patterns, Drawings, Dies, etc.

Patterns, drawings, dies, etc., are also self-explanatory and are stated separately because their value as an asset is very difficult of ascertainment; and in fact frequently merges into the last item of goodwill. While their use is continued they are worth their cost, but as soon as by changes in design they cease to be used, they are worth little or nothing; and yet they are an asset which every manufacturing business must have and which frequently represents large original expenditures.

As to all these items it may be stated generally that it is not usual for a corporation to take credit for a surplus, nor on the other hand is it necessary for it to charge itself with a loss arising out of a revaluation as long as the property valued is in actual use for the purposes of the business; but here it should be noted that if the business includes among its objects the purchase and sale of assets of this class, they should then be considered not as fixed but as current or circulating assets, being in fact stock in trade, the turning over of which is expected to result in profits or losses to the company. The fixed assets now under consideration are those which during the life of the business will remain, whether in their present or some other shape, in a permanent condition, provided that due provision is made for wear and tear or other waste due to operations.

Patents, Goodwill and Franchises

The remaining items, patents, goodwill and franchises, are very much akin to one another. Theoretically it would seem that if a patent be granted for a term of years, the amount paid for it should be written off against the profits earned during those years. But practically it is found that by the time the original patent has expired the owner may have built up a virtual monopoly, or at any rate such a lucrative business that the original cost of the patent is now replaced by the reasonable value of the goodwill. Moreover, it is seldom the case that one patent stands by itself; during its life probably many others have been taken out, representing modifications which extend the life of the original in an improved form, and these may have cost small sums as compared with the very much larger cost of the original.

Goodwill represents the value of the trade-name, business connection and organization of the undertaking. As long as the earnings of the business are maintainable at not less than the level contemplated at date of purchase, it is impossible to allege any depreciation of value or the necessity of any provision therefor. On the other hand, if any serious depreciation has taken place, the profits are probably so much reduced that it is not practicable to make such provision. Goodwill is in fact a fixed asset whose value is to some extent dependent upon the profits earned, its fluctuations being consequent upon and not a cause of the earning of profits, as are wasting or partially wasting assets, and not therefore to be taken into account in ascertaining them.

Franchises may be either perpetual or for a fixed term. In the former case, the same considerations would apply as in the case of goodwill. In the latter case, they may be renewed or terminated at the expiry of the fixed term, and prudence would dictate a reasonable provision each year by a charge to Profit and Loss account, although no definite amount may be ascertainable.

Provided, therefore, that the wise policy is followed of writing off at once all expenditure on new patents which do not turn out useful, or which supersede or modify older ones, and provided also that the principle is admitted of building up a substantial reserve fund against whatever portion of the capital is invested in this class of assets, it would seem reasonable to merge the three items into one and treat them as part of the permanent invested capital of the business, which may be left to continue at its original value as long as the business is a going concern.

Changes in Value of Capital Assets

It is necessary to recognize that there are causes at work, particularly in young and growing communities, which may render a statement prepared on the basis of cost of capital assets misleading and even prejudicial to the proper interests of present owners. Over a period of years changes in value due to rise or fall in prices may be sufficiently permanent to render it unfair to one business to maintain original cost values as compared with another whose assets have been created at widely varying costs. Moreover, even where constructed works may have fallen in value owing to depreciation or obsolescence which has not been provided for, there may be an offsetting increase in the values of land and its subsoil or other natural products due to the development of the community and consequent largely increased demand. It is true that from the point of view of earnings such increment can not be taken as in any way a proper offset to losses due to wear and tear, depreciation or obsolescence; but this does not alter the fact that in spite of an insufficient provision for depreciation on some assets, there may be an actual increase on the total value of all assets. In fact, there are well-known cases in which by far the larger part of the ultimate profits of a corporation over a long series of years has been due not to the results of its activities but to the large unearned increment on its capital assets. This condition must be recognized and is frequently met by means of careful appraisals of all properties, the resulting increase (or possibly decrease) being taken up as a special credit or debit to Profit and Loss account (or Surplus) and shown as entirely distinct from the operating results.

In the case, too, of the sale of a portion of the capital assets it may be entirely legitimate to take up any profit just as it may be necessary to provide for a loss. This may be done by means of an appraisal of the portion of the property remaining unsold, the difference between this figure and the book figure, after deduction of the sale price of the portion sold, being treated as the estimated profit or loss arising on the sale and appraisal. This being divided proportionately to the sale and appraisal figures, the former will represent the approximate profit or loss on the sale. It is undoubtedly more conservative to treat profits so arising as a capital reserve available to meet possible losses from further sales or ultimate realization, while losses if clearly ascertained would be written off either at once against past surplus or by instalments against future earnings. There are, however, cases in which a surplus exists beyond all reasonable doubt and no objection can be taken to treating at any rate a substantial portion thereof as realized and divisible. It is always difficult to come to a decision as to the best treatment in cases of this kind; as in many others, each must be considered on its merits, with due regard to safety in finance and justice to the varying interests of present and future owners.

In any case in which such a surplus on revaluation is credited to Profit and Loss account (or Surplus) it is most important that the amount be clearly distinguished from earnings from operations, with a full description of its nature.

(2) PERMANENT INVESTMENTS

This class of investment, which in the form of balance sheet submitted in Chapter II is considered as part of the fixed assets, may be generally defined as investments which control some essential part of the activities carried on. They may consist of actual ownership of stocks or bonds, interest in a partnership, or advances by way of loan or on current account to affiliated undertakings. The distinction between these and marketable investments, which latter are included among current assets, is that the former cannot be sold without in some way affecting the activities of the owner, while the latter representing merely the temporary deposit of surplus working capital can be disposed of at any time without in any way affecting such activities. The distinction is a most important one and has an equally important bearing on the financial position of an undertaking by reason of the fact that the investment in the former class of a portion of the current assets withdraws those assets from the general use of the business and prevents their use for the purpose for which current assets are intended, viz.: the conversion as rapidly as may be from cash into products for sale and so back into cash again. The conversion of any part into assets of a permanent nature diminishes the current assets and can only be offset either by reducing operations or increasing liabilities, unless of course the current assets are in the first instance more than sufficient for all needs. If permanent investments are included in current assets, it is impossible to get a clear view of the facts.

The ease of conversion of investments into cash is not the sole test that should be employed in distinguishing between permanent and marketable investments, the possibility of conversion without diminishing or hampering the business activities of the owner being an even more important one. The following instances of permanent investments will perhaps better elucidate this point.

Investments for Purposes of Control

The first class would include those held for the purpose of controlling the operations of another business and may consist of any interest therein which carries a majority vote; or even the whole interest with the exception in the case of a corporation of the few shares necessary to constitute a sufficient number of shareholders.

Where the interest owned is the whole, or substantially the whole, the best treatment is to consolidate the balance sheets of all such interests with that of the owner in the form known as a consolidated balance sheet, in which the assets and liabilities of all are aggregated under their proper headings, and the particular asset of "permanent investments," so far as those interests are concerned, disappears. This method which avoids many awkward questions is dealt with in some detail in Chapter VIII.

When the interest owned is less than a substantial whole but still a controlling interest, this treatment should not be adopted but the investment should then be treated as an asset. The controlling factor in its valuation is the actual cost which must be assumed to be the result of a bargain. Subsequent changes in this value, apart from additions to or withdrawals of the capital invested, will be due either to profits or losses made in its operations or to appreciation or depreciation of its assets due to other causes. The proportion of the former corresponding to the interest owned should always be taken up in the Income account of the owner; and this is best done by adding to or deducting from the investment the amount of such profits and losses and crediting or debiting the same to Income account. The argument in favor of this course is that the investment itself from an operating point of view is better or worse than at the commencement of the period by the profit or loss made. If dividends are subsequently declared and paid, they will be credited not to Income account but to the investment account for the reason that the investment itself is worth so much less on account of the assets thus withdrawn. Appreciation or depreciation due to causes other than operation should be treated exactly as in the case of that of other fixed assets already discussed; the data for such being obtained from a critical investigation of the property and other assets and of the liabilities of the particular sub-interest. The reason for adding profits to the investments instead of treating them as a current asset, is that there is no possibility of receiving them as profits until a dividend is declared; and further that for good reasons these profits may be employed in the extension of the business of the subinterest, leaving no current assets available 'for the declaration of a dividend.

Investments Controlling Facilities or Output

The second class of permanent investment would include those which are held to secure some portion of the output of the subinterest or other facilities, such as through routing of traffic of a railroad, which it is necessary for the owner to possess. The ownership in such cases may be only a small proportion of the total capital of the subinterest and may be readily saleable at any time to other owners or to outsiders; but its sale would cut off important connections and therefore interfere to a measurable degree with the owner's activities and for this reason it will, unless some change of policy takes place, be held permanently and not sold. It would clearly be misleading to treat such investments as current assets and in most cases they may be valued at cost rather than at market value. Full consideration is required of all the surrounding conditions in each case, and if there is reasonable doubt as to cost representing the present value of the facilities or connections which the investment controls, then proper reserves should be made. It frequently happens that no profits are made by such subinterests, the products being shared in proportion to the respective ownerships and charged to them at a price to exactly cover cost and fixed charges.

Minor Investments

The third class would consist of small interests owned for various business purposes. Such investments are in the ordinary sense "marketable," but for the very reason for which they are owned will not be marketed unless a change of policy occurs; therefore they should be treated as permanent. The rule for treatment of dividends and values would be the same as for marketable investments, although no great objection could be taken to carrying them at cost until realized.

Non-Income Producing Investments

The fourth class would consist of interests owned purely for business purposes but not producing income, such as stock exchange and board of trade memberships, and deposits with governments which must be maintained as long as the business is conducted on the same lines. These are usually of fixed cash values and have no dividends or other income accruing, except possibly interest on deposits, which would in the ordinary course be credited direct to Income subaccount. No special question arises in connection with such investments.

Advances

The fifth class would consist of advances made for the purpose of acquiring or constructing additional properties, the ultimate ownership of which is uncertain. They may eventually be absorbed entirely by the owner; they may be turned over to a separate corporation of which he will own the stock, and the outlays may be repaid out of proceeds of bonds issued by such corporation; they may become joint ownerships of some kind, or they may be finally disposed of altogether. Such advances are usually found in the first instance buried among accounts receivable, but it is evident that this is not a proper place for them, as whatever final disposition is made they remain a suspended asset for the time, generally considerable, necessary to complete the matter. They should be eliminated entirely from current assets and carried in permanent investments, or a subheading thereof denoted "advances," until such time as they are again converted into a liquid form. Frequently interest is added to such investments during the time they are carried and this course may or may not be legitimate according to the circumstances. In the case in which they represent actual new construction the rules as to the disposition of this interest are the same as in the case of any other capital asset; but if the advances are made to an operating property whose earnings are not sufficient to meet the interest, the amount so added should be carried to a credit suspense account until such time as it is earned and not to the credit of Income account where if earned it would naturally find a place. In the meantime, in preparing the balance sheet this credit suspense account should be treated as a reserve against the investment and deducted therefrom. All such advance accounts require continual supervision to insure that they are alive and represent property, and are not mere depositories for losses or expenditures which are of no permanent value and should be written off as incurred.

(3) INVESTMENT OF RESERVES

It is a common practice to make special investment of the funds set aside for the different voluntary reserves included under the main heading of surplus. As the variation in the value of the investments affects only the reserves themselves, and losses or profits can not be definitely ascertained until the reserves are required and the investments sold, it is common to maintain these investments at cost, ignoring any appreciation or depreciation. Provided that the fluctuations in value are of a temporary nature and of small relative amount, no objection need be taken to this proceeding; but any material or permanent change in value ought to be reflected in an adjustment both of the reserve and the investment.

Another question arises where these reserves, as is frequently the case, are invested in the securities, either stocks or bonds, of the corporation itself. There seems no reason to depart from the principle laid down for ordinary investments of the corporation (Chapter VI) that any investments of this nature should be eliminated both from the asset "Investment of Reserves" and from the liability on the particular class of security. The contrary treatment is frequently adopted on the ground that these investments are readily saleable and therefore immediately convertible into cash when required. It is impossible, however, to ignore the fact that until such sale is made the reserves are actually invested not in outside securities but in the undertaking and business of the corporation. This may be good or bad policy according to the facts or conditions, but it does not seem correct to maintain the fiction of an outside investment under such circumstances. It may easily be that when the reserves are most urgently required by reason of some sudden disaster these securities may be saleable only at a very heavy depreciation or even entirely unsaleable.

Generally, therefore, it may be said that "Investment of Reserves" should include only outside investments, with the addition to the heading of some such phrase as "In addition to . . . . bonds or stock of the corporation of a par value of $. . . . . . ."

II. WORKING ASSETS

Working assets are grouped under the following captions:

Stores and supplies for use in operations.

Money in hands of agents for business purposes.

Insurance, interest, taxes, royalties, etc., paid in advance of the period over which they accrue.

Working assets, as already stated, are those which are consumed in the activities carried on without themselves forming an integral part of the products. It follows that no questions of profit or loss should be involved in the ascertainment of their proper values except such as arise from changes of value due to fluctuations in prices or to depreciation. On the other hand, the quantities and money values are continually changing and must therefore be accurately determined whenever a balance sheet is prepared.

(1) STORES AND SUPPLIES

In any good system of bookkeeping, accounts will be kept for all the items included in the last two groups, and frequently also there will be a book account for Stores and Supplies; when no such account is kept an inventory of the latter must be taken. This inventory requires:

(1) An accurate determination of the quantities on hand, which involves no important question.

(2) A determination of the price at which the quantities shall be valued.

(3) A sufficient allowance for depreciation in value due to age, deterioration or obsolescence.

The price would in the ordinary course be the actual cost of purchase, which would also be the value at which the consumption would be charged to costs of operation in the future. This price, however, would be subject to adjustment if the market value had fallen below cost, although any adjustment in this respect is in the nature of a reserve in favor of the cost of production in the next period and is not a factor in the cost of production of the past. Such reserves should be made, therefore, specifically out of net profits, and actual cost maintained on the books and used in subsequent operation; the reserve being credited back to Income account in the succeeding period.

It is very important that reserves be made for unusable or damaged stock, preferably by a direct charge into costs, as deterioration of such character is an incident of production or operation. It is further important as a matter of economy of operation that the stocks carried be not allowed to accumulate beyond the needs of the business, as such accumulation is bound to lead to waste and loss by deterioration or otherwise. Such accumulations are frequently evidence of carelessness or even dishonesty on the part of those responsible.

(2) ADVANCES TO AGENTS

The caption of "Advances to Agents" should include all cash items or the equivalent which are permanently or temporarily locked up for business purposes and are not free cash; such as balances left in hands of agents for special purposes, which are in process of being spent and will not be accounted for until the purpose is accomplished; or deposits made in connection with bids made or contracts undertaken. These would all be entered at their book value subject to any known loss or depreciation. It is desirable that each of these items shall be cleared at a balance sheet period and the book balance adjusted to an actual asset value after writing off any portion that may have been expended. This practice should be adopted wherever practicable, but there are many cases where either the work involved would not justify the result or where for other reasons such a course is inconvenient. Provided that the accounts are all carefully scrutinized at short intervals and always at a balance sheet period, all known adjustments made and no accumulation of unexplained balances allowed, practical accuracy is obtained by leaving the remainder temporarily unadjusted and including them under this caption in the balance sheet. Such accounts being in the nature of suspense accounts, always require very special attention for the reason that they may if neglected become a receptacle for improper or fraudulent entries which might remain for a long time undiscovered. Independent evidence of the existence and character of the accounts, in the form of certificates or correspondence, is nearly always available and should be in the possession of those in charge of the accounts.

(3) Expenses Incurred in Advance of Accrual

The third class of items strictly consists of expenses which have been incurred in advance of accrual; they are treated as assets for the purpose of keeping the transactions of each period separate, and because they are to be met out of the profits on future operations. They will consist either of expenses paid in advance of due or accruing dates, or of those which are due and accrued but relate to operations not yet completed, although not part of the direct cost of such operations nor of the value of the resulting products.

It will be found in the next chapter that merchandise on hand should be valued at cost of production, not including cost of sale. There are, however, special cases in which it may be fair and reasonable to carry forward some proportion of selling expenses incurred to a subsequent period in which the results therefrom are expected. Thus the cost of advertising a newly started business may frequently be largely in excess of any immediate results expected or realized, and it may be desired to carry forward a proportion of such expenses as a charge against the results of subsequent periods. Interest or other charges incurred in carrying assets of any kind that require time for their full development and conversion into a shape in which they can be sold; charges incurred on account of operations pending and not completed, and the profit or loss upon which can not at the moment be ascertained, such as uncompleted voyages of ships; royalties paid in excess of mineral worked and recoverable out of any excess worked in future years over the minimum; these and many other similar items find their natural place in this category. In every case the greatest care is necessary to see that all items so carried forward are not only reasonable but safe, in that at least the amount carried forward will be recovered or provided for within a reasonable period.

The item of royalties deserves special consideration. It is a frequent custom to provide for the payment of a royalty based on the tonnage produced but with a fixed minimum payment. In the early years of development it may well happen that the tonnage mined is not equal to the minimum upon which royalties are payable, and provision is often contained in the lease that the excess royalty so paid may be set off against that due on tonnage worked in excess of the minimum in subsequent years. The value of this excess royalty paid will depend upon the quantity of workable mineral, the term of the lease, and the probable annual production; and unless there is a reasonable probability of working a tonnage in excess of the minimum during a sufficient number of years before the expiry of the lease to offset the shortages in earlier years, no value can be attached to the asset.

It is hardly practicable to lay down any specific principles upon which the assets which may be included under this caption should be valued. Each case must be considered on its merits and with regard to its reasonable and, above all, safe value, so that the risk of carrying an item at a value which can not ultimately be realized or provided for out of the margin of profits to be realized in the contemplated operations, may as far as possible be eliminated.

CHAPTER V

BALANCE SHEET ASSETS (Continued)

III. CURRENT ASSETS

(1) Stocks on Hand.   (Materials carried for sale or conversion, and products partly or wholly manufactured intended for sale.)

The enumeration and valuation of stocks on hand is a matter of considerable difficulty and involves many important questions.

Profits can only be made out of the sale or exchange of one commodity for another of a definite and realizable cash value.   The mere increase in the market value of an article which is not actually sold, can not be considered as a profit; for the reason that the article may never be sold at that price, and the paper profit may never be realized.   The object of the Profit and Loss account of a manufacturing or merchandising concern is to ascertain as closely as possible the profits which have been realized on sales actually made; and for this reason raw materials on hand, and products partly or wholly manufactured, but not sold, should be entirely eliminated.   In practice this result is obtained by valuing them at cost, no more and no less, and so exactly offsetting the charges to Manufacturing account for materials, labor and expenses, in so far as the result of their combination in manufacturing processes is still uncompleted and unsold.

On the other hand, a balance sheet is required to show the true financial position as a going concern. The inventory at actual cost may represent more or less than the market value, and, therefore, overstate or understate the assets; but to change the valuation would be to take up a profit or provide for a loss which might never be realized owing to subsequent changes in the market value. Sound commercial principles require that no credit be taken for profits until they are realized; but further, that if there is any possibility that what remains unsold may not realize its cost, a proportion of the realized profits on sales which have been made, should be carried forward to cover these possible losses. It is accordingly generally recognized as a correct accounting principle that if the cost value of the inventory exceeds the market value, a reserve should be created to bring it down to the latter value, while, on the other hand, if the market value exceeds the cost, no credit should be taken for the profits until they are realized by an actual sale. This rule is of considerable importance where the inventories at the end of successive years show a progressive increase. If they be valued above cost, profits are shown in each year, which are an anticipation of those of succeeding years, and a large asset is created which, on a subsequent fall in market prices, may prove unrealizable.

It should be noted that it is not essential, and in fact it would frequently be incorrect, to value materials and products on hand at the end of the fiscal period upon the same price basis as at the commencement of that period; all that is necessary or proper is that the basis of valuation—that is to say, the principles on which the values are arrived at—should be the same at the beginning and end of the period, the actual prices usually varying from one year to another. Unfortunately, in practice, many concerns are unable to ascertain the cost of their various products, with the result that their stock valuations are based entirely on estimates of costs made with more or less accuracy. There does not appear to be any legal obligation on a corporation to adopt any particular basis, provided that the price adopted is not in excess of that ultimately realized after deduction of any subsequent cost of completion, storage and sale; but the absence of knowledge as to the approximate cost not infrequently leads to disappointment to the owners, and even to serious financial loss. It is obvious that a constantly changing basis of cost must lead to serious inequalities in the profits shown between one period and another, but it is not equally obvious that an erroneous basis of valuation consistently adopted year after year, even if that basis be a conservative one and really below true cost, may result in large and unexpected discrepancies between the profits shown in different periods. For instance, if stocks be valued on a basis exceeding cost, and if the trade, and consequently the materials and products on hand, increase very rapidly for one or more years, the profits during those years of increase will be abnormally inflated; but when the trade settles down to a comparatively steady turnover, there will be a considerable drop in the profits as compared with the preceding year on the same amount of business done—a drop which the management as a rule will be unable to account for until an investigation discloses the true cause; viz., the cessation of the annual increase in materials and products on hand. On the other hand, if the stocks be conservatively valued considerably below cost, the profits of a year in which a small quantity of goods is carried over at the close of the year in comparison with the beginning, will be inflated as compared with a succeeding year, when an opposite condition prevailed, although the sales and profit thereon may have been the same in both years; thus entirely upsetting all the calculations and estimates of the managers.

Essentials for Ascertaining Correct Profits

The essentials for ascertaining correct profits so far as stocks on hand are concerned are:

(a) An accurate enumeration of the quantities on hand.

(b) An accurate ascertainment of the actual cost of the different manufactured articles, either completed or in progress.

(c) Accurate clerical work in calculating from (a) and (b) the money values.

(d) A specific reduction in the prices of raw materials and manufactured products of the amount by which the market valuations at the close of the fiscal period fell short of the cost.

(e) A proper provision for all stock which is old or depreciated or for any reason likely to be unsaleable.

The more exactly these different elements are ascertained, the more accurate will be the resulting statements of profits, and if the special reserves under (d) and (e) be made separately, it will be an easy matter usefully to compare one period with another.

Taking the Inventory

An accurate enumeration of quantities on hand is the most important of these elements, and is frequently a matter of much difficulty by reason of the necessity of making it as of a fixed common date for the whole stock. Where a plant can be closed down for such period as is necessary to take the inventory, this difficulty is largely eliminated; and it is entirely eliminated where running book inventories are maintained, which can be checked up with and adjusted to the actual quantity on hand at any time, within say twelve months, that the stock of each class is lowest.

In taking an actual count as of a particular date it is as

a rule impossible to make the count on that day, and the work must extend over a longer period. For this purpose it is necessary to keep careful record of everything coming in or going out from each class of commodity from the time it is counted until the final inventory date inclusive. It is also necessary to note on the original sheets any old, obsolete or damaged stock upon which reduced values should be placed. The ease and accuracy with which such a count can be made, will depend greatly upon the laying out of a systematic plan beforehand by which duplication can be prevented; incoming stock segregated until the count is completed; and outgoing stock selected as far as possible from that which has not yet been enumerated. Furthermore, the enumeration will be much easier in well-ordered stockrooms than in those in which no method prevails; and much time at stocktaking periods can be saved by arranging the storerooms with this among other objects in view.

When all possible counting and weighing has been done there will frequently remain certain important classes which can only be ascertained on an estimated basis, and for which, therefore, it is desirable that book inventories be kept even if these are not a part of the regular system of accounting. The quantities of bulk material such as ore, coal, coke, pig iron, logs and similar articles are always difficult of ascertainment as they are usually from their nature stored in irregular piles, the apparent contents of which will be affected by moisture or by irregularities in or sinking of the ground surface upon which they are stored. Measurements made under such conditions can hardly be more than an approximation to the true figure; although a sufficient degree of accuracy may be generally obtained if the estimates are made by two qualified persons independently of each other. It is important too that a limit should be placed upon the size or extent of the piles in which bulk materials are stored, so that by keeping even a rough account of the quantities put in and taken out from the time the pile is started until it is completely used up, a check can be had upon the accuracy of the quantities at comparatively short intervals; and the piles should not be too large, so that each may be worked out within some reasonable period.

The enumeration and valuation of unsawn logs present peculiarly difficult problems when, as is usual, they are floated down rivers or waterways to their destination at saw mills, pulp mills or storage points. The cut of a season in the woods can be measured with a fair degree of accuracy, particularly as the payments made for labor are often based on these measurements. It is seldom, however, that the whole cut of a season will run down the waterways during the period of high water, much remaining to come down in the following season from the cut of which it cannot be distinguished. There will also be some loss of logs which may be held up by obstructions at various points until they are partially or wholly damaged; and the breaking of a boom at a storage point due to flood or other causes, or the stranding of logs in inaccessible positions at periods of unusually high water may entail at times even serious losses; and to these may be added losses by fires in the forests after logs are cut and stacked. It is usual at intervals of several years to have what is known as a clean-up in the waterways, when a good many supposedly lost logs may be recovered, but even allowing for this, losses must occur which are difficult to estimate and can only be provided for by reserves based on experience in other cases. There is a natural tendency on the part of operating officials to underestimate such possible losses which in itself renders the creation of adequate reserves not only more difficult but more important.

Work in progress is another class involving special difficulties which can often only be satisfactorily overcome by keeping approximate accounts of the labor and material put in, and the finished products taken out, taking care at the same time that a proper allowance is made for wasted material, of which there must necessarily be some percentage.

Scrap material in theory can be weighed, but its quantity, weight and shape frequently preclude any such course and no really satisfactory method has yet been devised for arriving at the quantity on hand with any close degree of accuracy. The best method is to keep a book inventory of the scrap weighed out from the shop into the yard; to store the same in separate piles or in separate locations, and weigh out deliveries; so, by keeping a separate book account of each pile, to prove the quantities up as they are exhausted. A liberal deduction is required in any estimate of scrap stock to provide against possible overvaluation.

Cost Accounting

The importance of a valuation at cost emphasizes the necessity of such a system of accounting as will enable cost to be accurately ascertained and makes desirable at this point an outline of the principal points involved. The theory of cost accounting, which is fully discussed in Chapter IX, is merely an elaboration of ordinary bookkeeping, and its difficulty lies almost entirely in a correct ascertainment of the elements that enter into it. There is no theoretical difficulty in keeping a record of the number of hours, human and machine, and the quantity of material that enter into any process of manufacture; but practical difficulties arise from the large number of items involved, the chances of error in the tabulation of hours worked and quantities consumed, loss of weight in process and many other minor points, coupled with the necessity of an economical operation of the cost accounting system.

Even when the actual quantities of material and number of hours worked in the direct processes of manufacture are known, there are many other expenses which cannot be allocated to any particular operation and yet are essential to all operations, such as power, light, heat, taxes, insurance, clerical and general supervision; and the determination of the proportion in which these expenses should be distributed to the different processes is a problem which is incapable of an absolutely accurate solution. Almost every business differs in this respect, and various methods are adopted for arriving at an approximation to the result. The essentials are that the total amount absorbed in the cost over any period should not materially exceed, nor fall short of, the total of all such expenses incurred during that period; and that the method of distribution, once settled, should be consistently maintained regardless of the effect on the operations, unless and until a more accurate method can be substituted therefor.

Distribution of Expense Burden

The following are some of the methods most often used for apportioning these charges, which are generally described as "overhead expense," "burden" or "dead expense."

(a) They are apportioned each month in total over all the direct cost accounts, either in proportion to labor, or to labor and material, or to material only, or partly on one of those bases and partly on another, according to the nature of the expense.

One objection to this method is that departments that are more fully occupied are made to bear the expense of those not fully occupied or even not occupied at all, thus producing considerable inequalities between the results of any one department in different periods; and perhaps even showing losses on some one department which are usually attributable not to that department at all, but to the partial or total closing down of some other one.

(b) They are carefully allocated in the first instance between separate departments on the basis of one or more of the factors of space occupied, normal possible output, or normal quantity of power required, and then in each department prorated in proportion to labor and material costs as in (a).

This is a more accurate method in theory, and eliminates the error of charging one department with the results of slackness of work in others. It is more difficult to carry out in practice, and involves a good many assumptions in obtaining the division between departments. It is also still open to the objection that there is considerable fluctuation in the incidence of overhead expense between busy and slack periods, and costs are shown as higher in the latter than in the former.

(c) In machine shops the overhead expense is frequently apportioned over machine hours worked, each machine having a rating ascertained by experiment.

(d) As a result of careful estimates, certain fixed percentage rates on labor, or material, or both, based on a normal average output, are adopted.

In both of the last two methods the rates are at first independent of the actual expenses. The amounts added to costs are credited to certain accounts to which all expenses covered by that rate are charged, and the two should on an average approximately agree. If the difference accumulates, it is due either to errors in the rates which would have to be adjusted, or to an extra busy or extra slack period of operations. Such contingencies should be provided for by including in the burden a reserve based on experience, which, with the addition of the excess provision accumulating in busy periods, would suffice to meet the deficits due to slack periods. These methods would appear to be better in every way than the first two, as discrepancies in costs due to circumstances not in fact pertinent to the output are avoided and periods varying from the normal are regularly provided for.

All the methods here outlined involve much thought and skill in determining the proper classification of expense accounts and their effect on various parts of the operations.

Allocation of Expenses

A further difficulty lies in the fact that it is not always possible to draw a hard and fast dividing line between expenses directly chargeable to manufacture and expenses not so chargeable. There are expenses of supervision and bookkeeping, and general expenses, which cannot be specifically divided between the different departments of manufacture, sale, collection, and general management. The expense of the first department only would enter into the cost of manufacture, while that of the second and third would be chargeable only against the gross profits resulting from the sales, and that of the fourth would be chargeable against the profits of the whole undertaking.

A thorough understanding of the business, a careful analysis and apportionment of the duties of individuals, and a general knowledge of the manner in which each item of expense affects the different departments are necessary to arrive at even an approximate division, and at best the basis adopted is somewhat arbitrary.

Selling Expenses as Part of Manufacturing Cost

It is legitimate, though not usual, to take into account a proportion of the selling expenses as part of the value of the stock on hand when those goods are sold in advance of manufacture. Even then there always remain expenses of delivery and for miscellaneous purposes to be incurred on or before completion, and it is generally considered more conservative to allow the profits realized on goods sold and delivered to pay for all selling expenses, and to ignore those that may perhaps apply to deliveries not made. There are, however, exceptions to this usually salutary rule which depend on special conditions and must be considered each on its merits as they arise. When it can be clearly seen that expenses not appertaining to cost of manufacture have been incurred specifically upon certain classes of goods which for good and proper reasons have not been delivered, no valid objection can be raised to carrying forward these expenses as part of the cost for inventory purposes.

Status of Interest

The question continually arises whether interest in any form should be considered as part of the cost of manufacture. It is true that manufacture takes time and involves the lock-up of money for certain periods, and that this money for those periods should be earning interest. On the other hand, it must be remembered that interest is only one form of profit, that the object of any business is to earn profit, and that each operation, as well as each department, is only one in a series, none of which is complete in itself, and the whole of which is necessary to the complete process of manufacture and sale out of which alone can any profit be earned. To charge interest into costs is in effect to add to those costs a certain amount of profit before it has been made, and is, therefore, against sound commercial and accounting principles. It is sometimes claimed that as interest on loan capital, from the point of view of the owner of the business, is an expense, it therefore should be treated as part of the cost of manufacture; but this contention loses sight of the fact that such capital is raised for the purpose of conducting the business, and is remunerated by a strictly defined share of the profits earned in that business. It is true that interest is usually payable whether there are profits earned or not, but it is merely one of the incidental conditions of the loan that the lender is to be paid his share of profits at regular dates, and frequently in advance of any such profits being earned. This subject is considered at greater length in Chapter IX.

Increasing Value of Seasoning Material

There are, however, certain classes of products in which time is a more than usually direct part of the essence of their manufacture by reason of the fact that the raw material or finished product must be kept for a certain time to season before it is available for sale. If such material or products were purchased in a seasoned condition a higher price would undoubtedly be paid, and it is difficult to resist a claim that the interest cost representing the time occupied in seasoning should be considered as part of the cost of manufacture for inventory purposes.

This principle is, however, one which, if adopted in practice, should be employed only with the utmost caution, for the reason that any subsequent fluctuations tending to large reductions in selling prices might have a much more serious effect if profits had been previously paid away on the basis of inventories valued at a figure including such interest; whereas, in the contrary case, nothing more serious can occur than the postponement of a declaration of profits until the carrying charge represented by this interest has been recovered by a sale of the products. It may frequently happen in practice that the carrying charge is in the form of interest on loans made for the purpose of carrying stocks of materials during the seasoning period, and in such cases the interest actually paid is a good measure of the amount to be carried forward as an asset; where no money, or a part only, is so borrowed the most conservative practice would be against making any addition, although when the interests of present shareholders would be prejudicially affected for the benefit of the future, no serious objection could be taken to a reasonable addition for carrying charges, the credit for which would be made to the profits of the period under consideration. It should be noted that in a steady regular business it is only on increasing quantities of seasoning materials that an addition for carrying charges will affect profits, and in older countries, where the tendency is toward a steady average business over a long series of years, this question is of little or no importance and such additions are in consequence usually omitted. In a comparatively new country, such as the United States, the tendency of business is toward progressive increase, and the question assumes greater importance often by reason of the desire to show sufficiently large profits to attract the further capital necessary for a rapid increase in the volume of trade. It is just for this reason that the utmost caution is necessary in the application of the principle. If business were increasing at a moderate rate the increasing profits might be sufficient to provide the increased working capital necessary, and nothing would be gained by inflating inventory values and profits by the addition of carrying charges which would only remain in the business; nor on the contrary could the addition of these charges have any bad effect. Where the additional capital required is raised by loan or fresh issues of stock, and the carrying charges are added and employed to increase dividends, elements of danger are present, and a too general application of the principle might conduce to excessive inventories and to speculation in raw materials which would show increasing profits arising out of inflated inventories and eventually, if the speculation turned out badly, would cause large losses.

Treatment of Carrying Charges

It is sometimes suggested that this same principle of adding carrying charges should be employed where large stocks of material not requiring a seasoning period are accumulated for any purpose, speculative or otherwise. This, however, is an entire misapplication of the principle as no question of cost of manufacture is involved. The purchases are made with the idea of ultimate profit by their resale in the same or a converted state, and on such resale a profit or a loss is made. To make additions for carrying charges in such a case is merely to anticipate profit which may or may not be earned, and is just as incorrect as to anticipate profit under any other conditions.

Where it has been decided to treat as an asset any carrying charges, it is on the whole preferable that in the balance sheet these charges should be included not in the caption of "Inventories" as part of cost, but under the classification of "Working Assets" as a "Deferred Charge" to be met out of subsequent profits. In this way more attention is called to the policy adopted, and any undue increase in the amount is more likely to be disclosed.

Profits on Work in Progress

The extent to which it is permissible to anticipate profits on work in progress forms another important consideration in the valuation of inventories. When work is being carried out under definite contracts extending over long periods of time, and when it may perhaps reasonably be contended that at any rate some portion of the profit is earned at the time when the work is performed, it is quite a frequent practice to estimate and bring into account some portion of the profit proportionate to the cost for any period, and there does not appear to be any objection in principle to the adoption of this practice. On the other hand, it is undoubtedly more conservative not to take credit for any such profit until the whole contract is completed. An added reason for the latter course is that unforeseen contingencies are continually arising during the progress of the work, with the result that what was originally expected to realize a profit may in the end result in a loss. It is true that the more conservative course may cause large inequalities in the amount of profit shown for successive periods; but if the accounts are stated on a basis of total work completed less cost thereof, the reasons for the fluctuations, as well as the advantages of more rapid completion, are apparent.

Conditions may exist which would render such conservative treatment inequitable to certain classes of stockholders, as for instance when part of the capital stock is of the non-cumulative preferred class, the dividends upon which are dependent entirely on the profits of each year. In determining profits, due regard must be had to such interests so that no substantial injustice may be done them.

If, however, estimates of profits on pending contracts are to be taken into account, it is of the utmost importance that such should be made on an ultra-conservative basis, and further, that estimated losses should also be fully provided for. Even where it is not the practice to take up any part of the profits on contracts not completed, it may be necessary to provide for losses of an exceptional character likely to arise on similar contracts; neglect to take this precaution may easily result in subsequent disaster by the distribution over a series of years of dividends in excess of profits.

While, therefore, under certain conditions no objection can be taken to the inclusion in a profit and loss account of profits on work in progress, a sound conservative policy would be against such a practice unless in very exceptional cases on the ground:

(1) That the best estimates are misleading.

(2) That such profits are not in most cases yet realized and cannot therefore be employed in payment of dividends, except by a corresponding increase in working capital.

(3) That the asset of work in progress is unduly swelled by an addition that may perhaps never be realized.

Reserves for Contingencies

Of somewhat more importance than the question of profits and losses on contracts, is that of reserves for future expenses on contracts which are apparently completed. These expenses may represent general supervision during a certain period after installation; claims for non-fulfillment of stipulated provisions, either under guarantees of satisfactory performance extending over a definite period or otherwise; or other small adjustments; and on the other side there may be bonuses due after a certain period of satisfactory working. The only really safe way to provide for such expenses and claims is by the creation out of profits of a contingency reserve, either by charging to each contract a certain percentage, or by setting up specific reserves based on an examination of the results of similar contracts. Reserves so made should be carried as a current liability of the business, and not as a free reserve. Bonuses should not be taken credit for until actually earned by the completion of the specified conditions.

Book Inventories

The accuracy of the periodical statements of earnings of manufacturing concerns depends to a large extent upon that of the inventory, both as to quantity and value. Without correct information as to the value of the stocks, it is impossible to ascertain the earnings; and yet the delay and expense involved prohibit the frequent taking of physical inventories, which in most cases would necessitate the closing of the works for a period of some weeks, and a consequent loss of business. Up to comparatively recent times, it was the practice to take such inventories once a year, closing the works at a suitable date for that purpose; but the demand for more frequent statements of earnings has necessitated some method of arriving at the approximate value of stocks on hand without the expense and delay involved in a physical enumeration thereof. There has by degrees been evolved a system of book records, continuous throughout the year, of materials, work in process, and manufactured products, which enables a book inventory to be obtained each month so accurately that the closing down of large works for this purpose is now very unusual.

These book records consist of accounts, both of quantity and value, kept for each class of material and manufactured product, based on accurate returns of the quantities received and consumed and of the labor expended, and balancing with the principal books so far as money values are concerned. The money value of labor worked is obtained from the analyzed pay-rolls, frequently based on a large number of slips made up either by the individual workmen or by the foremen. These slips form the basis of the entries to the debit of different order numbers in the cost records, and the total of all such debits is balanced with the factory pay-roll. The quantity and values of materials received are obtained from the original bills, analyzed, and charged to the respective stores accounts. The production records are thus obtained from a very large number of small individual records of time and material expended in the various productive operations, which are collected, classified and summarized, and charged and credited to the Production, and Material, and Labor accounts respectively on ordinary bookkeeping principles; with the result that the balance left on any material account should represent the stock on hand, and the balance on any production account, after crediting the finished product, should represent the cost of the completed or partially completed work.

It might be supposed that reports made up by working men, often illiterate, and with no idea of the purpose for which the records are required, would be so inaccurate as to be useless for practical purposes, but a little consideration will show that, apart from any deliberate attempt at falsification, errors would tend to offset each other, and the resulting difference should be comparatively small in proportion to the totals involved. In fact, as in so many other problems of everyday life, the principle of averages obtains, and if ordinary precautions are adopted, the final results are as a rule found to be surprisingly accurate.

Physical Verification of Book Inventories

As any particular material in stock is reduced to a low point, a physical inventory thereof is easily taken, and any discrepancies found on a comparison with the book records are adjusted. In this way the whole of the material accounts are verified physically at least once in the course of each year without any interruption to the ordinary business. In the case of large bulk stocks, such as ore, pig iron, etc., already referred to, the problem is a more difficult one, because it may be, and frequently is, a period of some years before the piles in which these articles are kept are reduced to a sufficiently small quantity to enable any accurate inventory to be taken. In these cases, however, it is usual to allow a small extra percentage on the consumption to cover waste or loss, with the result that in practice the physical test more often shows an excess over the book record than otherwise.

Material in process of manufacture can often only be physically verified when the process is entirely completed, which may be after weeks, months, or, in large contracts, even years. But by a subdivision of accounts into different processes and small units, the book records are being continually verified at each end; that is, by the labor and material which is known to have gone in, and by the processed or finished product which is known to have come out, and provided that the values at which the material is charged in, and the product credited out, are approximately in accordance with the facts, the resulting balance of work still in progress must be substantially correct also.

Monthly Charges

In all these accounts the month is the unit of time most usually adopted, and the value at which a month's consumption of material should be charged out is of some importance. The safest rule is to assume that the stocks on hand at the beginning of the month are first exhausted, and to value the stock at the close at the average cost of the month, except where such stock is greater than the total receipts for the month, in which case the excess should be taken at the price at which the commencing stock was valued. Having thus obtained the value of the inventory at the close of the month, the consumption for the month should be credited to the material account, and charged to the proper cost accounts, at a figure which will leave a balance on the material account equal to such inventory value. But this rule requires to be followed with care, because it might happen, for exceptional reasons, that the cost for the month was either very much above or very much below the average, and in such a case the stocks should be adjusted to a more normal valuation.

Contracts of Purchase

Contracts of purchase made for future delivery form another class of items that call for consideration in connection with inventory valuations. As long as such contracts are made in the ordinary course of business for the purpose of supplying its actual needs as they accrue, no question need be raised in connection with a balance sheet as of a date prior to the date of delivery. In many concerns, however, these future contracts form a business in themselves, being made either as a simple speculation or to protect legitimate dealings in a highly speculative market. Such contracts must be taken into consideration in the preparation of the balance sheet, and the losses shown by a comparison between the contract price and the market price for similar future deliveries at the date of the balance sheet provided for. The differences on such contracts may amount to very large sums, and their omission from the balance sheet will then give a most misleading view of the position. This condition usually applies only to those classes of commodities which are dealt in on produce exchanges and in which there is a free market for contracts in future deliveries; and for the proper ascertainment of the profits or losses a thorough knowledge of the methods and rules of the exchanges is essential.

Inventory Credits and Liabilities

In close connection with the subject of inventory valuation is that of proper provision for all liabilities in respect of the commodities included in the inventory, and on the other hand for the proper inclusion in the inventory of all commodities for which liabilities have been taken up. Commodities may frequently have been delivered for which no bills have yet been rendered; and on the other hand they may be in transit from the point of shipment and only received subsequently to the enumeration, while the bills, by the terms of shipment or to take advantage of discount, may have been rendered and paid prior to that date.

A similar condition may arise also with sales which may for one reason or another have been billed to the customer while the goods are still on hand.

Any good accounting system should provide for such conditions automatically; but good systems are more rare than they should be, and serious errors in balance sheets and profits may easily arise through neglect of proper precautions to guard against such omissions.

Accuracy of Inventory Valuations

Enough has been said to show the vital importance to a correct balance sheet of accurate inventory valuations. Practical experience has reduced to a comparatively simple routine the methods for guarding against possibilities of error, and the serious ones that occur are generally due either to ignorance of both principles and routine on the part of those concerned, or to deliberate fraud in the certification of quantities or values.

There are, however, other causes of shrinkage in value which it is more difficult to provide for. A fall in market prices, a sudden cessation in the demand owing to panic, war, or other disturbing causes may at any time quite unexpectedly either entirely prevent the realization of stocks on hand, or so depress prices as to render such realization only possible at a sacrifice. For such reasons as these it is prudent to build up a reasonable reserve in good times to provide for contingencies that may arise in less prosperous ones. Such reserves, while deductible from the inventory in the balance sheet, should be quite separate from and independent of the inventory itself, and should not be made up by reducing the valuation or prices of specific parts of the stocks on hand.

(2) ACCOUNTS AND BILLS RECEIVABLE

The items appearing under this heading should all be liquid and current, and in the aggregate realizable at their total face value within a definite term, dependent on the nature of the business carried on. It follows, therefore, that full provision should be made for all accounts which are or may become bad or doubtful, and for all losses that can reasonably be anticipated from fluctuations in foreign exchange when the debts are contracted abroad. Accounts in the nature of advances to enable other parties to carry on their business—which are not therefore currently recoverable— should not be included under this heading, but under that of permanent investments, and similarly advances made for business purposes and forming part of the working assets, such as balances on working funds in hands of officials or agents, should be eliminated from accounts receivable and included under the proper subheading of working assets. The idea underlying this caption is that it represents a class of asset that is being continually day by day and in the ordinary course of business converted into some more liquid and available asset such as cash, and may therefore safely be counted on as a source from which corresponding liabilities may be met as they mature. The term within which payment is to be made will, of course, vary with the nature of the business. Collections may be made, according to the custom of the particular trade, monthly or quarterly, and amounts not so collected may be considered overdue and subject to necessary reserves, or, in extreme cases, such as notes taken from farmers by agricultural machine manufacturers, the term of payment may normally extend over several years before such conditions arise. In determining, therefore, the class of accounts which may be properly included under the present caption, it is essential that full consideration be given to the nature of the business.

Present Values of Accounts and Bills Receivable

Bills receivable will not be due until a date subsequent to that as of which the balance sheet is prepared, and should therefore be reduced to a present value. If the bill is for a fixed sum with interest, its present value is its face value. Usually, however, commercial bills are drawn for a fixed sum payable at a certain date without interest, and in such cases provision should be made to reduce the face value to present value by charging to Income and crediting an interest or discount reserve account with the interest on each bill from the date of the balance sheet to the due date.

Accounts receivable are often subject to a discount for cash in addition to the trade discount, which latter is or should be always deducted when the charge is made on the books. When this cash discount is a material amount it should be provided for, being offset to a certain extent by similar discounts to be obtained on creditors accounts. This reserve is frequently considered to be covered by that for bad and doubtful accounts, but the point should not be overlooked.

As a rule there is little expense, other than the cash discounts allowed, attached to the collection of accounts and bills receivable, and it is not customary to make any provision for such expense as may be incurred. If, however, the cost of collection is likely to much exceed the normal amount that would be necessary in, say, a good wholesale business, this question must be considered. In some lines of business dealing with large numbers of small customers over a considerable extent of territory, such, for instance, as harvester machine companies, fertilizer companies, etc., the expense incurred before the accounts and bills are finally collected, may be considerable. So far as bills are concerned there is usually an asset of the accruing interest which may only be credited to Income as received, and this will to some extent offset the collection cost.

Generally wherever it may appear that there must, before final collection, be a material shrinkage in the face value of accounts and bills, due to cost of collection, sufficient reserve should be made by charges to Income account each year to provide therefor.

(3) INVESTMENTS

The classes of investments which should be grouped under this caption, as has already appeared from the discussion of permanent investments, are either those which represent the temporary disposal of surplus cash, or those acquired in payment of debts, or otherwise, and held for realization at a suitable price. Such investments have no relation whatever to the business, and can be disposed of without in any way interfering with its earning capacity, other than the loss of the dividends thereon.

Unissued Stock or Bonds

For reasons fully explained in the next chapter, it is not proper to include under this caption, or indeed as an asset at all, stocks or bonds of the corporation itself when these are merely held in the treasury for future issue; and, moreover, there may be grave danger in so including these, in that, if stated at par when the market value is less, they may be seriously overvalued; while, if stated at market value, not only has an apparent loss or profit to be provided for, which is purely a capital item relating only to capital liabilities, but also the market price probably could not be realized if it were attempted to make any considerable sale.

Issued Stock or Bonds Held in Treasury

This principle should strictly be extended to temporary purchases of the corporation's own stock or bonds, for whatever reason made, or at any rate such holdings should be separately stated. In the majority of cases, however, it has been customary up to the present time to treat such holdings as ordinary investments, and when they are small in amount and readily saleable at market price, there is no serious objection to such course from an accounting standpoint. Moreover, there is a good argument for making a distinction between such stocks held in treasury, unissued, and those bought in the market, in that the former can only be legally issued at par or over, while the latter can be sold at any price obtainable. The most careful consideration, however, is required before the inclusion of a corporation's own stock or bonds in current assets should be permitted, for the reason that abuses may easily be concealed from stockholders and investors by such means.

Valuation of Investments

Investments should be carried on the balance sheet at cost unless the market value is below cost, when they should be written down to market value. An objection to an actual market valuation in the balance sheet is that profits and losses are thereby created which cannot be definitely ascertained until the investments are realized; but when the amounts are small and not very material to the true statement of the assets, a cost valuation may be permitted, provided that any depreciation in value is disclosed.

Another method of dealing with fluctuations in the value of marketable investments is to create an investment fluctuation reserve, either out of estimated or realized profits on investments, or by a charge to Profit and Loss, of such an amount as may be necessary to prevent this reserve from showing a debit balance; and by charges or credits to this reserve to maintain the asset at market value.

Life insurance companies in the United States are now required to value their investments in bonds on an amortization principle. Taking into consideration the purchase price, nominal rate of interest, term, and price of redemption, the corresponding true or effective rate of interest is ascertained. This rate, on the cost, is carried to the Income account in the first half year, and the balance of interest, which may be a credit or debit, is deducted from or added to the investment cost, giving a new figure for the latter, on which the income for the next half year at the effective rate is calculated, this proceeding being repeated each half year until redemption or sale. In permanent investments this is a correct method, but it ignores fluctuations in value due to the varying credit of the borrower or to changes in market interest rates, and if sales are made before maturity there may well be a balance of profit or loss to be provided for which is not covered by the effective interest rate which has been adopted. A word of caution is necessary as to the application of this principle of amortization to bonds purchased at a discount. The discount may be due to the difference between the nominal rate of interest on the bond and the average market rate; or it may be due to the bad credit of the issuing company. In the former case it is reasonable to suppose that the bond may be held until payment at maturity; but in the latter a contingency of risk exists which may render the application of the amortization principle unwise. If the amortization method is adopted, it is desirable also to set up a reserve to provide for such possible further fluctuations.

(4) CASH

The statement of cash in a balance sheet usually presents little difficulty.   It will consist of three main items, viz. :

(1) Cash on current account with bankers.
(2) Cash on deposit with bankers or others under varying conditions.
(3) Cash in hands of officials of the concern.

Cash on Current Account

Cash on current account should represent the actual amount shown by the banks' accounts to the credit of the customers, less any checks which the customer may have drawn and issued before the closing date but which have not been presented to the bank for payment; and with the addition of any drafts or other negotiable instruments which are at the closing date in the hands of the banker for collection but have not been collected.   Sometimes, with a view either of showing smaller amounts due by debtors or to creditors, or a larger balance of cash, the cash book is not closed on the proper date, but is kept open and entries of receipts and payments are made of a date later than, but relating to the transactions prior to, the closing date.   This practice is entirely incorrect and should never be permitted.   The object of closing the books on a given date is to ascertain the position on that date, and the balance sheet cannot accurately show this position if items of accounts receivable and payable are shown as if they had been received and paid respectively on or before the closing date, when as a matter of fact this is not the case.

Outstanding Checks

The important consideration in the case of checks issued is whether certain portions of the bank account have, by the issue of orders in favor of creditors, been disposed of on or before the closing date, and this cannot be so unless the checks have actually been mailed prior to that date.   If they have actually been so mailed, the mere fact that at that time the amount is still at the credit of the bank account is not material, because it is no longer disposable. Until the checks are actually mailed this cash is disposable, because the checks can always be cancelled and withdrawn. It may be said that until the check is actually presented to the bank and paid, the amount is disposable, because payment can always be stopped. Technically, this is so, but in practice a check once issued is rarely stopped, except to protect the creditor against loss in the mail or otherwise, so that this contingency need not as a rule be considered.

Restricted Cash Balances

In stating bank balances in the balance sheet, it is important that any amounts that are not free for all purposes should be stated separately with an explanation of the nature of the restriction on their use. Some of the purposes for which these restrictions may exist would be the following:

> Cash received on account of new issues of securities and only available for capital expenditure.
>
> Cash deposited with trustees for payment of bonded or other debt or interest thereon.
>
> Cash deposited on an agreement that it will not be withdrawn before a certain date.

It is also preferable to divide the free cash balances so as to distinguish between currency on hand and balances at banks bearing interest and not bearing interest respectively.

(5) FOREIGN EXCHANGE

Important questions relating to accounts arise where assets are situated, or expenses or liabilities are incurred, in a foreign country having a different currency from the home country. In the statement of current assets it is necessary to consider the value in terms of the home currency. When the fluctuations in exchange are merely those due to the varying rate for bills of exchange between two gold standard countries, a fixed par of exchange can be adopted in ordinary commercial, as distinct from banking transactions, with safety and substantial accuracy. Between countries which do not have the same metallic standard, and one or both of whose currencies are depreciated and subject to daily fluctuation due to causes other than the supply and demand for bills, it is necessary to adopt different methods.

On operations carried on in the foreign country, the object should be to obtain as nearly as possible an exact equivalent at cost in the home country for all assets or liabilities created and all revenue earned or expenditure incurred in the foreign country. So long as a transaction originates and is completed in the foreign country, no question of exchange comes into the calculation. Where, however, it has created an asset or liability, or is incomplete at a closing date, or in the process of its completion passes from one country to another, a change in the basis of value occurs, which must be reflected in the accounts.

Assume that an American firm or corporation carries on a manufacturing business in a country, such as China, having a silver standard currency.

At first money may be remitted to China for construction of works and will realize a certain sum in silver; machinery and other materials for construction purposes may be purchased in the United States in gold and shipped to China, and other purchases may be made in China in silver. The capital cost of construction should be stated at the actual United States money expended, which will be represented by (1) cash remitted to China, and (2) cash payments in the United States for purchases, freights, etc. As long as the whole business done consists of construction chargeable to Capital account, and the principal books are kept in United States currency, no question of exchange arises. But if the books are kept in Chinese currency (taels), it is important to consider what rate of exchange should be used.

So far as cash remittances are concerned the actual amount realized in Chinese currency should be taken; for payments in the United States an arbitrary basis must be adopted, and the most accurate would be the equivalent in Chinese currency of the United States invoice at the rate of exchange on the date of shipment. The United States office should keep a current account with the Chinese office, showing in one column the dollar and in another the tael equivalent for each transaction.

When the construction period is finished, charges from the United States may consist of stores and supplies, or materials for repairs and renewals of machinery shipped, and other payments made by the United States for the Chinese office. All these inter-country transactions should be put through the current account in United States currency, with the equivalent in Chinese currency at the current rate of exchange on the day of shipment for shipments made to the Chinese office, and on the day of payment for payments made for it. Similarly the Chinese office will put through its current account with the United States office in taels, and at the exchange of the day in dollars, all transactions between the two offices which originate in China. As long as the business is confined to construction this method requires no modification; but when construction and operation are carried on concurrently, the basis on which materials, stores and supplies should be charged out requires consideration.

If these materials are taken up in the Chinese books at the tael equivalent on date of shipment from United States, and between that date and the date of consumption there is considerable fluctuation in the rate of exchange, then the charge to the respective construction and operating accounts will be greater or less than the true value, according as the rate of exchange is lower or higher, for the reason that the number of Chinese taels representing the materials, etc., consumed is now worth either more or less than the number of United States dollars at date of shipment, while the intrinsic value of the materials in United States dollars is, so far as exchange questions are concerned, unchanged. The most satisfactory method of dealing with this condition is to keep the accounts of materials, stores and supplies originating in the United States in United States currency until they are used, and then to charge them out to the accounts concerned—whether construction or operating—at the rate of exchange current on the date of issue for consumption; in other words, these materials, etc., while in fact in China, are deemed to be in the United States until issued for consumption, and are only then passed through the current accounts between the two offices.

The business being an American one, it is desirable that its results should be expressed in United States rather than in Chinese currency. This involves the periodical conversion of its capital and current assets and its current liabilities from taels into dollars. Assuming that the capital assets are kept in the Chinese books in taels, it is important that the rate used for conversion should be that at which the expenditures were originally incurred. If a higher or lower value of the tael be adopted, the asset will be correspondingly understated or overstated in dollars. To obviate this result it is necessary that the dollar and tael equivalent of each construction item as on the date of the first charge to construction account be both kept in parallel columns continuously, and only the dollar equivalent so shown be taken for purposes of accounts as the value in United States currency. This result is of course better obtained by transferring all construction expenditures directly to the United States books as soon as charged; and in practice this may be done with substantial accuracy by so transferring all charges for a month at the average rate of exchange for that month. Construction expenditures having been thus transferred through the current account between Chinese and United States books to the latter, this account will, by comparison of all Chinese and American equivalents, for the year or other period for which the accounts are being stated, give an average rate of exchange for that period; which, applied to all remaining items in the Chinese books, including earnings, expenditures, current assets and liabilities, will convert them at this average rate of exchange into an exact equivalent in United States currency.

If construction expenditures are maintained in the Chinese books, then there will be on conversion a loss or profit representing the difference between the actual United States figures as shown by the dollar equivalent at time of expenditure, and the equivalent at the current average rate, and this difference can only be debited or credited to the United States Income account.

There will also be a further debit or credit to Profit and Loss account for the difference between the United States equivalent of the Chinese value of the current assets and liabilities at the average rate of exchange and at the current rate at the date as of which the accounts are being prepared; it being necessary in the case of these current assets and liabilities to state them at their actual value at the date of the account.

Such an elaborate method of dealing with foreign transactions is not often found necessary in practice.

Most of the important countries of the world now have a gold standard, and any difference in exchange due to the employment of the fixed par value of the gold standards will usually be a small one and can be absorbed in the Income account without inquiry as to its origin. It may, however, happen even in such cases that by reason of remittances for capital purposes, at a rate differing materially from the par of exchange during the whole of a construction period, a considerable difference on exchange may be shown, and in such a case the profit or loss in exchange should be treated as a capital item. Even in dealings with silver-using countries substantial accuracy may be obtained by apportioning any profit and loss on exchange between Capital account and Income account on some arbitrary basis determined by the relation of capital to other expenditures.

The two important points to be remembered in this connection are: firstly, that capital outlays should be represented by the actual amounts of cash in the home currency expended thereon; and secondly, that all current assets and liabilities should be converted at the rate current on the date of the balance sheet. Further, it should be noted that the exchange on this date may be so exceptionally favorable and unlikely to be maintained that it may be wise policy to adopt a less favorable rate, thus setting up a reserve against possible future unfavorable fluctuations, remembering that an exceptionally low value of the foreign currency will be a favorable one for liabilities and an unfavorable one for assets.

Dealings in Foreign Exchange

The problems so far considered have relation entirely to commercial accounts. Others arise when operations in exchange are carried out by bankers or brokers for the purpose of earning profits out of daily fluctuations in exchange rates due to the demand and supply for money or bills. Such operations necessarily involve interest as well as exchange. The transactions being all in effect for cash payable or receivable now or at some short future date (being then represented by bills of exchange), each one has its exact equivalent in the currency both of the originating and the foreign country. If it were not for the element of time which enters into the question, the determination of the profit on any series of transactions contained in one account would be made as already described in commercial accounts, viz.: by converting the outstanding balances at the close of the period at the rate current on that date. Inasmuch, however, as at any closing date there will be items not due until a subsequent date, these must be reduced to their present value at the closing date, and this present value converted at the current rate of exchange on that date. The balance on that account will be the profit or loss thereon, which by custom among bankers is usually considered as arising partly from interest at either market, or some customary rate, and partly from fluctuations in exchange. In order to show these two profits separately on any one account, it is necessary to calculate interest on every item up to the closing date, or at the customary rate adopted for all transactions. The balance of these interest items will be the interest profit or loss, and the remaining balance, after closing the account as already described, will be the exchange profit or loss.

The subject of foreign exchange is an exhaustive one and there are various methods in force for carrying out in practice the principles laid down. For further explanations on this subject, reference should be made to the various text books.

CHAPTER VI

BALANCE SHEET LIABILITIES

(1) CAPITAL STOCK

Capital stock of a corporation is firstly authorized by its charter or constitution; secondly, created by resolution of the board of directors; and thirdly, issued to the stockholders either for cash or for other valuable consideration. This statement, however, requires modification. According to the law of most of the United States, and of Great Britain, capital stock cannot be issued except for value; but this legal difficulty is avoided by issuing it in accordance with a contract in the body of which is contained a statement as to value conformable to the stock or other securities to be issued, and the excess of this value over that of the actual tangible assets acquired is often euphemistically entitled goodwill. In effect, as is shown by the market quotations for such stocks, they have frequently been issued at a discount, *i. e.,* to a par value in excess of the true value of the concern.

While this fiction has so far maintained its legal sanction, it still remains doubtful how far an issue of stock for a cash consideration clearly less than its par value is legal, or whether if so issued the purchaser or holder is not liable to pay up the whole of the discount, at any rate on liquidation of the corporation. This is the law in England—with the exception that it is now legal for a corporation to pay a reasonable commission for services in placing its stock—and it is also the statute law of some of the United States, notably New York. Discount on stock would therefore either be an asset of the corporation recoverable from some person or persons and not chargeable to profit and loss, or the liability on the stock would be the amount actually paid for it. Premiums on stocks issued may be a source of surplus to the corporation eventually, because they are cash received in excess of the authorized capital which must be maintained intact, but they are not profit on operations and should not therefore be credited as such to Income, although they may be applied to make good depreciation in fixed assets, or exceptional losses, where such depreciation or losses do not arise out of the ordinary business of the corporation.

In the case of both discounts (if permissible) and premiums, the proper view would seem to be that the stock is sold for whatever it will fetch, and that any discount or premium should be considered as a deduction from or addition to the par value of the stock on the face of the balance sheet.

Capital Stock Without Par Value

This view is reflected in a law recently passed by the Legislature of the State of New York which permits incorporation with shares having no specific par value, the shares of stock representing shares in the surplus of assets over liabilities and being sold from time to time for whatever they will bring. Objection has frequently been taken to the absence of a par value for the reason that it might provide opportunities for improper manipulation by unscrupulous promoters. In reply to this, it may be urged that in other states where a fixed par value is maintained and where the law provides that it must be paid in cash, there are many known legal methods of evading these provisions by means of contracts, and unscrupulous promoters find no difficulty in carrying out their schemes while the legitimate plans of more scrupulous people are hampered. It is difficult to see how the absence of a par value can give more opportunities for fraud than are available under existing laws, and the power to incorporate on this plan will enable shares in an undertaking of uncertain or speculative value to be issued or sold on their merits.

As long as stock has a fixed par value it is better, theoretically, to treat premiums thereon as receipts on capital account, but no serious objection can be raised to crediting them to profit and loss surplus, preferably under a separate subheading.

Redemption of Capital Stock

Provision is sometimes made for the redemption of certain classes of capital stock out of profits. Such a provision, if redemption is made at par, acts as an allocation of profits to capital purposes and does not effect a reduction in surplus. There is no difference whatever, so far as the financial results are concerned, between the application of profits to increase fixed assets or to reduce capital liabilities. The proportion of the profits so expended is—at any rate temporarily—locked up and capitalized, but may at any time be made available by raising further capital. When stock is redeemed at either a premium or a discount, an actual loss or profit has been realized—which can only be met by a charge against or credit to profit and loss—resulting not from the business activities but from a change in capital. In fact the value of the shares of the remaining stockholders has been depleted or added to by the transaction, where the premium (or discount) is not the exact proportion of the surplus (or deficit) belonging to the shares redeemed.

Treasury Stock

An important question arises as to the treatment of stock of a corporation held in its own treasury. Many corporations still treat this as an investment asset, either under a special division of the balance sheet or among the current assets.

The Interstate Commerce Commission in its railway balance sheet makes the same requirements, but in the steamship balance sheet, more recently issued, requires that the correct accounting methods detailed below be followed. A little consideration will show that such a practice is entirely erroneous and misleading, and moreover, that it also raises difficult questions of valuation. The capital stock represents the manner in which its property and assets are distributed among those who constitute the corporation. If one of these owners disposes of his share to the corporation, he withdraws therefrom, taking with him what he considers his fair proportion of the asset value, and leaving the rest to be divided among the remaining owners. Assuming that the seller gets full value, the value remaining to the others is neither more nor less in fact than it was before, although if the stock is actually worth more or less than its par value, there will be an apparent profit or loss on the transaction; the effect of which may be thus illustrated. A corporation has a capital stock of $1,000,000, divided into 10,000 shares of $100 each, and represented by assets of equal value. The holders of 1,000 shares withdraw, i. e., sell their shares to the company at the book value, which in this case is par. The stock is thereby reduced to 9,000 shares, i. e., $900,000, and the assets are similarly reduced by the payment of $100,000 to $900,000. There is clearly no reason whatever for pretending that there are still 10,000 shareholders and assets of $1,000,000, when as a matter of fact there are only 9,000 with assets of $900,000, and the position of these 9,000 is entirely unchanged.

A similar result would appear if the capital stock was originally only $800,000, with assets of $1,000,000, and therefore a surplus of $200,000. If holders of 800 shares withdraw, taking $100,000 of cash or other assets, i. e., the book value of the stock, the position of the remaining stockholders is unaltered.

If more or less than the book value of the withdrawn shares is paid, then the remaining shareholders have on paper sustained a loss or realized a profit; but whether or no this is a real loss or profit depends upon the intrinsic value rather than the book value of the shares. This paper or book profit or loss is rightly charged or credited to Profit and Loss account as a special item. There is no possible variation from this result in the most complicated cases; but lawyers have devised clever legal fictions for pretending that the stock which either has not in effect come into existence, or has in effect gone out of existence, still exists. These are mainly designed to evade the law that capital stock cannot be issued at a discount; and while in many cases no doubt they are harmless in their results, in others they are made use of for improper purposes. As an instance of such a device, it is found that on the purchase of an undertaking by a corporation a large block of stock is issued to the vendor, of which a proportion is returned to the corporation as a gift. In effect this stock so returned acts as a reduction of the purchase money, and both cost of property and capital stock should be correspondingly reduced. In practice, the stock having been apparently legally issued at par, subject to the very doubtful possibility of any attack being made on the validity of the contract, can now, when it returns to the corporation, be sold at a discount below par, and if, as may well happen, the stock has been taken onto the books at a figure well below par, the ultimate effect is that, in spite of the law to the contrary, the stock is sold by the corporation at a discount and the discount charged to cost of property, which is thus considerably inflated. The effect of this device is clearly the sale of the stock at a discount, but this is concealed from stockholders, and it would undoubtedly be much better if the stock had no par value and were issued at whatever price it would fetch on the market, without the necessity for such juggling as now frequently takes place. The accounting rule should be that all stock in possession of the corporation which issues it, should be deducted from the liability shown on the balance sheet so as to truly set forth the number of shares in the undertaking which have really been issued to and remain in the hands of the public at the date of the balance sheet.

Another objection to treating such stock as an asset is that, not being held as necessary for the purposes of the activities of the company, it cannot be treated as a permanent asset and maintained at cost, but must be written down to market value, if below cost, thus in effect unduly reducing the surplus if the value is below par, or unduly increasing it if the value is above par.

As a matter of convenience small amounts of such stock are carried as marketable investments when the same are held temporarily; but even this practice is open to criticism as lending itself to a use of the funds of a corporation for influencing the market in its own stock, which is not one of the purposes for which it is permitted to exist. A desirable amendment to the existing law would be one that would make it illegal for a corporation to own its own stock, a provision which is already in force under the rules of the New York Stock Exchange.

Treasury Stock—English Rule

It is interesting to note that it is now settled law in England that a corporation cannot acquire its own stock. In the well-known case of Trevor v. Whitworth, the House of Lords held that a corporation could not acquire its own stock on the general grounds—

(1) That the corporation cannot be a member of itself;
(2) That the purchase of its own shares is a reduction of capital in a manner not sanctioned by the various Companies Acts;
(3) That such a purchase is a return of a part of the capital to the stockholder in a manner not authorized;
(4) That such a purchase is not incidental to the objects for which the corporation is formed;

and, underlying the above grounds,

(5) That the capital stock paid up is the fund to which the creditors are entitled to look to protect them against loss, and that no diminution of this fund, except in the manner specifically provided in the statutes, can be permitted.

(2) Bonded Debt

The most important questions which arise in connection with bonded debt have relation to the premiums and discounts on issue and redemption thereof, the methods of redemption, and the proper treatment of funded debt held in the treasury of the debtor company.

Effective Interest Rate of Bonds

Premium or discount on bonds is a deduction from or addition to the nominal rate of interest which the bond carries; that is to say, there is a rate known as the true or effective rate at which any corporation can place its bonds at par; if it elects to place them at any other rate the bonds will sell at a premium or discount as the case may be; but the effective rate remains the same and this effective rate is the proper charge to Income account. Hence the premium or discount should theoretically be spread over the term of the bonds, and the annual instalment thereof credited or charged to Income account each year.

It should be remembered that the effective rate must be applied not to the par value but to the cash value at time of issue of the bonds; *e. g.,* for bonds issued at 90 the effective rate will be calculated on $900 for each $1,000 bond, and not on $1,000.

Annual Income Charges

Having ascertained this true or effective rate on the basis of the terms of issue, it is still frequently a difficult matter to determine the charge that should be made to Income account under the conditions which may actually exist in the future.

If an issue of bonds be made for a fixed term of years at a certain nominal rate of interest, with provision for the redemption of a specified amount each year at fixed prices, it is a comparatively simple matter to determine the present value of all the repayments, and thence—by an inspection of annuity tables—the equivalent theoretical interest rate on the basis of the fixed present value and term.

Varying Conditions Affecting Annual Charge

In accounting for the charge to income where the effective interest method is adopted, these cases must be considered:

(a) Bonds issued at a discount and redeemable at par. When the bonds are first issued the full par value would be credited to the liability account, while the difference between this full value and the cash received would be charged to a discount on bonds account. The full effective rate of interest would be charged to Income account, while so much of it as represents the nominal interest would be credited to Interest Accrued, and the balance to Bond Discount, thus gradually reducing this account over the life of the bonds.

(b) Bonds issued at a premium and redeemable at par. The conditions are exactly the reverse of case (a). Discount on Bonds account will become Premium on Bonds account with a credit balance; the effective interest charge will be less than the actual, leaving a charge to Bond Premium account in reduction of the balance on that account.

(c) Bonds issued at par, redeemable at a premium. This case is in substance identical with (a), but in practice the treatment is different, as there is neither discount nor premium at the date of issue. The charge to Income account will exceed the interest accrued, and the difference will be credited to Bond Premium account and accumulated there until final redemption, all premiums paid on redeemed bonds being charged to this account.

(d) Bonds issued at a discount and redeemable at a premium. This combines cases (a) and (c). The excess of the effective rate will be credited to Premium and Discount account, and will gradually convert the debit balance on that account into a credit sufficient to equal the amount of all premiums payable on final redemption.

In practice it is often found that bonds are purchased in the market at prices varying from, and generally less than, the specified redemption prices, and then transferred to the trustees of the sinking fund at the specified prices, and a saving thus effected which must be taken into account in determining the annual charge to income. Or again, the redemption dates may be anticipated for a whole or part of the issue, and further disturbing factors thus introduced.

The saving on the purchase of bonds in the market at prices below those fixed for redemption, may be dealt with in one or other of the following methods:

(1) Credit the amount to Income account each year, thus finally disposing of it.

(2) Credit the amount to discount (or premium) on Bonds account, thus eventually producing a surplus on this account, which would ultimately be transferred to Income account.

Neither of these methods is theoretically accurate; but in view of the impossibility of determining what the market price will be in the future, theoretical accuracy is impossible.

The treatment in the case of anticipation of redemption dates is a more difficult matter, for, if carried out on at all a large scale and not accompanied by an equitable reduction on the redemption price, the effective interest rate will be materially increased. The only sound method would appear to be to recalculate the effective rate on the basis of the bonds still outstanding and the new redemption terms. If this is not done, there may be a considerable shortage to make up at the date of final redemption. This fact is frequently overlooked, although it should be recognized as an important factor, particularly in any refunding or redemption plan.

Methods of Determining Charge to Income

There are various methods in use for determining the proper interest charge to be made to Income account under the varying conditions that arise.

The first and most correct method, which may be called the effective interest method, consists in charging to Income account the effective interest rate calculated from the known conditions of issue upon the whole amount outstanding during the year, with an addition or deduction of an amount equal to the excess or deficit of the amount paid for redemption during the year as compared with the fixed amount provided. For instance, if the conditions of the issue provided that $100,000 of bonds be retired during the year at 105, and as a matter of fact they are purchased at 95, the true interest on the bonds bearing interest during the year would be reduced by $10,000, representing the saving on bonds retired during the year as compared with the price therefor assumed in determining the effective rate. The tendency of this method would probably be to increase gradually the annual charge to Income for interest and sinking fund until the limit price of redemption was reached; for, as the amount of bonds outstanding diminished, the market price might be expected to rise.

The second and more common method, which may be called the equal instalment method, is to ignore altogether the effective interest rate; to charge to Income account each year the interest actually paid, together with a proportionate part, according to the whole term of issue, of the discount on issue or premium on redemption; Income account being also credited with any savings made by purchase of bonds in the market.

A third method, which may be called the bonds outstanding method, and which may safely be adopted where, by reason of complication in the terms of issue and redemption, it is difficult or impracticable to determine the true interest rate, is to distribute the discount or premium over the period in the proportion that the bonds outstanding for each year bear to the sum of the bonds outstanding for all years of the currency of the loan. Any saving made by the purchase of bonds in the market is credited to Income account.

When a large accumulated surplus is available, the practice is frequently adopted of charging the whole discount on issue to Profit and Loss account, taking up any profit or loss on subsequent redemption at a discount or premium to the credit of Profit and Loss account as it arises, and leaving the nominal interest on the bonds actually outstanding each year as the only charge to Income account. A great objection to this practice is that thereby the true rate of interest paid on loans during their currency is entirely lost sight of; current fixed charges against earnings are understated; and the portion representing the discount is charged against surplus arising out of previous operations, instead of against income from current operations which should meet it. Any savings on bonds purchased in the market are a credit to Income account.

Operation of the Various Methods of Determining Annual Charge to Income

In order to show the effect of these various methods, it may be well to consider a specific case as follows:

An issue of $1,000,000 of bonds is made at 90, carrying interest at 5 per cent, and redeemable at the rate of $50,000 each half year, at 100 for the first five years, and thereafter at 105. Calculations made on these premises show that the effective rate of interest is approximately

8 3/16 per cent. Bonds are redeemed each year as specified, but they are purchased in the market at the following prices, viz.:

1st Year...................... 92
2nd "   93
3rd "   95
4th "   97
5th "   98
6th "   100
7th "   102
8th "   104
9th and 10th drawn at.......... 105

The tables that follow give all the essential figures.

In the table on page 140, the last four columns show the charges to Income account on the basis (5) of the effective interest method; (6) of the equal instalment method; (7) of the bonds outstanding method; and (8) of charging all discount and premium to surplus; in each case crediting to Income account the surplus arising from purchasing bonds at less than the fixed redemption price.

If the latter be credited direct to surplus, or carried in the Bond Discount account until all discount has been written off by the operation of these credits and the balance of the effective rate, then, at the end of the 11th half year in the first case and at the end of the 15th half year in the second, the discount will be extinguished and thereafter only the actual interest paid, less surplus on market purchases, will be charged to Income.

Determining Annual Charge When Proportionate Discount is Written Off

The charge to Income account on the bonds outstanding method is arrived at as shown in the table on page 141. It is so close to that given by the effective interest method that for all practical purposes it may safely be adopted.

Period ½ Year.	(1) Payments for Interest at 5% p.a. (a).	(2) Effective Interest charge at 8 3-16% p.a. (b).	(3) Discount provided for (2) — (1).	(4) Surplus on purchase at less than redemption price.	(5) Charge to Income on effective interest method.	(6) Charge to Income on equal annual Instalment method.	(7) Charge to Income when Discount written off on Bonds outstanding method.	(8) Charge to Income when Discount charged to Profit and Loss Account.
1	$25,000.00	$36,843.75	$11,843.75	$4,000.00	$32,843.75	$27,250.00	$32,905.00	$21,000.00
2	23,750.00	35,001.56	11,251.56	4,000.00	31,001.56	26,000.00	31,060.00	19,750.00
3	22,500.00	33,159.38	10,659.38	3,500.00	29,659.38	25,250.00	29,714.00	19,000.00
4	21,250.00	31,317.19	10,067.19	3,500.00	27,817.19	24,000.00	27,869.00	17,750.00
5	20,000.00	29,475.00	9,475.00	2,500.00	26,975.00	23,750.00	27,024.00	17,500.00
6	18,750.00	27,632.81	8,882.81	2,500.00	25,132.81	22,500.00	25,179.00	16,250.00
7	17,500.00	25,790.63	8,290.63	2,500.00	24,290.63	22,250.00	24,333.00	16,000.00
8	16,250.00	23,948.44	7,698.44	1,500.00	22,448.44	21,000.00	22,488.00	14,750.00
9	15,000.00	22,106.25	7,106.25	1,500.00	21,106.25	20,250.00	21,143.00	14,000.00
10	13,750.00	20,264.06	6,514.06	1,000.00	19,264.06	19,000.00	19,298.00	12,750.00
11	12,500.00	18,421.88	5,921.88	1,000.00	15,921.88	16,250.00	15,952.00	10,000.00
12	11,250.00	16,579.69	5,329.69	2,500.00	14,079.69	15,000.00	14,107.00	8,750.00
13	10,000.00	14,737.50	4,737.50	1,500.00	13,237.50	14,750.00	13,262.00	8,750.00
14	8,750.00	12,895.31	4,145.31	1,500.00	11,395.31	13,500.00	11,417.00	7,250.00
15	7,500.00	11,053.12	3,553.12	500.00	10,553.12	13,250.00	10,571.00	7,000.00
16	6,250.00	9,210.94	2,960.94	500.00	8,710.94	12,000.00	8,726.00	5,750.00
17	5,000.00	7,368.75	2,368.75	.....	7,368.75	11,250.00	7,381.00	5,000.00
18	3,750.00	5,526.56	1,776.56	.....	5,526.56	10,000.00	5,536.00	3,750.00
19	2,500.00	3,684.38	1,184.38	.....	3,684.38	8,750.00	3,690.00	2,500.00
20	1,250.00	1,842.19	{ 1,232.80	.....	2,482.80	7,500.00	1,845.00	1,250.00
(c) Extra		640.61						
		1/20th = $6,250.00	$125,000.00	$34,000.00	$353,500.00	$353,500.00	$353,500.00	$228,500.00

(a) Interest at 2½% for each half year on $1,000,000, less $50,000 each half year.
(b) Interest at 4 3-32% for each half year on $900,000, less $45,000 each half year.
(c) Balance due to approximation in effective rate.

Period ½ Year.	Bonds Outstanding.	Proportion of Outstanding Bonds to total Bonds.	Amount of Discount Instalment.	Interest Payment.	Profit on Bond Purchase.	Annual charge to Profit and Loss.
1	$1,000,000	100/1050	$11,905	$25,000	$4,000	$32,905
2	950,000	95/1050	11,310	23,750	4,000	31,060
3	900,000	90/1050	10,714	22,500	3,500	29,714
4	850,000	85/1050	10,119	21,250	3,500	27,869
5	800,000	80/1050	9,524	20,000	2,500	27,024
6	750,000	75/1050	8,929	18,750	2,500	25,179
7	700,000	70/1050	8,333	17,500	1,500	24,333
8	650,000	65/1050	7,738	16,250	1,500	22,488
9	600,000	60/1050	7,143	15,000	1,000	21,143
10	550,000	55/1050	6,548	13,750	1,000	19,298
11	500,000	50/1050	5,952	12,500	2,500	15,952
12	450,000	45/1050	5,357	11,250	2,500	14,107
13	400,000	40/1050	4,762	10,000	1,500	13,262
14	350,000	35/1050	4,167	8,750	1,500	11,417
15	300,000	30/1050	3,571	7,500	500	10,571
16	250,000	25/1050	2,976	6,250	500	8,726
17	200,000	20/1050	2,381	5,000	...	7,381
18	150,000	15/1050	1,786	3,750	...	5,536
19	100,000	10/1050	1,190	2,500	...	3,690
20	50,000	5/1050	595	1,250	...	1,845
	$10,500,000	1050/1050	$125,000	$262,500	$34,000	$353,500

Discount on Bond Issues Not a Proper Charge to Capital

Under no ordinary circumstances is it correct to treat discount on bond issues as a charge to capital. It does not represent any property; for it is clearly incorrect to consider that the cost in cash of a piece of property varies according to the credit of the purchaser or constructor. Hence, where any such discounts have been charged to capital assets, it is essential for a proper understanding of the balance sheet that this fact should be clearly set forth. In effect, in corporation finance such discounts are frequently included in capital expenditure, as are many other fictitious items which represent either a sanguine estimate of future gains, or mere "water"; and this is done by the fiction of the sale of the property to a new company at a largely inflated value, for a price including the par value of the bonded debt; the intermediaries in this sale then selling the bonds at the market price. This principle has been extended also to cases of reorganization effected without any sale of assets, where the discounts on bonds, as well as bonuses of capital stock issued to facilitate the completion of the reorganization, have all been capitalized. These exceptions must not be taken as a justification for a similar treatment in ordinary cases of financing; and, in fact, there is no real justification for their adoption in any case, beyond that of expediency. The whole system has led in the past to many and serious abuses, and the more strict supervision of capital issues which is now being extended over certain classes of corporations, will tend to put a stop to it in all cases. The objection to charging discount on bond issues to Capital account must not, however, be held to include such a charge of the annual instalment of discount for the period of construction during which interest also is charged to

Capital account. The rate of interest chargeable to capital should be the actual cost of the money, *i. e.,* the effective rate, and any approximation to this rate obtained by including that proportion of the discount which belongs to the period would be a permissible charge to capital.

(3) AVAILABLE CAPITAL RESOURCES

Corporations frequently express a desire to include created but unissued stock and bonds held in treasury as assets, on the ground that these represent available capital resources and are therefore of value.

It is submitted that the value lies not in the par or other value of these securities, but in the fact that certain formalities necessary to their issue, and involving expenditure of both time and money, have been complied with, and that the sale alone remains to be made. It is true that in some cases this sale may be merely a matter of a few minutes' talk with a banker, but in other cases it may be difficult if not impossible. In reality it is only on final sale that these securities become of any real tangible value to the corporation; and the intangible value resulting from their mere creation, or even their use as collateral security, is not properly represented by treating it as an asset at par or market value.

This can better be shown in the schedule of capital liabilities given in Chapter II, (p. 35), and the total of the "Amount in Treasury" column for both stocks and bonds might well be inserted as a memorandum in the balance sheet after the main heading of capital liabilities, but should not be included in the totals.

(4) CURRENT LIABILITIES

The subheadings given in the *pro forma* balance sheet

in Chapter II are almost self-explanatory and call for little additional comment.

Current bank loans and commercial paper should include only seasonal advances, i. e., those made during the part of the year when outlays are heaviest, and repaid in due course each year as the proceeds of sales are collected. It is frequently difficult to draw a clear distinction between current loans and those made for capital purposes, particularly when working capital is provided in this way, but indications generally exist in the manner in which repayments are made which will permit of a proper classification. For instance, loans made against accounts or bills receivable, and repaid as they are collected, would clearly be current loans even though they are immediately and continuously replaced to a greater or less extent by further loans against other accounts and bills. On the other hand a continuous bank overdraft by arrangement with the bank, not of fixed amount, but varying only according to the payments and the withdrawals made in the ordinary course of business, would more properly be considered as a loan for capital purposes. Such overdrafts are very common in England, and are entirely different from temporary overdrafts resulting from financial difficulties, which latter should be treated as a current liability.

Such items as percentages retained on contracts and accounts for goods invoiced and at risk of purchaser, but not received, should be included under trade accounts; but where there is a trade custom to invoice goods for new season's trade some months before the same are used and before payment is due, both the liability and the asset (under the head of stock in trade) are frequently omitted. While there is the justification for this practice that the transaction is made largely for the convenience of the seller, who is anxious to save storage space, and not for that of the purchaser, who would be just as willing to take delivery at a date nearer to his requirements, it is submitted that the true position of the purchaser would be better shown by including the amount on both sides of the balance sheet.

Under the heading of miscellaneous accounts payable should be included all salaries, wages, and other payments accruing and due from day to day and payable at short intervals, while other items accruing but not due until some subsequent date, such as interest, taxes, etc., would appear under the next heading of accrued items.

A difficult question frequently arises as to the period to which assessments of taxes apply. Generally speaking, if the taxes—although not accrued or even ascertainable —become a charge or lien on the property at a particular date, they should be provided for as of that date, at any rate by estimate.

The confusion in the same state and even in the same city is frequently great, and it is difficult to ascertain the facts as to any particular tax. The only safe rule is to err on the side of providing too much rather than too little.

Provision should always be made for all known liabilities, even when the exact amounts are not ascertainable. Some sort of approximate estimate can always be made, and should be included under the heading of current liabilities and not under that of surplus or reserves, for the reason that a real liability exists and should be provided for -in order to show the true position.

(5) CONTINGENT LIABILITIES

This term is used to denote a liability which may or may not arise out of transactions entered into in the past, and in the former event will result in a corresponding addition to the assets. This addition will as a rule be of equal value to the liability, but it may be either more or less.

The most usual contingent liabilities are the following:

(1) Liability on bills discounted, being the obligation arising from the indorsements on the bills when discounted to take up the bills at their face value if the maker does not do so. In this case the liability is a definite fixed value, while the corresponding asset depends on the ability of the maker of the bill to pay, and this ability must be judged and valued in the same manner as his ability to pay accounts or bills not discounted.

(2) Liability on shares in corporations not fully paid up, being the undertaking to pay up the par value of the shares when called on. As this payment increases correspondingly the assets of the corporation, the asset value will as a rule equal the amount of the call. It may, however, happen that the call is made to make good lost assets, or pay the creditors, and in such case it may represent no value at all, and a corresponding reserve will be required.

(3) Liability on guarantees of principal or interest of loans to other persons or corporations. If such loans are fully secured and the guarantee has eventually to be made good, at least an equivalent in property value would be acquired. If not, a reserve might be required.

Two other classes of liability may be considered under this head which are of a somewhat different character.

(1) Liability on contracts to make good defects in work done or goods supplied. This must always be a matter of expense without any corresponding asset, and a reserve to meet such contingent liabilities must always

be provided in full of all expected claims. In fact, this class of items should not appear at all under contingent liabilities but under current liabilities.

(2) Liability on contracts for purchase or sale for future delivery. These contracts are of two kinds: (a) those in products dealt in on produce exchanges at prices which fluctuate from day to day—or speculative contracts; and (b) those made at fixed prices for future requirements of the business.

The measure in the former case is the difference between the future price at date of contract and date of valuation, and this may represent either an asset or liability, which is only contingent in that it differs from the asset or liability value that will ultimately accrue. It properly belongs in either current assets or current liabilities, and has no place under the heading of contingent liabilities.

The latter class of items may be and are usually ignored altogether, on the ground that the contracts are made in the ordinary course of business, and that no liability really arises until the other party to the contract performs his part of it; and inasmuch as, until performance, the actual value of the corresponding asset may usually be taken as equal to the liability value, this treatment is safe. Circumstances might arise—as in the case of wide fluctuations between the contract price and the value at the date of the balance sheet—which would require the creation of some reserve or even justify an asset value in excess of the liability.

The usual method of treatment of contingent liabilities is by a footnote to the balance sheet under this heading, no values being carried into the totals of either assets or liabilities, and inasmuch as in the majority of cases values cannot be definitely stated, this method seems the most satisfactory. Alternatively, however, (1) both assets and liabilities are increased under the respective headings by the liability value; or (2) main headings of "Contingent Assets" and "Contingent Liabilities" are created in the body of the balance sheet, and the values included in both totals. In the case of bills discounted a satisfactory method is to state the full amount of all unmatured bills among the current assets, deducting therefrom on the face of the balance sheet the amount discounted.

(6) SINKING FUND RESERVES FOR REDEMPTION OF DEBT

Sinking Fund or Debt Extinguishment Reserves are not in theory a charge against Income, for the reason that they do not represent a loss or expense, but the extinction of an existing liability. Inasmuch, however, as in most cases the only source out of which such redemption reserve can be provided is the surplus earnings, it is quite usual to insert a provision in trust deeds that the sinking fund reserve is to be provided out of the profits of the year. The discharge of liabilities involves either a corresponding reduction in assets, or the accumulation of other liabilities or surplus. A reduction in current assets or the accumulation of other liabilities as a substitute for bonded indebtedness, is clearly objectionable, and it is therefore desirable that the amount applied each year to sinking fund purposes should be offset by the retention in the business of a corresponding amount of profit, which should be transferred either to a special reserve, or in reduction of some fixed asset account by way of provision for depreciation or otherwise. In the latter case it must be remembered that the provision for depreciation will be to that extent represented by capital instead of current assets, and while there is no theoretical objection to this if the depreciation account is sufficiently large, the latter necessarily ceases to be available in cash for one of its principal purposes, viz., the renewal of various capital assets from time to time. If, however, part of the fixed assets is of a wasting character, the sinking fund reserve may be quite safely applied in reduction of the book value thereof, or it may with equal propriety be applied in reduction of the book value of goodwill or patents.

It is important to note that there is no relation whatever between the amount of sinking fund instalment and the annual depreciation charge; it is therefore still necessary to calculate the latter on the usual principle, and then to consider to what extent the sinking fund instalment may be properly considered as available to meet this provision. The considerations here involved will appear more clearly in dealing with the subject of depreciation.

(7) Other Provisions or Appropriations

In considering reserves it is important to distinguish between voluntary reserves and necessary reserves; the former being mere allocations of surplus while the latter are either an actual liability or a deduction from the book value of an asset.

No balance sheet can set forth clearly the true position of affairs unless all reserves have been provided which, at the time of the preparation of the balance sheet, may be found necessary for contingencies that have actually arisen at or prior to the date to which the balance sheet relates. Such reserves are:

(1) For bad debts either known, or estimated on the basis of past experience.
(2) For depreciation of plant.
(3) For exhaustion of minerals.
(4) For reduction in value of goods on hand to cost or market price.

(5) For damage claims in respect of events which have happened, the resulting money value of which can only be estimated.

(6) For expenses incurred but not definitely ascertained in money value.

The first four of these should in preparing the balance sheet be deducted from the assets to which they relate, while the last two would be included as current liabilities.

On the other hand, there is no obligation to provide out of profits for contingencies that have not arisen but may arise in the future. Such provisions are evidence of prudent foresight, but have no present effect upon the surplus as a whole, and if made they should be set up as a subdivision of the general surplus account, as in the form of balance sheet given in Chapter II. Such voluntary reserves, in addition to sinking funds already dealt with, would consist of:

(a) Provision for insurance against future possible losses from fire, etc., or other insurable risks.

(b) Provision for losses due to accidents that may occur in the future.

(c) Provision for capital outlays representing an application of profits either in the past or future to the creation of fixed assets.

(d) Provision for equalizing dividends in the future; or,

(e) Provision for special expenditures to be incurred in the future.

(8) Secret Reserves

There is a general consensus of opinion that an over-statement of profits knowingly made is improper; but the opposite proposition as to an understatement of profits has so far received little consideration, and yet it is of considerable importance. Corporations are the property of the stockholders; and therefore primarily anything which the stockholders or the directors elected by them may approve, may be considered to be within their power to decide as they like, provided that it is within the law; and it has not been suggested that there is any general law which would prohibit an understatement of profits, as it would undoubtedly prohibit an overstatement. But inasmuch as the stocks of the majority of corporations are quoted on the stock exchanges throughout the country, the corporation is in some sense the property also of the public. It becomes, therefore, a great question to what extent it is legitimate or proper that it should publish a statement of its earnings or its position which materially underestimates either; though it is clearly within the discretion of the managers or directors to make reserves to meet possible contingencies, and the constitution and by-laws of most corporations give them such powers.

Secret reserves may take several forms, as writing down to a comparatively small figure valuable assets, providing excessive depreciation, providing excessive reserves for bad debts, or contingencies, valuing stocks of materials and products on hand at values largely below either cost or market, or including special reserves for future contingencies under the head of accounts payable. Inasmuch as the majority of industrial corporations do not publish their gross earnings, such reserves can easily be made, and are made continually in a form in which they do not appear in any way in the published accounts, and are known therefore only to the directors and managers.

Each case must be judged on its own merits. Where the directors or managers have exercised a wise discretion in providing in advance for contingent losses, incident to the nature of the business, which cannot, from a reasonable point of view, be considered as in excess of the amounts which a wise foresight would provide, it would seem that no exception should be taken to the undisclosed provision thereof. This would apply particularly to cases in which the business conducted was of a fluctuating or speculative character, or in which its success was largely dependent on the maintenance of very high credit, such as a bank. Reserves in such cases may well be larger than in others where such conditions do not exist, provided that they are made on the same sort of basis continuously and not merely spasmodically. In all such cases the sudden disclosure of heavy deficits or losses which are clearly incident to the nature of the business but only occur at irregular intervals, may easily be disastrous to the interests of the stockholders by unduly depressing the market price of the capital stock, and it would seem to be not only the right but the duty of directors to protect them against such contingencies by making ample secret reserves when profits permit. Where, however, reserves are made largely in excess of any possible contingencies, the amounts provided should be disclosed in the Profit and Loss account and probably also in the balance sheet, so that all those interested may be in a position to form a reasonably correct opinion as to the financial position. So far as the majority of corporations and businesses are concerned, publicity in such matters is undoubtedly most desirable; and all reserves to meet contingencies which may occur in the future, but have not yet occurred, should be fully disclosed.

CHAPTER VII

REPAIRS, RENEWALS, DEPRECIATION, AND NEW CONSTRUCTION

In order to insure a correct statement of the earnings and position of any business, it is essential either that its property should be fully maintained at the same standard as at the date of acquisition, or that proper provision should be made foi any falling off from that standard. A little reflection will show that the first alternative is impossible in the case of a new property. After a plant has, within a short period of its original construction, reached its state of fullest efficiency, it is continually wearing out; and even though it may be a long period before the wear and tear reaches such proportions that actual renewal expenditures are either necessary or desirable, yet the shrinkage in value resulting therefrom is going on all the time, and must be reflected in the accounts. The provisions necessary either to maintain the property values, or to compensate for any falling off from the original standard, consist of repairs, renewals, and depreciation, the latter including both that due to wear and tear and that due to obsolescence.

By reason of the fact that frequently the property is maintained by expenditures on additional construction to take the place of that worn out or abandoned, the consideration of construction is also involved in that of maintenance; and further light may be thrown on the whole question by first considering which class of expenditures may be legitimately added to capital account, the natural inference being then drawn that all other expenditures must be provided for in some form out of income.

(1) PROPERTY EXPENDITURES

Classification

Expenditures on property may be broadly divided into:

(a) Actual additions to the property, such as new buildings, new engines or new tools, which did not exist before, or additions to existing articles of this class. All such expenditure would be at once admitted as a proper charge to Capital account.

(b) Alterations to capital assets resulting in increased capacity or reduction in expenses of operation, or both. The treatment of this class of expenditure must depend largely on the circumstances surrounding each case. As a rule that portion of the expenditure which has resulted in additional property or increased capacity may be properly charged to Capital account, while the portion representing reconstruction of a plant to keep pace with modern operating conditions, to prevent deterioration in the effective operating value, or to offset the increase in costs due to the rise in the price of labor and material, would usually be chargeable to Income account either directly or through the renewal or depreciation accounts, discussed later.

(c) Expenditures necessary to rehabilitate and restore to a normal working efficiency a property which has been purchased in a depreciated condition. These may include outlays which under normal conditions could only be considered income charges, but under the special conditions existing may properly be treated as capital.

(d) Finally, we have ordinary replacements, repairs and renewals, recurrent either at long or short intervals, and resulting neither in increased capacity nor in saving in operating expenses. Such would always be a charge against profits, either through the depreciation account or direct, according to the nature of the outlay.

In one sense, it may be said that all expenditures on assets which deteriorate from the wear and tear incidental to operating, are in the nature of deferred charges to operating, and must be written off completely during some fixed term applicable to the particular plant under consideration. This view may be admitted as a true one of individual machine units; but a whole plant remains in existence over long terms of years as a complete entity, and to all intents and purposes—so far as waste due to operating is concerned—may be better considered as a permanent investment, which must be kept in good and efficient going order by means of expenditures on repairs, renewals, and depreciation.

Reconstruction and Improvements

It may frequently happen, as for instance in large reconstruction and improvement works resulting in some partially new structures, and in others substantially repaired and renewed, that it is a difficult matter to determine what proportion of the charges should be made to income and what to capital. The proper rule is that an amount which will fairly represent either the original cost or the value now (according to the general method adopted*) of the property abandoned together with the cost of all alterations, shall be charged to Income account or to credit accounts created out of income; the excess may fairly be capitalized.

Interest and Overhead Charges in Capital Outlay

A difficult problem in the proper determination of the cost of additions and improvements to property is involved in the matter of overhead charges and interest. In the case of expenditures chargeable to profits this question is of

---

*See page 159.

little importance, because the credits to profits in respect of such charges are offset by the debits contained in the charges. In the case of capital expenditures, however, any arbitrary addition for overhead charges and interest involves a credit to and increase in profits corresponding to the addition to capital expenditures. In a going concern a conservative course is generally adopted, and no charge is made beyond the labor and material cost for expenditures of moderate amount on additions to the property; but, on the other hand, if a new and distinct plant were in course of construction, and producing no earnings from operation, the whole of the administration expenses and the interest paid on loans raised for this special purpose would be charged to construction account; and rightly so, being necessary elements of completing the work.

This at once suggests the argument that what is reasonable and proper in the latter case should also be reasonable and proper in the former. The safe rule is, however, that no charges should be made to construction for overhead expenses which would have been equally incurred if there had been no such construction, and would in that case have been charged against profits; but that, if special loans have been raised to provide funds for construction purposes, or a special staff of employees maintained for this sole purpose, the interest paid on such loans and the salaries of the special staff may properly be charged to construction account until the work under construction is in effective operation. Any other method might result in the creation of fictitious profits, which could not be realized as long as the property was operated, and might never be realized on its ultimate sale.

Profits on Construction Work Not Permissible

Managers of the operating departments of a factory frequently claim that they should be allowed to charge a profit on construction work carried out for their own mills, on the ground that, if the work were done outside, they would have to pay a profit, and at the same time would set free their own facilities to carry out additional work at a profit for outside customers; and they even go so far as to say that, if they can not charge a profit on construction work so carried out, they will in future have the work done by outside contractors. It must be admitted that this is a plausible argument, but a little further consideration will show that it is fallacious.

There is here a confusion between a profit and a saving. The reason that a concern undertakes its own construction work in place of letting outside contracts therefor, is that it can by that means effect a saving in its expenditure by taking advantage of its own capital and facilities to carry out the work, instead of using the organization and the capital of others, upon which it would have to pay a profit. The saving so effected is of considerable advantage, in that it reduces the amount of capital invested, and future earnings will represent a larger return on the investment. Moreover, it is seldom true in a well-managed going concern that the use of its facilities for construction expenditure involves giving up profitable work for outsiders, which would otherwise have been undertaken; the situation will have been foreseen and arrangements made so that its organization may, almost automatically, expand sufficiently to provide for any increase in its operations which is likely to be thrown upon it. In the contrary case it would be difficult to find justification for increasing costs of construction because of the lack of foresight of the management. Moreover, if a sum be added to the cost of construction and credited to Income account, to represent the profit which would have been earned by the company if the work had been done for outsiders instead of for itself, this profit can only be made available for distribution by increasing the amount of capital contributed for new construction work; and it can hardly be considered good financial policy to increase indebtedness or take in new partners merely for the purpose of paying dividends. The only sound principle that can be adopted is to charge to construction all costs and expenses which are directly attributable to that construction, together with a fair and moderate proportion of necessary indirect expenses and of interest actually paid, but no further amount to represent profit.

It should be noted that in England the Companies (Consolidation) Act, 1908,* now provides that when any shares of a company are issued to provide money for construction purposes, the company may, subject to certain regulations and to the approval of the Board of Trade (a government department), pay interest on such shares to the stockholders at a rate not exceeding 4 per cent per annum during the construction period; and that the interest so paid may be added to and form part of the cost of construction. This provision does not permit of the addition to construction cost of any interest which is not actually paid out in cash.

So far this question has been considered in reference to its bearing on the determination of profits. There is, however, the other aspect of its bearing on values. If an asset is created by construction without including in the charge all the elements which an outside contractor would charge, the value based upon market prices will clearly be low. The saving so effected is of undoubted benefit, in that less capital has been employed upon which profit has to be earned, but the asset value is understated. On the ground already stated that no profits should be made out of construction, this difference in value cannot be considered as a profit arising out of operations; but there can be no objection to treating it as surplus appropriated to capital purposes,

*See Appendix IV.

provided always that the total book value of all assets together is not in excess of actual value.

(2) Maintenance Expenditures

Turning now to the consideration of maintenance expenditures, it is apparent at the outset that there are two distinct theories upon which this problem can be properly considered.

Under the first method, capital is considered to have been invested, once for all, in property which is permanent and must be kept up at the expense of income, no additions being made to the capital account except for entirely new and additional property, and all expenditures on maintaining or replacing the existing property, irrespective of the relative values at the time of construction and of replacement, being charged to Income account.

Under the second method, each unit of property is followed from its construction to its removal or destruction; upon abandonment its original cost value is written off to income and the cost of the new structure which takes its place is charged to capital.

Under the first method changes in price levels are reflected in the Income account, while under the second method they are reflected in Capital account. Over a long period of years, where prices are rising and falling alternately, there will be little difference between the results of the two methods in this respect, provided that one or the other is consistently followed throughout for each class of assets; and provided that proper provision is made under the first method for dealing with property abandoned and not replaced. If, however, prices are continuously rising or continuously falling, the first method will give greater or smaller charges, respectively, to Income account, than the second, and the latter will tend to keep the Capital account nearer to the current level of prices than the former. The first method perhaps brings out more clearly the problem with which operating officials have to deal—namely, the maintenance of the property entrusted to them for the purposes of operation—and avoids the confusion which frequently arises between depreciation due to wear and tear (which sooner or later will have to be made good by cash expenditures), and appreciation arising from circumstances entirely outside the operations, which can never be realized so long as operations continue, and which should be dealt with as a separate question.

Treatment of Maintenance Expenditures by Railroads

The two methods are well illustrated by the present practice of railroads where both are in use for different portions of the property. It should be noted that from the earliest days the treatment by railroad companies of renewals, replacements, and depreciation, has differed from the practice general among commercial concerns. Prior to the revision of the classification of railroad accounts by the Interstate Commerce Commission beginning in 1907, railroad accounts were kept on the theory that the capital and revenue accounts were distinct, and that the only charges to be made to the latter should be for the cost of replacing property as and when replacements were made, no provision whatever being made for property abandoned. This difference in treatment was fostered in England by the legislative enactments in regard to railroads; but from an accounting standpoint it was never regarded as resting on very solid ground, and from a financial standpoint its results did not prove satisfactory. After the panic in 1893 and the numerous railroad reorganizations which followed, whilst the methods above noted were continued, their harmful effects were largely counterbalanced by the practice, which became general, of charging to income or profit and loss large sums which might properly have been capitalized.

In the classification promulgated by the Interstate Commerce Commission in 1907, provision was made for writing off property abandoned, whether replaced or not, according to one or other of the two methods described. In allocating charges for replacement of equipment the second method is followed, and the cost of the original unit going out of service (less salvage) is required to be provided for out of income, while the entire cost of the new unit, which replaces it, is to be charged to capital; so that not only the increased capacity but any variation in the price of equipment is carried to Capital account. Provision is also to be made year by year through a depreciation account for the estimated wear and tear accrued during that year, and in advance of the time when it becomes necessary to make good the depreciation by maintenance expenditures.

In the case of all other replacements the first method is followed, the classification providing that the cost of replacing abandoned property must be met out of income by charging thereto "the cost, at the current prices of labor and material, of renewing such property by the construction or installation of other property substantially similar in capacity, service and accessories, and having a physical condition and an expectation of life in service equal to that of the replaced property when acquired, or, if improved after acquirement, when in its best condition." If the replacement is accompanied by an addition or improvement properly chargeable to capital, the cost of replacing the abandoned property as defined above must be estimated, and this estimate of cost is not to be "based upon the current prices of material identical with that of which the thing abandoned was constructed, particularly when such material is no longer obtainable except at prohibitive prices and would not be used if a renewal of the property without betterment were undertaken."* Under this ruling no provision is made for shrinkage in value due to wear and tear of the property until it becomes necessary to make good the depreciation by actual expenditures.

In the case of property (other than equipment) abandoned and not replaced, the cost (estimated if not known), less salvage, is to be charged to Profit and Loss account, and it is also provided that by consent of the Interstate Commerce Commission reserves for the estimated loss on abandonment may be made by charges to operating expenses, *i. e.,* Income account, in advance of abandonment. It thus appears that in respect of a great part of the property of a railroad, no provision is required, or in fact permitted, for depreciation due to wear and tear or obsolescence in anticipation of expenditures. Such practice, while at present binding on railroads, and owing to special conditions more defensible for such companies, does not form a safe guide for other undertakings, and it is noticeable that the best electric railway and lighting companies, and other public utility companies which for many years followed the railroad practice, have tended steadily away therefrom, and now provide for depreciation along the lines followed by commercial concerns.

Classification of Maintenance Expenditures

Having disposed of these important questions, the methods of providing for the maintenance of property may be considered. Maintenance expenditures consist of:

(1) Repairs.

(2) Renewals.

(3) Improvements which cannot be capitalized.

---

*The words quoted are extracted from the general instructions for dealing with expenditures for additions and betterments issued by the Interstate Commerce Commission under date of July 1, 1910, and they give a good description of the first method of providing for maintenance of Capital account.

There are also improvements which might legitimately be capitalized, but which conservative policy desires to provide for out of profits; this class may be at once disposed of inasmuch as, being legitimate capital, they should be treated as such; charged to capital, and credited to profits appropriated for capital purposes.

The first class of expenditures will occur continuously and will usually be charged against Income as and when incurred, although occasionally repairs and renewals are grouped together and treated on the basis now to be described for the latter. It is difficult to draw a hard and fast line between these three classes, as one naturally merges into the other, but the following has in practice been found satisfactory when applied with reasonable intelligence to doubtful items.

(1) *Repairs.* This should include all current expenditures recurring from day to day and from month to month on the general upkeep of the existing property without the renewal of any substantial part thereof, and generally all periodical repairs which are necessarily undertaken within, say, one year.

(This caption will, of course, include certain renewals of small parts, etc., such as would be necessary to continue the useful life of any unit of building, plant or machinery over the estimated period of its life.)

(2) *Renewals.* This should include all expenditures incurred in renewing, in whole or in part, any unit of building, plant or machinery, which tend to extend its useful life beyond the average term. These expenditures would in general be those which would only occur at long intervals of two or three years, and whose effect would last for a number of years afterward.

(3) *Improvements.* This should include any expenditures made upon existing buildings, plant and machinery,

other than those covered by the terms "Repairs" and "Renewals."

(3) RENEWALS AND DEPRECIATION

General Considerations

In practice it is difficult, and perhaps hardly necessary, to draw any hard and fast line between renewals and improvements. Renewals of plant generally carry with them some measure of improvement, and while for management purposes it is as well to distinguish between the two classes of expenditures, both of them must be considered as making good or arresting depreciation which has taken or might take place; and for this purpose provisions for such improvements as can not be charged to Capital account will, as a rule, be made out of the fund provided to take care of renewals and depreciation as now to be described.

Renewal expenditures being incurred only periodically —and in the case of a new plant only after a period of several years—while the wear and tear goes on continually, must be provided for each year by an estimated charge based on the best available information as to the life and character of the particular plant. Involved therein is the ultimate replacement of each separate unit of plant when, by reason of excessive wear and tear, want of efficiency, or obsolescence, it ceases to be economical to operate it. There is some difference of opinion as to whether depreciation due to obsolescence on a large scale—for instance, as in the conversion of horse street railways into cable or electric railways, or of an ordinary steam electric generating plant into a steam or water turbine plant—should necessarily be met out of earnings, on the ground that the savings in future cost of operation will pay for the charge. This, however, seems to be an argument in favor of providing for the loss on the change out of future rather than past earnings, for there can be no doubt that certain property has ceased to exist. The result of such a policy was well seen in the case of the Metropolitan Street Railway system in New York, which, largely for want of proper depreciation charges, was practically ruined and forced into the hands of a receiver; the reorganization involving a considerable reduction in the capital values of the property.   Another objection to the postponement or abandonment of charges for accruing renewals and depreciation is to be found in the lessened operating costs and greater profits thereby shown, which, in these days of rate regulation of public service companies, must, if continued, inevitably lead to demands for reductions in rates.   If an insufficient provision has been made in the past, and the resulting profits have been distributed in dividends at a full and reasonable, or even excessive rate, it is difficult afterwards to maintain, as an argument against rate reductions, that the provisions for depreciation, etc., have been insufficient in the past and must be largely increased in the future.   In the case of Knoxville v. Knoxville Water Company, the United States Supreme Court held that the water company, having failed to provide for depreciation in the past, could not, therefore, claim a value for its property on the basis of cost to reproduce, without deduction for depreciation.

The only sound principle would seem to be that no profit can be properly said to have been earned until full provision has been made on the best available data both for accruing renewals and for depreciation due to obsolescence or other causes; and, if such full provision is not made, it should be clearly understood that eventually, except for possible appreciation of property due to entirely extraneous causes, part of the capital will be lost, or will have been distributed in dividends.

It remains to consider how such provisions for renewals

and depreciation should be dealt with. In the early life of a new plant, there will be little or no expenditure upon renewals, and a consequent accumulation to the credit of Depreciation account. After some years renewal expenditures to be charged against this account will increase, but there should always remain, if the provisions have been sufficient, a credit balance which will represent the difference between original cost and average efficient value; *i. e.,* the value below which the plant cannot be allowed to fall without becoming inefficient. It might at first be thought that the factor of obsolescence would not begin to operate until an even later period, and in some extreme cases this may be true; but as a rule, owing to the continuous progress of science and invention, obsolescence will be as continuous as renewals, and after an increase of the Depreciation account to a figure which cannot be definitely stated but may, for the sake of example, be put at from 25 to 33 1/3 per cent of the original plant cost, expenditures will, on the average of a few years, keep pace with the addition to the Depreciation account and there should be no further accumulation.

The charges to the Depreciation account will vary according to which of the methods of maintaining the Capital account—as fully defined on page 159—is adopted. Under the first method all expenditures, both for renewals and replacements, will be charged to Depreciation account, no charge will be made for property abandoned and replaced, but a charge should be made for property abandoned but not replaced. Under the second method all expenditures on renewals, as above defined, will be charged against the Depreciation account, as well as the book value of all property abandoned and not replaced, the charge to operating expenses consisting of (1) repairs as defined above, and (2) depreciation; while the cost of new property, to replace that abandoned and charged to the Depreciation account, will be charged to Capital account.

(4) METHODS OF PROVIDING FOR DEPRECIATION

One, and the most simple, method of providing for depreciation, for which little or no justification exists, is by the charge of arbitrary sums from time to time, either to income or to profit and loss, as earnings and surplus permit, and upon no definite basis.

Any scientific system necessitates in the first place a detailed plant inventory, divided into groups according to the estimated life, assuming ordinary repairs to be made. From these data can be calculated the amount which must be provided in a definite number of years to make up the difference between cost and scrap values at the time when the unit may be expected, in the ordinary course of events, to become obsolete. It must be noted that all such calculations are purely estimates, based on past experiences so far as available; and periodical revisions of all the elements involved are necessary if the result is to work out with any degree of accuracy.

There are four methods by which the amount required for depreciation as thus ascertained may be provided.

(1) The annuity method; *i. e.,* setting aside each year a fixed annual sum which, accumulated at compound interest at some assumed rate, will provide the amount required at the end of the agreed life.

(2) The straight line method, by which an equal proportionate part is charged each year; *i. e.,* on an outlay of $1,000,000 with a life of twenty years, and a scrap value of $300,000, the annual charge would be $35,000.

(3) The diminishing balance method, under which, in the case of an outlay of $1,000,000 with a life of twenty

years and a scrap value of $300,000, an annual sum of 6 per cent on the balance at the beginning of each year—after deducting the depreciation of the previous year—would be provided.

(4) A combination of the first two methods, by which an annuity is provided for so much of the depreciation as represents the drop from new to normally efficient value, and the straight line method is provided for the balance, which represents renewal expenditures which will have to be incurred.

Annuity Method

Objections to the annuity method are that it does not take into account that expenditures are continually being incurred to make good the depreciation accrued; that these expenditures must be taken out of the fund; consequently that the fund will not remain intact during even a small part of the assumed term and that it cannot be accumulated to the estimated required amount at the end of the term. Furthermore, by the addition of interest it becomes an increasing charge against profits each year, unless, which is unlikely, the fund is specifically invested; and it would be difficult for the owners to resist the temptation to reduce the annual contributions in later years if profits were insufficient for their needs. In fact this sinking fund method does not take into account the essential character of a depreciation fund—viz.: a fund set aside not for the sole purpose of providing the value of the plant at the end of a term, but for the much more important purpose of keeping the plant up to the highest standard of efficiency, and leaving it at that standard at the end of the term by continuous expenditures during the term.

A further and perhaps even greater objection to the annuity method is that the accumulations are small in the early years and large in the later years, whereas the actual fall in value of the plant will usually be greatest when it is new, and gradually decrease as it gets older. Consequently if depreciation is provided on the annuity method, even assuming that it makes good the whole value at the end of an assumed term, the apparent net property value will, throughout the whole of that term, be in excess—and in the earlier years largely in excess—of the actual. If the property changes hands on a valuation basis, the amount of depreciation accumulated on the annuity basis will be found entirely inadequate.

This principle came up for consideration in the purchase by the British Government of the National Telephone Company in Great Britain. The company claimed a depreciation deduction on the annuity basis, while the government claimed the larger deduction provided by the straight line method. After hearing testimony on the subject the arbitrator decided in favor of the contention of the government.

Straight Line Method

The second, or straight line method, has been found on the whole the most satisfactory for a going concern in an average condition, but for a new plant it results in a considerable accumulation during earlier years while the plant is getting down to its average, say 75 per cent condition, and this accumulation will in all probability not require to be expended on renewals.

This method lends itself readily to a sliding scale adjustment by which, as is proper, the provision for depreciation may be varied in accordance with the amount of business done. If a plant is working at only 50 per cent of capacity and is thoroughly maintained, the depreciation due to wear and tear is undoubtedly much less than if it were working at 90 per cent of capacity, while that due to obsolescence is unchanged. On this basis, for any particular plant a sliding scale of depreciation, according to used capacity, may be prepared which will be just to both present and future owners, subject always to the necessarily estimated character of all depreciation allowances.

Diminishing Balance Method

The third method is objectionable in that it ignores to some extent the spending feature of the fund. When, however, renewals made are added to capital each year and the depreciation deducted, and the depreciation for the next year is calculated on the balance so resulting, this method would give results not widely different from the second, but the rate would require to be higher. The method as thus carried out is confusing; the original plant value is lost sight of, and the accumulated depreciation unexpended and available for future renewals is not clearly shown.

Combination Method

The fourth method is a new and untried one which has been the subject of some discussion. In a quite new plant it has the advantage of diminishing the depreciation charge in the earlier years, and, provided that the annual instalments are invested outside at the assumed rate and maintained as an investment, it might be found satisfactory. If the accumulations are invested in the business, the charge against profits each year will increase so that eventually it will be quite a serious item in poor years, and there will be great temptation to draw upon it in favor of profits. The objection already noted to the annuity method, viz.: that it overstates property values, applies equally to this modified form of it, for the depreciation actually accruing within the early years in respect of the fall from a new to a normally efficient value, will only be provided over a much longer term and more towards the end of that term than at the beginning.

Treatment of Interest on Accumulated Depreciation

Any of the methods described will result from time to time in the accumulation of funds in excess of necessary or economical expenditures for renewals and replacements, and this accumulation at once raises the question of interest. The annuity method automatically provides for this, but in the other methods no interest charge is usually considered. The accumulated funds may either be held as unexpended cash balances on current account or on deposit, or may be invested in outside interest-bearing securities, or may be invested in the undertaking—which is the most usual case. Strictly speaking, interest on the accumulated funds should go in reduction of the annual charge to operations to the extent earned, and if earned in the business this credit to operations would be offset by a debit to Income account as a distribution of profits. When only stockholders are interested in the profits there is no necessity to take into consideration interest on these balances, as, if earned from outside sources, it forms a credit to Income account, and if not so earned, it forms part of the profits on the business just as does surplus not distributed in dividends. In cases, however, where outsiders are interested in operating profits, such as in profit-sharing agreements between public service corporations and a state or city, it is important that this principle should be carried out, as otherwise the stockholders alone will obtain the benefit of the use of the accumulated funds. The only difficulty is as to the rate of interest to be allowed; in theory this should be that proportion of the net profits—before paying interest or dividends—which the accumulated balance of the depreciation fund bears to the total capital stock, bonds, surplus, and all other funds actually invested in the business; or the rate may be taken at some figure on the average approximating thereto.

Exhaustion of Minerals

Thus far depreciation has been considered in respect of assets which are used for operations; there is another class of depreciation consisting of the actual consumption of subsoil products which reduces the original property value. This is more generally known as provision for exhaustion of minerals.

The product taken out of the land becomes stock in trade as soon as it is extracted, and whatever the land was worth before its extraction, it is clearly worth an appreciable amount less thereafter. The provision to be made should be on the basis of the quantity extracted, having regard to the total available, and to the realizable value of the property after the products have all been extracted. The same principle would also apply to timber lands where no provision is made for reforesting. The contention is sometimes raised that no provision need be made for exhaustion of subsoil products where the amount known to be in a definite tract at the end of any period is largely in excess of that which had been discovered at the beginning of the period. This argument can not, however, be admitted except as a reason for reducing the rate to be provided. As a general principle, whatever there was in the ground, whether known or unknown, has been reduced during the period under consideration by whatever amount has been extracted; and while the new discoveries may be accepted as reducing the necessary rate of provision for extinction from, say, one dollar to one cent per unit of quantity, the original principle that provision must be made, holds good on the smaller figure, whatever it is. It may be, of course, that the provisions made in earlier years have been sufficient to cover a number of future years on the basis, from the commencement, of the rate subsequently found to be sufficient in view of the new discoveries; and in this case there would be no necessity to provide further for extinction until the total production at the new rate is equal to the total amount written off.

It may happen, as in oil fields and gold mines, that it is impossible to obtain any reasonable basis upon which to calculate depreciation, and in such cases it is customary to state profits before making such provision, and either to apply a proportion of the profits in purchasing or developing other areas, or to return the whole to the owners with the clear understanding that the amounts they receive represent a return of capital as well as a distribution of profits.

Amortization of Leaseholds

The term depreciation is frequently applied to the amortization of properties of which the lease only and not the freehold has been purchased. It is not, however, a correct term to apply in such cases; for the so-called purchase money, being merely rent paid in advance over the term of the lease, is the present value of an annuity for that term, the annual instalments of which should be charged against profits in due course. In practice the straight line method is frequently adopted in these cases also, and an equal annual instalment (in the case of a twenty-year lease) of one-twentieth of the purchase money is charged into operating expenses.

Conclusion

The present discussion of this whole subject is far from exhaustive and deals merely with the general principles involved. Volumes have been, and may still be, written on the detailed application of the various methods to different undertakings, and to these volumes— and to papers on the subject appearing in the many technical journals—reference should be made.

A word of caution may not be out of place as to the essential part played by estimates in all schemes for providing for current wear and tear and future renewals. The only test is actual expenditures, together with a skilled examination of the physical properties. Few schemes have been in force for a sufficiently long period to provide a test of their accuracy; and organic changes by sale, reconstruction or destruction, as well as the rapid growth of land values, have all tended to confuse the issue. A few cases in special industries have tended to show that provisions for depreciation have been inadequate in these cases to provide for necessary changes; and there are other cases in which excessive and evident liberality has produced an opposite result. Conservative policy would, under these circumstances, aim at ample provision in years of good profits, while maintaining the estimated minimum in hard times; such a policy builds up ample reserves which will often be useful in tiding over long periods of depression, and generally conserving and strengthening the business against unforeseen contingencies which may easily bring less conservative concerns to disaster. While a greater approach to scientific accuracy in all such matters is much to be desired, real safety lies rather in an ample provision than in a strictly accurate one.

CHAPTER VIII

SPECIAL POINTS IN CORPORATION ACCOUNTING AND FINANCE

(1) ACCOUNTING FOR HOLDING COMPANIES

The now common practice of forming large aggregations of capital on the basis of a control by one corporation of the whole or the majority of the stocks of a number of others, raises important accounting questions.

It has generally been considered that the balance sheet of any corporation, prepared from its books and records properly kept, would disclose its true financial position; but the development of this system of control has shown that such a balance sheet will no longer suffice for this purpose.

It is important in this connection to realize the difference between an investment in a company when this investment represents only a small proportion of its capital stock, and an investment representing the whole or practically the whole, and carrying with it the absolute control of the operations. Thus, corporation "A" may own the whole stock of corporation "B," both carrying on a similar business. Stockholders in "A" may know this fact, but have no means of ascertaining the real position of corporation "B." "A," having the control of "B," may turn over to "B" all its unremunerative work, with the result of showing large profits on its own accounts, while the accounts of "B" show correspondingly large losses. Corporation "A" in its balance sheet may carry its investments at cost, probably merged under the general head of "Cost of Properties," with all its other capital assets. Corporation "B" may obtain loans from corporation "A" which largely exceed its current assets, and may be expended in construction work, or even lost in operations, while corporation "A" may carry in its balance sheet these same loans as current assets recoverable on demand.

The Consolidated Balance Sheet and Income Account

By reason of the misleading character of the ordinary balance sheet in such cases, there has been evolved the consolidated balance sheet; the basis of which is the recognition of the common-sense fact that a network of companies connected with each other by control of stockholdings, is still in effect one undertaking, and that if the stockholders in the holding company are to have before them a clear statement of its position, legal technicalities must be brushed to one side, and the position of the holding company shown in its relation, not to these subcompanies, but to the general public. The position of the holding company can only be changed by outside influences affecting itself or its constituent companies, and not by any change in the relation between itself and these companies, or in the relations among the latter. The consolidated balance sheet represents the true position of the whole group of the constituent companies to the outside world, and is thus not the balance sheet of a corporation, but of a condition after eliminating all the relations of the constituent companies one to another. Debts due by one company of the group to another; stocks of one company owned by another; earnings of one company at the expense of another—are all eliminated. The amount by which the value of the stocks of any company on the books of another exceeds or falls short of the par value thereof, represents an addition to or diminution of the asset of goodwill in the final balance sheet; and as a result the capital assets in the consolidated balance sheet consist of the total physical assets of all the companies (that is, land, buildings, plant, machinery, etc.), and in addition an item of goodwill represented by—

(a) The goodwill asset in the balance sheets of the separate companies, and

(b) The amount by which the aggregate book value to the holding company of the stocks of subsidiary companies exceeds the par value of that stock and the surplus at the date of acquisition.

Similarly, the capital liabilities represent the stocks and bonds of all the companies in the hands of the public, those owned between companies being eliminated.

The consolidated earnings account is made up on the same principles. Profits resulting to one company out of sales to another are eliminated. Only sales and purchases to and from the outside public are included, so that no profits are considered such except those made on deliveries outside the organization.

In other words, the whole organization is considered as merely a series of separate works under the same ownership; and the same accounting principles which would apply to a corporation owning several factories, are applied to the one owning the whole stocks of a number of subsidiary companies, which in turn own the stocks of other subsidiary companies, all the companies in the group themselves owning and operating their own factories. It will readily be understood that in practice the preparation of a statement of earnings exactly on the basis here laid down is a difficult matter; but inasmuch as a neglect of these principles, so far as the Income account is concerned, only means the swelling of the totals both of gross earnings and cost of operation, it is not of so much importance; provided that the valuation of the stocks of goods on hand is made on the basis of actual labor, material, and expense involved therein, without including any proportion of the profit of the different companies in the organization through which these products may have come, and provided also that capital expenditures do not contain any intercompany profit.

A balance sheet of a corporation, whose only or principal assets are stated to be investments in other companies, should be looked upon with suspicion, unless the names of the other companies are given, and clear statements are also given of their financial position; and even then a collection of balance sheets can not show the true financial position of the whole group until they are all combined into one and the intercompany interests eliminated.

In respect of the earnings of such a consolidation similar considerations prevail. Legally, the earnings consist of the results of the operations of the holding company, together with any dividends which may be declared on the stocks which it owns in the subsidiary companies; and so long as those stocks represent only minority interests in companies which are not in any way controlled or operated by the directors of the holding company, an Income account prepared in such a way would be a correct and proper statement from an accounting as well as from a legal point of view.

Under the conditions, however, of majority or complete ownership, as they so commonly exist, no statement of earnings can be considered correct which does not show in one account the profits or losses of the whole group of companies, irrespective of whether dividends have or have not been declared thereby. If this principle be not insisted upon, it is within the power of the directors of the holding company to regulate its profits according not to facts, but to their own wishes, by distributing or withholding dividends of the subsidiary companies; or even to largely overstate the profits of the whole group by declaring dividends in those subcompanies which have made profits, while entirely omitting to make provision for losses which have been made by other.companies in the group.

Legal Status of Consolidated Balance Sheet

It is doubtful whether there is any existing law which could legally require a corporation to make up its statement of profits on the basis here suggested; but possibly it may eventually be found that the ordinary rule, of a reasonable valuation of assets, may be made to cover this point, for the following reasons. It is clear that whatever the value of an investment in a corporation may be at a particular date, its value at any subsequent date (other things being equal) must be greater or less by the amount of the profits or losses made and not distributed during the intervening period. Even if other conditions at the two dates are not the same, and—quite apart from any consideration of the earnings or losses during the intervening period—there is a considerable appreciation or depreciation in the investment, that appreciation or depreciation must undoubtedly be more or less, respectively, by reason of profits earned or losses incurred. The change in value of the asset is at any rate partly due to the result of the operations for the purpose of which the investment is held. On the general principle, therefore, that an Income account should take into account all profits or losses resulting from the trading operations, but should not take into account the profits or losses arising from a revaluation of capital assets, it may eventually be held, on legal as well as on accounting principles, that the statement of earnings presented by a holding company is not correct unless it takes into account, by way of either a reserve or a direct addition to or deduction from the capital value of the investment, the profits or losses made in operating the subsidiary companies.

Intercompany Profits and Accounting

In a large consolidation, when the subsidiaries are carrying on business as separate entities, and contracting and dealing with each other as independent concerns, the elimination of profits on sales or transfers between companies is a somewhat difficult and complicated matter, particularly having regard to the fact that each subsidiary company is legally entitled to take up the profits on such sales, and, if there are substantial minority interests outstanding, has no right to exclude them. This difficulty has been overcome by means of an elaborate system of accounting which provides for carrying the intercompany profit through the operations as a separate item from the original cost, until such time as the finished product is sold to parties outside the consolidation. The method by which this result is accomplished may be shortly outlined as follows:

Company A produces a raw material and sells it to company B at a profit of, say, 10 per cent; company B converts this raw material into a partly finished product and ships it over a railroad C, owned by the consolidation, to company D, by whom it is further manufactured and finally sold to outside parties. Company A produces material to the cost value of $100,000, and sells $20,000 of this to outside parties, $60,000 to company B, and has the remaining $20,000 in stock. Company B buys material from company A, costing $60,000, for $66,000; spends $34,000 in further manufacture; ships $70,000 of the manufactured product over railroad C to company D; sells $20,000 to outsiders, and has $10,000 in stock. Company D purchases products from company B, costing $70,000, for $77,000; pays $5,000 freight to railroad C—which costs the latter $3,500;

expends $18,000 in completing its manufacture; sells $80,000 of the finished product to outsiders, and has the remaining $20,000 in stock.

The books of company A require no special entries.

In company B's books its Manufacturing account will stand as follows:

	I. C. Profit	1st Cost	Total
Cost of material....	$6,000	$60,000	$66,000
Manufacturing cost.	.....	34,000	34,000
	$6,000	$94,000	$100,000
Cost of Sales:			
To outside parties	1,200	18,800	20,000
To Company D..	4,200	65,800	70,000
Balance in stock....	$600	$9,400	$10,000

In company D's books the Manufacturing account will be dealt with similarly, as follows:

	I. C. Profit	1st Cost	Total
Cost of material per Company B....	$11,200	$65,800	$77,000
Freight	1,500	3,500	5,000
Manufacturing cost	.....	18,000	18,000
	$12,700	$87,300	$100,000
Cost of Sales:			
To outside parties	10,160	69,840	80,000
Balance in stock...	$2,540	$17,460	$20,000

The subsidiary companies will take up in their Income accounts the whole of their profits on their sales, and will declare dividends in the usual way. Out of the dividends it receives, the holding company will set up $600 in respect of B's profits, and $2,540 in respect of D's profits, or a total of

$3,140, which will be credited to an inventory reserve. In this way, all stocks on hand of all companies are, on the consolidated balance sheet, carried at net cost within the consolidation, and the consolidated income takes up no profit except on sales made to outside parties. If any of the product is used for construction work within the organization, the net cost only is used, so that no profit of subsidiary companies enters into capital expenditures.

The actual process, by reason of the magnitude of the business and number of transactions, is necessarily more complicated than the simple example given, which, however, is sufficient to show the principles involved.

What is a Constituent Company?

One other difficult point is the determination of what is or is not a constituent company whose Profits and Losses or Assets and Liabilities should be brought into account in this manner. It is suggested that this depends partly on the proportion of stock owned, and partly upon the degree of control exercised by the holding company. When the latter owns at least a majority of the stock, operates the company, dictates its policy, and practically treats its property as its own, subject only to the right of the minority stockholders to receive a share of the profits, the conditions would appear to be such as to require the proportion of profits and losses corresponding to the stock owned to be taken up. In order to justify a consolidated balance sheet, in addition to the other conditions just mentioned, the ownership of at least the common stock should be substantially complete; or the balance not owned should consist either of shares left in the hands of managers or others for business purposes, or of shares the ownership of which cannot be traced. On the other hand, a mere majority ownership of stock without any effective control of the management and operation, should properly be treated as a permanent investment, subject to the same rules as other investments of a similar character.

The conditions under which any stock of a subsidiary company remains outstanding are of some importance, not only in determining whether the ownership of the holding company is sufficient to justify or require consolidated accounts, but also in determining what proportion, if any, of the surplus should appear on such a balance sheet as appertaining to the minority stockholders. The proper practice is to take up as a liability the par value of the outstanding stock, together with its relative share of surplus; but when the amount involved is small, the proportion of surplus is not always set aside.

If minority stock is left outstanding by deliberate intent, as, for instance, to give managers of the company a substantial interest in its results, then a share of any undistributed surplus clearly appertains to this outstanding stock, and the liability to be taken up, therefore, is the par value of the stock, together with the proper proportion of the accumulated surplus.

Other Forms of Consolidated Statements

While the consolidated balance sheet already discussed is on the whole the best method of stating the accounts of a holding company with a group of controlled subsidiaries, it is not necessarily the only one. It must be remembered always that the object of accounts is to show facts, and that any form of statement which discloses all material facts is equally permissible and proper; whether one or other of these forms should be adopted, is largely, but within limits, a matter of individual preference.

Such statements are frequently prepared in a form in which there is shown, as one item in the balance sheet of the

holding company under the heading of "Investments in Subsidiary Companies Controlled," the total cost to the holding
company of the stocks of its subsidiary companies. This is
supported by a columnar statement, each separate column
of which contains the assets and liabilities of one subsidiary
company under the usual and proper headings; while the
total column contains a summary of all the detail columns,
eliminating intercompany items, and adding or deducting
the amounts by which the prices paid by the holding company
for the stocks of the subsidiaries exceed or fall short of
the par value of their stocks and surplus.

The consolidated balance sheet shows to shareholders
of the holding company the position of the interests they
own or control through these shares, but it does not perhaps answer this purpose so well for either creditors of, or
minority stockholders in, subsidiary companies. The consolidated balance sheet, being a grouped balance sheet, does
not distinguish between the liabilities of different companies
in the group, and does not show separately the assets to
which the creditors must look for the discharge of these
liabilities. Similarly, the stocks outstanding in the hands
of the public are shown as representing all the assets in the
consolidation, and no separation is made of those appertaining to the stocks of any particular subsidiary company outstanding in the hands of the public.

Such objections apply in a lesser degree to the balance
sheet of any single company which has different classes of
bonded debt, each secured on separate assets. The objections in the case of the consolidated balance sheet, as in the
case of any ordinary balance sheet, can be met by subsidiary
schedules giving the information required, or by publishing
the balance sheet of each separate company as well as the
consolidated one.

(2) Profits Earned Before Date of Consolidation

A question of considerable importance in its bearing upon the determination of profits in a holding company, or in any corporation which has acquired a going business, is that of the proper disposition of the profits of the consolidating companies, or of the purchased business, earned prior to the date of consolidation. There is a clear rule of common sense, and probably also of law, that a corporation cannot earn profits before it exists; when, therefore, a corporation at its organization purchases an undertaking, together with the profits accrued from a certain prior date, the whole of such profits earned prior to the date of purchase must be treated as a deduction from the purchase price, and not as a credit to Income account available for dividends.

This proposition is the more evident if it be remembered that these profits exist in the form of assets included among those purchased, and that any realization thereof is merely a return to the purchasing company of a portion of the purchase money, *i. e.,* of the capital of the corporation. Similar reasoning will show that where a holding corporation purchases the stocks of several others, all profits of the purchased corporations accruing up to the date of the purchase must be treated by the holding corporation as a deduction from the price paid. The subsidiary corporations can legally declare dividends therefrom; but these dividends, when received by the holding corporation, are merely a transfer to it of some of the assets included in the value of the stock it purchased, and are therefore a return of capital; and dividends declared and paid by the holding corporation to its stockholders out of such profits would clearly be paid out of capital. It is important to note that the date of purchase should be taken as the date of the contract for purchase, and not the date of completion. If the purchasing corporation was in existence at the date of entering into the contract, it is to be presumed that the price fixed had relation to the conditions existing at that date, and that the corporation is entitled to treat as profits all earnings of the subsidiary corporations subsequent to that date, less any consideration, such as interest, given for those profits. But if the holding corporation had no legal existence until a later date, it is submitted that, as it cannot earn profits when it is not in existence, it is only entitled to distribute as dividends profits of the subsidiary corporations earned subsequent to its own incorporation, or to the purchase of the property, whichever is the later date.

(3) Questions Arising on the Organization of a Corporation

Initial Surplus

It frequently happens that a corporation contracts to purchase property at an agreed price, which on the face of the contract is declared to be its value, and that by another clause in the contract, or by another contract, the vendors agree to provide, in addition to the property, a certain sum in cash for working capital or even for free surplus. It is sometimes maintained that this free sum so provided is a profit or surplus of the new corporation available for payment of dividends if the directors so determine. It is submitted that this contention is entirely unsound. Vendors are men of business, and it is not their practice to give something for nothing. A contract must be assumed to be the result of a bargain between purchaser and seller, and whatever the purchaser is to receive under the contract must be set off exactly against what the vendor is to receive; and although, in the formation of a large number of modern corporations, the vendors and purchasers, through the intervention of syndicates, are one and the same, the only safe and sound method of accounting is to assume that the same principles apply as in the case of an ordinary sale. It is difficult to believe that, if such a contract formed the subject of legal proceedings, any other view could be taken than that the so-called gift for working capital was merely a return to the purchaser of a portion of his purchase money, and should be so treated in the accounts. If the reverse principle were upheld, and this gift were treated as a clear profit to the corporation and distributed in dividends, it would seem that a portion of the subscribed capital would in effect be returned to the stockholders.

In a few exceptional cases properties are transferred to corporations at appraised values, and for some reason the stock and other securities issued for the properties have an aggregate par value less than the appraised value of the properties and all other net assets. Assuming that the appraisals are genuine, it would seem that in such a case the corporation commences business with a real surplus, which, however, is clearly a capital and not an income one. Such a condition can only exist when the appraisals cover substantially all the assets.

Losses on Current Assets Acquired

Other accounting questions relating to the formation of consolidating corporations have relation to losses that may occur on current assets taken over from the vendors. The valuation of inventories for purposes of transfer from a vendor to a purchaser is frequently made on a higher basis than would be usual for a going concern, the vendor in effect stipulating for some profit on his unsold product. The excess over the fair, going value of the inventory must in such cases be considered as an addition to the fixed capital investment in the shape of goodwill.

Similarly, if debts and liabilities, as is sometimes the case, are taken over without any guarantee from the vendor, and a loss occurs on final realization and payment, this loss may also be treated as an addition to the amount paid for goodwill. These principles are in accord with those heretofore laid down, that profits and losses of a corporation are such as arise out of its operations subsequent to the date of its formation or of the purchase of its properties, and that profits and losses appertaining to a period prior to these dates are capital items.

Adjustment of Inventories on Purchase and Sale of a Business

It frequently happens that the vendors have many contracts in force for the purchase of materials or supplies or manufactured articles, at prices differing widely from the market price at the date of sale. It is, therefore, fair both to the vendor and the purchaser in such cases that some regard should be paid to such contracts. If the vendor has made advantageous contracts a long way ahead at a time of low prices, the purchaser is certainly getting something more than the mere business contracted for; on the other hand, if such contracts for purchase are above current market prices, then the purchasing company is in a worse position than it otherwise would be. It is, however, doubtful whether it is a fair proposition as between the vendor and the purchaser that the market price on the date of the transfer should necessarily form the basis of a settlement between them. Some allowance must be made for the good judgment of the purchasers, and they should not be required to take over large quantities of materials on the fixed date of acquiring the property, at prices which in the ordinary course of business they might not have considered, when the transfer of such an inventory at the top market price may have a considerable effect on the future prosperity of the business.

It is certainly, therefore, a material fact to the intending investor that he should be clearly informed on what basis of price the inventories will be acquired, and what contracts for purchase of materials or manufactured articles have been entered into at prices differing from those current. Another material factor is the amount of orders on hand for future delivery, and the prices therefor, and the proportion such orders might bear to the possible capacity of the works. As a rule a large number of orders on hand may be regarded as a source of strength if they have been obtained in the ordinary course of business and at reasonably remunerative prices. It is, on the other hand, an easy matter to obtain orders if no regard be paid to the prices, and it might happen that an unscrupulous promoter had built up a large prospective business, at totally unremunerative prices, for the sole purpose of transfer to the purchasing company. Even without any fraudulent intent it may be that, owing to a considerable rise in costs, either of raw materials or labor, or both, the vendor concern may have on hand contracts taken when the range of prices was much lower, which can be filled only at considerable loss to the purchasing company. Similarly, orders on hand—to be completed by a fixed time—to an amount largely in excess of the actual or contemplated factory capacity, might easily be a source of loss rather than of profit to the purchaser.

These are some and perhaps the more important of the questions that may arise in practice when a new corporation is formed to take over one or more businesses as going concerns.

CHAPTER IX

SOME THEORIES AND PROBLEMS IN COST ACCOUNTING

The subject of cost accounts is one of the widest importance, and on its practical side calls for a fuller treatment than is possible in a general work on accounting. The economic theories involved in determining the cost of any given article of manufacture, together with an outline of the general methods of cost accounting, and some of the more important problems involved therein, form the subject of this chapter.

The term "manufacture" used in its widest sense comprises every operation necessary to render a natural product available for use, and by so doing to give it a value based upon cost in excess of that which it had in its natural state.

The elements that enter into the process of manufacture are:

(1) The natural product itself—or material.
(2) The subsistence necessary for the labor or service employed in converting it to use in the place where it is required, and during the time occupied in this process—or labor.

In these elements nothing in the nature of profit is involved, for the reason that profit is represented by the difference between the actual cost of labor and material, and the value which the combination of labor with material has given to the finished product, this being dependent on the demand for and supply of the particular article. The resultant value so determined may at any moment be more or less than the cost of the primary elements, and if it exceeds this cost there is a profit, which is divisible among—

(1) The individuals whose joint efforts have brought this natural product into the shape for which and to the place at which the demand exists, i. e., labor.

(2) The owner of the natural product and the owner of the accumulations which provide for the subsistence of labor during the period of manufacture, i. e., the capitalist.

If, on the other hand, the selling value falls short of the cost, the loss must fall upon the capitalist; labor merely going without profit, except to the extent that the condition of the labor market may enable it to obtain in advance a definite sum, in lieu of its share of the prospective profit which may or may not be eventually realized.

Nature of Plant

At first sight it may appear that this elementary description loses sight of the important part which land, buildings, plant and machinery play in the process of manufacture. A little consideration will show that this is not so; but that these too fall naturally into the elements already given, each item involving the use of a natural product, and its conversion by means of labor over a period of time necessitating the provision of subsistence by a capitalist. For instance, the conversion of ore into manufactured steel involves the following operations:

(1) Natural products consumed, i. e., ore, coal, timber, etc.;

(2) Natural product used but not consumed, *i. e.,* land upon which to carry on operations;

(3) Labor—

    (a) Extracting ore in some very primitive way;

    (b) Smelting this ore in some equally primitive way, and with the use of fuel of some sort, both these processes being carried out as by savages with no provided facilities;

    (c) The manufacture of some kind of tools by using the natural products so far developed, and so, gradually and over long periods of time, constructing plants suitable for manufacture;

    (d) The actual manufacture of the articles which are of use to the community and have an exchangeable value out of which profit can be realized.

A more detailed consideration of the elements of material and labor will serve to bring out the principles involved in their determination.

Constituent Elements of Cost

Material cost consists in the first instance of the labor employed in obtaining possession of the material in its natural state, but the value is fixed from day to day on the basis of estimates of the probable supply and demand, and of the difficulties and cost of making it available. The purchase price so fixed is in practice accepted as the cost, although it necessarily involves profit to the original possessor and to subsequent owners through him, who are able, by virtue of the limitation in quantity available at any time, to demand a sum down rather than wait for the uncertainties of future profit. The purchase price thus forms part of the cost, and should be recouped on sale before any profit can be ascertained.

Labor is a direct element of cost, represented by the provision of at least subsistence to those who perform it, and its recompense varies, by reason of the supply of or the demand for labor of different classes, from the bare cost of living to a comfortable sum in excess of that cost. In effect, then, whatever share of ultimate profits the workers might eventually receive, is in most cases compounded for by a payment in advance, leaving the entire surplus profits to accrue for the benefit of capital, which, on the other hand, also has to suffer the loss, if any.

The capitalist provides from his accumulated savings either natural products for temporary use, such as land, or natural products for consumption, such as material or subsistence. The latter, being consumed, are an element of cost; the former, remaining unchanged, are not; the consideration given to the capitalist for permitting his accumulated savings to be temporarily used or consumed is a share of the ultimate profit, or interest, which in theory is not therefore an element of cost. In practice the demand for capital, like the demand for labor, is such that the capitalist is frequently able to stipulate for a fixed immediate return for the use of his accumulations; thereby, as in the case of labor, compounding for his share of the ultimate profit and leaving the balance, with the whole risk of loss, to the borrower.

Conditions Affecting Cost

The amounts so paid by way of composition for the shares of profit to labor and capital may thus become a part of the cost to those who continue to take the risk; and it follows that the commercial cost of two identical articles, the absolute or theoretical cost of which would be identical, may be widely different because of the different conditions under which the processes of manufacture have taken place. As an instance, in the manufacture of a complicated machine the following alternative conditions may exist:

(1) The manufacturer may own iron, coal, and other mines, and may at his own factories produce everything up to the finished product. In this case his costs will include no profit except that accruing to labor.

(2) He may purchase all his natural products but carry on all manufacturing himself at his own factories. In this case his costs will include the profits of the owner of the natural products as well as those of labor.

(3) He may purchase from other manufacturers the whole or a portion of the parts that enter into his finished machines. In this case his costs will include not only the profits accruing to labor and to the natural products, but also the profits of any number of other manufacturers who have preferred to limit their risk at a certain point of the manufacturing process, leaving to the final manufacturer of the complete finished product the whole of the ultimate profit or loss.

It is easily seen that in the first case the manufacturer's costs are very much lower and his profits very much higher than in the other two. On the other hand, he has a greater capital investment, and is taking risks by reason of the longer time involved in the manufacture and the consequent greater chance of eventual fluctuations in demand and supply. A practical illustration of these conditions may be found in a comparison between the United States Steel Corporation, which owns its ore and other mines, and converts these materials into finished structures, and a contracting company which buys all its finished material and itself only erects the building or plant.

Purposes of Cost Accounting

Turning now from the economic to the commercial

aspect of cost accounts, the principal objects to be attained by a modern cost system may be stated as follows:

(1) To ascertain the cost of the same product at different periods in the same mill or at the same period in different mills, and so to remedy inequalities in cost by reducing all to the results shown by the best.

(2) By an accurate ascertainment of the cost of output, to maintain running book inventories, which will show at any time, without a physical inspection, how much of each class of materials, supplies, etc., is on hand, rendering possible a reduction of stocks and capital invested to the lowest level consistent with efficiency; and at the same time avoiding the delay, expense and interruption to business consequent upon the old method of taking a complete physical inventory at a specific date in each year.

(3) The preparation of statistical information as to costs of parts, quantity, and variety of output; relative efficiency of different classes of labor; and relative costs of labor and material, between different mills and periods.

(4) The preparation of periodical statements of income in a condensed form, readily giving directors all material information as to the results of the business. This is, perhaps, the least important of all the objects aimed at; and it may safely be said that the cost of a system designed merely to produce periodical statements of income, without providing for the other and far more important objects set out above, may be considered as money thrown away.

Constituent Elements of Commercial Costs

The elements involved in commercial cost accounts are usually somewhat as follows:

Material—

(1) That to which manufacturing processes are applied to convert it into some different form;

(2) That which is used or consumed in the processes of manufacture,

    (a) Directly;

    (b) Indirectly.

Labor—

(1) That employed directly upon the materials under process of conversion;

(2) That employed indirectly in operations necessary for the manufacture but not a part of it, such as upon repairs to and upkeep of machinery, buildings, or equipment.

Expenses—

Consisting partly of material and partly of labor, which are incidental to the carrying on of a manufacturing business, but have not any direct relation to the process of manufacturing.

Wear and Tear—

Or the gradual consumption of the buildings, machinery, and equipment employed in the manufacturing process — more commonly known as depreciation.

Distribution of Overhead Expense

The object of any system of cost accounts being to ascertain the cost of manufacture of each article or class of articles, it is clear that in a factory producing many classes of product some method must be adopted for distributing many of the items of cost over these different classes.

Material in process of direct conversion and labor directly employed in such conversion present no difficulties, being easily chargeable to the process; and the same is true of auxiliary material consumed in the process or of auxiliary labor which can be segregated at the moment.

There is, however, a large class of items which cannot be distributed exactly, and yet are a necessary and integral part of the cost. These comprise part of the items of material and labor, and the whole of the items of expense and wear and tear, and are usually grouped under the term "overhead expense" or "burden," and distributed on a more or less arbitrary basis among the different products. This distribution involves difficult questions; and the adoption of an erroneous method may easily appear to show that certain articles are manufactured at a cost well below their selling price, while a more accurate distribution would show a reverse condition. The most usual method of distribution is by a straight percentage on the direct labor cost, and where all products are of the same nature this may give fairly accurate results; but it is not scientific. On the other hand, a more scientific system of distribution based on an exhaustive examination of processes, with a view to determining what share each operation should bear of each class of overhead expense, and requiring an elaborate analysis thereof, may involve so much expense as to be prohibitive; and the final result may be found not to differ materially from the more simple and ready method of a percentage division.

Modern factories are usually operated by departments, between which there are well marked divisions. Each department within its own limits occupies a certain floor space, involving light and heat proportionate thereto; uses an amount of power which can be estimated within reasonable limits; and has certain labor and other costs for general assistance, cleaning, stores, and superintendence, which belong entirely to its operations in total. All these can be charged to the department and serve to determine the burden of that department. Some items, such as insurance, heat and light, may be charged to the department on the basis of floor space; others, such as steam or electric power, on the basis of horse-power hours worked; others again, such as general labor, on the basis of the direct labor pay-roll; and others, such as superintendence and general expenses, on the basis of labor and material costs combined. This main division is a comparatively simple one, although the circumstances of each case require careful study in order to determine the most nearly correct method; and if the industry is such that each department is carrying out only one class of operation, easily measured on some unit basis, the division of this burden over unit costs presents few difficulties. It is in cases where the operations in a department are of a varied and complicated nature—such, for instance, as a large machine shop—that almost insuperable difficulties arise; and in such cases it may well be doubted whether any really accurate distribution is possible.

Selling Costs

In considering the item of overhead expense, it is necessary to emphasize the distinction which must be made between expenses necessary for the production of manufactured articles in a form in which they are ready for sale, and the expenses incurred in offering them for sale to the public and in carrying through the sales when made. The former item, as has already been shown, is an essential element of the cost of manufacture; the latter item is an element of cost only from the point of view that without such expense the products could not be sold and the profits could not be earned. Strictly speaking, therefore, these selling expenses should be deducted from the price ultimately obtained for the product, and the difference only should be considered as the amount realized for the manufactured article. In practice this same result is often achieved in a different way by distinguishing between manufacturing

cost and selling cost; manufacturing cost alone being
employed for the purpose of valuing the product which
remains on hand unsold at the time of taking an annual
inventory, and selling cost being dealt with only in memorandum form, in order that those engaged in selling the
products may know the limit below which they should not
be disposed of.

Importance of Accurate Cost Keeping

The necessity for accurate cost keeping by commercial
enterprises lies in the fact that without such cost keeping,
whether it be of a highly scientific nature or merely by rule
of thumb, it is impossible for a manufacturer to know
whether the price at which he decides to sell his articles will
or will not yield a profit. The objection to rule of thumb
methods is that they are generally quite inaccurate, except
where manufacturing processes are relatively simple. In the
most usual cases, where the process of manufacture is
divided over a number of separate departments, each representing a different set of operations, any such methods can
only lead to serious errors and frequently to ultimate loss.

It should be noted that, while the ascertainment of accurate costs is essential, it does not necessarily follow that no
profit can be realized by selling at a price which appears to
be below such cost. In any factory equipped for a certain
volume of production, the overhead charges will remain
practically stationary, whether the factory be operated to its
full extent or to only a small proportion thereof. It will
follow, therefore, that the unit cost of manufacture, including overhead expense, will be much higher when the factory
is partly operated than when it is fully operated; and consequently a manufacturer can earn profits for himself by
increasing his output and selling the increase at a reasonable
margin over and above the direct cost excluding overhead

expense, thereby reducing his unit costs and making more profit than he would have made on the smaller output. It is, however, safe to say that it would be dangerous to attempt to carry out any such procedure without an accurate knowledge of direct, overhead and selling costs.

Relation of Interest and Rent to Manufacturing Cost

One of the most important questions involved in cost accounting has relation to the propriety of including interest and rent in costs of manufacture.

It must be premised that the object of the investment of money in any undertaking is to realize a profit. The inducement to an individual to invest his capital in an industry, rather than in the purchase of stocks or bonds, is largely the fact that by so doing he not only can obtain remuneration for his own services, but can also obtain a higher return or rate of interest on the capital invested, although at the same time he takes increased risks. The old theory of economists has been that there is a certain rate of return on money which eliminates all elements of risk, and that this rate only should be termed interest, all additions thereto being considered as compensation for the risk involved; but no economist has yet been able to say what this minimum rate is, and even in the case of what is perhaps the lowest rate known—namely, that yielded by United States Government bonds—it can not be said that the element of risk is entirely absent. The impossibility of determining this pure rate of interest apart from risk goes to show that there is in effect no such rate, but that all returns upon money invested, whether in bonds or stocks or other business enterprises, are the profits realized on the use of that money.

Nature of Commercial Investments

Those who invest money in business enterprises frequently, and in fact generally, make arrangements by which they join in partnership with others who also wish to invest, giving to these others a share of the resulting profits as remuneration for the capital employed. This share is determined by reference to the risk which the different parties to the enterprise take; some prefer to take security in the shape of a first charge upon the whole property, and to compound for their share of the profit by a fixed annual payment, this fixed annual payment being that which is commercially known as interest. Others are willing to take a somewhat greater risk, but do not wish to take the whole of it, and they limit their risk by taking for the capital which they contribute a preferential charge upon the earnings or profits of the business, leaving the whole of the balance available for those who take the ultimate risk; the remuneration of both these classes being known commercially as dividends. There is still another class who do not contribute capital in the ordinary sense of the word, but provide the business with facilities, such as buildings, machinery, etc., compounding with their partners by agreeing to accept a fixed annual payment in lieu of the share of profits to which their contribution to the capital would entitle them; such payments being generally known as rent. All, however, whether consisting of interest, dividends or rent, are merely a division of the profits resulting from the business, and in the long run can only be met out of those profits either directly, or in some cases, owing to the nature of the relations between the different parties, by certain of them suffering an actual loss of a proportion of their share of the capital in order to carry out the bargain made with their partners.

Interest and Rent Not a Manufacturing Cost

The profit or return consists of the difference between the sale price of the product and the cost of producing and selling that product. It is clear, therefore, that interest or rent, or any other item in the nature of return upon capital invested, should not form a part of the cost of product, the ascertainment of which is a first essential to the determination of the yield or return which the business gives, and out of which the divisions of profits are to be made.

It is true that, as between the contributors to capital, those who take the ultimate risk may advance or commute the share of profits of others; but this is merely a bargain between the different classes of contributors, and should not in any way affect the cost of product.

If interest and rent are treated as cost of product, then the extraordinary result is shown that the cost of making a certain article (other things being equal) in a business in which the contributing interests are divided between (a) the owner of the factory, (b) the owner of capital taking a small risk, and (c) the owner of the residue of the capital, will be greater than in an exactly similar case where the residuary owner provides the whole of the capital required. It seems clear that the relations between the partners or contributors should not in any way affect the cost of the product; and furthermore it would not be reasonable that a manufacturer who had, by hiring his factory, raising loans, sharing profits with his employees, and such kindred operations, distributed a considerable portion of his profits, should then raise his prices to an amount in excess of his neighbor's who had decided to provide all his own facilities and not to share his profits with anybody.

The principle that rent and interest are a distribution of profits is recognized in the form in which railroad accounts are now prepared, where both rentals of leased lines and interest on borrowed money of all kinds are treated as a charge against the income from operations after the same has been ascertained—that is, as a distribution of profits.

Rental Charges

In the case of manufacturing companies no such clear recognition of this principle is found; and rent for factories, etc., where paid, is treated as an item of manufacturing cost or expense, while interest, an exactly similar item, is more usually treated as a charge against, or division of, profits. This method of charging rent as an expense has led to a claim that it is properly so treated, and that therefore, when a manufacturer owns his premises and pays no rent, an estimated amount corresponding to the value of the use should be charged into and considered as part of the cost thereof. This sounds plausible; but it is believed that a nearer approach to theoretical accuracy is to be found in the railroad practice of considering all rentals, at least when there is a natural division between rent and other service, as a charge against or division of profits.

The question of rent serves to show the difficulty, if not impossibility, in practice, of laying down any hard and fast rules based upon economic principles, which are to so great an extent theoretical. Rent has so far been considered only as relating to the provision of manufacturing facilities, land, etc.; but an industry exists in which capitalists erect buildings, and let them out in whole or in part to others for offices, residences, and other purposes incident and necessary to business enterprise of all kinds. Rent of a factory is clearly a distribution of profit, but it is difficult in practice to make the same claim for office rents, and yet the arguments seem almost identical. A general distinction may perhaps be made between rent paid for the use of premises which form a direct and integral part of the manufacturing operations, and that paid for premises which are merely incidental thereto; and a further distinction lies in the frequent inclusion in rent of a charge for other services, such as light, heat, cleaning, or elevators, or for depreciation, etc., all of which involve labor and profit, just as these items are involved in the purchase of material. No general rule can be laid down, beyond suggesting that wherever an item of rent appears to consist mainly of a direct division of profit, it should be so treated, and only considered as part of cost when it seems to be mainly a composite item of labor, material and profit representing service rendered.

Difficulties of Including Interest as a Manufacturing Cost

Turning to another aspect of the interest question, it is necessary to consider what rate should be adopted if it should be granted for the sake of argument that interest should be charged into costs. Is it to be the rate which should be obtained on capital invested absolutely without risk, or is it to be the rate obtained by investments in stocks or bonds, and, if so, of what class, inasmuch as the rates on these vary all the way from 2 per cent on United States Government bonds, up to 10 per cent and 15 per cent, and even 25 per cent and more, on mining and other investments? Or is it to be the reasonable rate which the particular business should return on the money invested therein? It has been generally assumed by the advocates of this course that interest at the rate of 5 per cent or 6 per cent should be charged into cost, but these rates mean nothing in themselves; they have no bearing whatever upon the particular industry or on the rate which money can earn in specified investments outside; they are arbitrary standards which those in the commercial community have set up in their own minds. The only rate which could be justified in argument, assuming that it be correct to include any interest at all, would be the rate which the owners of the business thought they ought to obtain on the money they had invested in it. The adoption of such a rate would at once raise the question: To whom should the profit earned over and above the rate so charged belong? The argument would seem to be that, inasmuch as the capitalists have charged into costs and obtained for themselves the rate which they think they ought to realize on the whole business, the balance of it—which under such procedure would be called profit—does not belong to them at all, but to those who purchase goods from them or to the general public or the Government. This is a conclusion which would hardly be desired by any manufacturer. The impossibility, therefore, of determining a rate which could be successfully defended, affords another ground for the conclusion that interest is not a proper charge to costs.

Some advocates of the inclusion of interest in cost propose only to include interest on the fixed plant employed in manufacture; but obviously such a course may in many cases be absolutely misleading. If, of two plants turning out the same product, one requires the employment of fixed assets of a value of $10,000 for thirty days, and the other the employment of fixed assets of $5,000 for sixty days, the interest charge introduced upon this principle will be the same in both cases, whereas the process which takes sixty days to complete will obviously involve a longer investment of working capital. But if an attempt is made to allow for interest both on fixed and working capital, the adjustment will inevitably be a very complicated and difficult one to carry out. Where interest on fixed assets alone is considered, the calculation of the charge is not free from difficulty. The amount of capital employed and the time for which it was employed may perhaps be easily determined; yet, unless continuous production throughout the year is possible, the interest charge based thereon will be inadequate, and any calculation to be correct must allow for the time during which the plant will normally be unemployed.

Some confusion in relation to the items of rent and interest is found in the relation of the profits of a corporation or an individual to the profits of the business which is carried on. The latter should be identical under the same conditions of manufacture, whatever the financial arrangements may be, but the former are affected materially by the share of such profits which is distributed to others in the shape of rent and interest, as well as in commission or other payments dependent in any way upon profits. The inclusion of these distributions as a charge, before determining the ultimate profit accruing to the corporation or the individual manufacturer, does not thereby justify their treatment as part of the cost of product.

Suggested Treatment of Interest in Connection with Costs

Although it cannot be conceded that interest is a proper element in the cost of product, there is an undoubted demand for some form of statement which will give effect to the interest element, at any rate for comparative and statistical purposes.

The most usual objects sought may be grouped into three classes:

(1) Cases in which the lapse of time is a necessary part of the cost of production, and materials consequently have to be stored for long periods while a seasoning process is completed, e. g., lumber or tobacco.

(2) Cases in which it is desired to give effect to variations in the amount of capital employed and the term of employment in the production of different articles, or the same articles by different methods or factories.

(3) Cases in which capital is expended in additional facilities with the view of cheapening cost of production, and it is desired to set off the interest on the new capital against the savings effected.

In the first case, there is a substantial and necessary lapse of time between the purchase of materials and the date when they become useful or productive—as, for instance, in the case of seasoning lumber; and the selling value of the product, apart from market fluctuations, increases by reason of the lapse of time to an amount more than sufficient to provide for an interest charge. The arguments already adduced apply equally against treating as part of cost, any interest that may accrue on money borrowed for the purpose of carrying the product until it matures. In fact, the stockholders, in compounding with the lenders for interest at a fixed rate payable at a fixed time, have in effect made an advance out of their share of the profits pending realization; and while this advance can not properly be treated as part of the cost, it may, as an asset, properly be carried forward as a deferred charge against profits under the category of working assets.

In the other cases, the correct way of arriving at the desired result is not to charge into the cost interest at an arbitrary rate—which means little or nothing—but to compare the margin between the sale and cost price, or in other words the return upon each product, with the capital invested, in order to secure that return. This comparison would be a true one, would show exactly how much the capital invested really earned, and would be a good guide as to whether too much or too little capital was invested. Moreover, the adoption of the arbitrary rate defeats its own object, for, according as the rate adopted varies from the true rate, if there be such, so the comparisons deduced from the results will be erroneous. If the capital invested in a mercantile business should yield from 15 per cent to 20 per cent on the investment, then it is clearly erroneous to say that the operations resulting from the use of a certain machine, in which a certain definite proportion of that capital had been invested, should be charged with interest on that capital at 5 per cent, or 6 per cent, or some other rate entirely different from that which it is really expected to yield. As between two different kinds of machines used to produce the same product, but having different capital values, the conclusion reached by comparing the cost including interest at 5 per cent will be entirely different from the conclusion reached by including interest at 10 per cent, and neither of these rates will be anything more than a guess.

Statistical Comparisons between Production and Capital Invested

The demand for statistical statements of comparison between production and capital invested requires consideration of the following factors involved in profits:

(1) The labor, material and expense cost of a unit of each class of article;

(2) Facilities used in manufacture, such as land, buildings, machinery, tools, stocks on hand and other working capital, all segregated between the different classes of articles;

(3) The time during which such facilities are in use for a unit of each class;

(4) The selling price of each unit of each class.

If these elements be known, comparisons can be made between different articles produced in the same factory, or between the same articles produced in different factories, as to the amount of fixed capital employed in different processes, and the time for which it is employed; as to the amount of working capital constantly maintained and used; and as to the effect of further expenditures on additions and improvements with a view to cheapening cost of production. The first of the above four factors should alone enter into the general accounting books and form the basis of inventory valuations, and so of the actual profits earned;

the remaining factors should be dealt with only in subsidiary statistical records. The difference between the sum of all selling prices (4) and of all costs (1) will agree with the gross profit in the accounting books; and a comparison of this figure with the total capital employed, including not only fixed but circulating capital necessary for manufacturing purposes, will give the rate of return yielded by all classes of articles. The cause of any variation in this rate of return, as compared with a previous period, or of the varying rates of return on different articles in the same factory, or of the same articles in different factories, will be obtained from the detail figures. Such variations may be due either to—

(1) Higher or lower cost of labor, material and expense;
(2) Greater or smaller amount of facilities used;
(3) Longer or shorter time during which these facilities are used;
(4) Lower or higher selling price.

If interest at an arbitrary rate is included throughout in labor, material and expense costs, it means that the fluctuations in profit due to the first three of these variations are merged into one and can not without considerable labor be again segregated. The best measure of factors (2) and (3) would seem to be the value of the facilities used, multiplied by the fraction of the year during which they were used, and divided by 100, which product would be equivalent to interest at 1 per cent per annum; the actual margin between selling price and cost of labor, material and expense divided by this product, would thus be the actual rate of return yielded by any particular class of articles, the average of such yields corresponding to the yield shown by the principal accounting records.

Unused facilities would under this system appear as a factor in reducing profits, either by lack of sufficient business to employ them, or by excess facilities in one portion of the plant as compared with another. The product factor corresponding to these unused facilities would form part of the divisor in obtaining the average yield.

Comparative costs of separate operations will be reached by a consideration not only of the actual labor, material and expense cost in different periods or in separate factories, but also by a comparison of these costs with the facilities employed. Thus the estimated savings to be effected in any operation by additional expenditures on construction account, should be found reflected in the reduced cost of these operations.

Such a plan as that here suggested gives proper weight to all the factors entering into profits without introducing any arbitrary rate of interest; it will be no more complicated in its working than are cost systems which are in constant use, and its complications will vary with the number of different articles produced for which separate costs are required.

Profit-Sharing in Its Relation to Costs

The question is frequently raised whether distribution of profits made to employees under profit-sharing schemes, or contributions to special funds, for their benefit, are proper items to include as part of manufacturing costs. This question must be answered in the negative. Labor has already received its subsistence, and this is properly included as cost; any further distribution to labor, whether by way of a share of profit or a provision for old age or sickness, unless it be a contractual or compulsory payment entirely independent of profits, represents a further share of labor in the profit. Contractual and compulsory payments not dependent on profits, compensation for accidents and casualties arising in the course of manufacture, and pensions to retired employees are, however, clearly proper elements of cost. All voluntary distributions to labor not called for by contract or law, or arising directly out of the process of manufacture, must be considered as a further share in profits given to labor.

Cost as a Price Basis

Contracts are frequently entered into on the terms that the price is to be fixed at actual cost plus a percentage thereon, and disputes sometimes arise as to what constitutes cost. These disputes are almost always due to carelessly drawn contracts, the parties thereto and their legal advisers frequently having a very loose idea of the principles involved. The importance of a clearly drawn contract is evident, in view of the conflicting views on such subjects as rent, interest, bonuses, commissions to employees, and many other similar items; and if a proper form of contract exists no dispute is likely to arise. In the contrary case, however, the elementary principles of costs may be relied upon to solve the difficulty. If a manufacturer enters into such a contract, it must be assumed that he has all the facilities necessary for carrying it out, and no charge for the use of those facilities, other than actual wear and tear and depreciation thereof in the course of carrying out the contract, can be allowed as an item of cost. Similarly, no charge can be allowed for rent or interest, or other items, which, according to the theory laid down, represent a share of profits on the operations. It is on these items that disputes generally arise, rather than on the more complicated questions of proper distribution of burden, upon which manufacturers and contractors are usually much better informed.

CHAPTER X

THE DUTIES AND RESPONSIBILITIES OF THE PUBLIC ACCOUNTANT

In preceding chapters a statement of accounting principles and methods has been set forth, and it has clearly appeared that in order to insure their correct application a careful study must be made of all the facts in each particular case. This critical examination is commonly undertaken by the public accountant, who is qualified for this purpose by his training and experience, and who undertakes certain duties and responsibilities in interpreting, advising upon, and certifying to statements of account for various purposes.

These duties and responsibilities may be divided as follows:

(1) Those in respect of the prospectus, or the preparation and certification of accounts of past results for the purpose of the sale of a business or the issue of new securities.

(2) Those in respect of audit, or the examination, audit, and certification of the annual statements of accounts.

(3) Those in respect of liquidation and reconstruction, involving the preparation of statements and reports upon the condition of a business which, by reason of financial difficulties, is put into bankruptcy or into the hands of a receiver; and the preparation of further statements and reports for the purpose of its reorganization.

(1) In Respect of the Prospectus

Necessity for Accountants' Certificates

The application to the public to subscribe to stocks and bonds of a corporation is generally termed a "prospectus." In Great Britain, where the value of the services of public accountants is more generally recognized, it is the almost universal custom that the prospectus should contain a certificate by a chartered accountant as to the earnings of a period of years, and frequently also as to the financial position.

In this country this certificate is still frequently replaced by a letter from the vendors, or from the president or directors of the corporation, or from the bankers who recommend the investment, stating the results of operations and the present condition. As has been already shown, the questions involved in the determination of profits are often highly technical; those relating to the proper valuation of inventories at the beginning and end of any specified period, the provision made for maintenance and repairs, and the distinction between renewals, improvements and construction, are of vital importance; and a departure from correct principles in these and other matters may easily make what is really a losing business appear as a comparatively profitable one.

The proprietors or chief officers of the vendor concern must to a large extent rely upon their subordinates for the facts which they furnish to the bankers or to the public. They have not, as a rule, the necessary skill in accountancy to detect errors, whether of principle or of detail, in the statements submitted to them; they do not properly appreciate the distinction between facts and estimates, which might perhaps be more properly described as "expert guesses"; and finally, they are interested in putting the best possible complexion upon the general state of affairs, and will naturally, and not necessarily improperly, be biased in cases of doubt in favor of the view which is most to their own interests.

The main desire of some bankers has been to sell the stocks or bonds which they are offering to the public, and make a quick profit on the turnover. Their reputation and standing requires them to take every reasonable precaution to satisfy themselves that the investment they are offering is a thoroughly sound and reliable one; and while it is doubtful if letters from or facts supplied by the vendors are sufficient precautions, yet, as long as the public demands no more, there is no reason why bankers should offer more. In the meantime the natural bias of the promoter helps the banker with a favorable statement, and the verification by a public accountant might show a less favorable condition and diminish the banker's profit. It may be added that the neglect of such obvious precautions by the honest promoter makes the task of the dishonest one comparatively easy, and in the interests of commercial morality and for the better protection of the public it is interesting to note that a change is in progress in this respect, and that the certificate of a reputable public accountant is becoming a much more common feature in prospectuses, and will no doubt soon be as universal here as in Great Britain.

English Requirements as to Prospectuses

The English practice, with reference to the issue of prospectuses, is worth a reference. Under the English Companies (Consolidation) Act, 1908,* every company inviting subscriptions for capital is required to file with the Registrar of Joint-Stock Companies a copy of its prospectus, or, if there is no prospectus, a statement in lieu of the prospectus, containing the following, among other information: the names and addresses of the directors; the minimum sub-

---

*See Appendix III.

scription upon which the company may proceed to allotment; the names and addresses of the vendors of the property purchased or proposed to be purchased or acquired; the purchase price, distinguishing the amount paid for goodwill; the amount of commission payable for procuring subscriptions for any of the capital offered for subscription; the estimated amount of the preliminary expenses; the amount paid or to be paid to any promoter, and the consideration for such payment; the dates of and parties to every material contract, and the time and place at which such contracts may be inspected; the names and addresses of the auditors; and particulars of the nature and extent of the interest of every director in the promotion of the company or in the property proposed to be acquired. In addition, it is the regular practice in all cases, except that of an entirely new business not yet established, to incorporate in the prospectus a certificate of a chartered accountant, as to the earnings for a period of years, and frequently as to the value of the net current assets, where these are to be taken over.

The Act also provides, in Section 84, that every director or promoter, or other person who has authorized the issue of the prospectus, shall be liable to pay compensation to all persons subscribing for shares on the faith of the prospectus, for any loss or damage they may have sustained by reason of any untrue statement therein, unless it is proved that there was reasonable ground for believing such a statement to be true; or, if based on a report of an expert, that it fairly represented such report and that those responsible for the prospectus had reasonable ground for believing that the expert was competent to make the report.

Period to be Covered by Prospectus

In addition to such accounting questions as are directly involved in the determination of profits, there are others of equal, if not greater, importance to which due attention must be given if the prospectus is to fully disclose to the intending investor all the material facts necessary to enable him to form a judgment upon the value of the securities offered to him.

Perhaps the most important preliminary matter for decision is the period for which results should be given in the prospectus. Those of one year, especially if that year happened to be an exceptionally good one, can under no circumstances be considered a fair basis. Generally it may be said that the longer the period taken, the better, with the qualification that the results should be brought down to a date as close to the publication of the prospectus as the circumstances will permit, and that greater prominence should be given to those of the last three or five years. It has frequently happened that an undertaking has been offered for sale just at the zenith of its prosperity, or even just after the tide has turned and it is commencing to show less satisfactory results, so that figures of past profits were not a fair criterion of future prospects. On the other hand, owing to general depression of trade or other special causes —such as excessive competition—which will be avoided under the scheme proposed, it may have shown within the last year results which are less than a fair measure of its earning capacity. The responsibilities thrown upon the accountant are thus onerous. He must consider that his duties are primarily to the investor, and must be careful that the years selected and the manner in which the results of these years are grouped will disclose the real facts; and yet in so doing he must remember that he has a duty also to the vendor, and must not make his selection in such a manner as to reflect, as permanent, conditions which are really temporary. Generally it may be said that no period of less than three years can usually be considered as giving a fair basis, and that one of five years is better; and while the results of a longer period are always a useful guide to the past history of the undertaking, they are not such a good indication of the actual condition at the present time.

Treatment of Unusual Profits or Losses

In setting forth the results it is imperative that extraordinary profits or losses not arising out of operations nor in the ordinary course of business, such, for instance, as those resulting from sales of portions of capital assets, should be either eliminated or stated separately. Particularly should regard be had to any contracts or other arrangements in force during the period examined resulting in excessive profits or excessive losses, which, from the fact that these contracts or arrangements have since been terminated, may not recur. Such profits or losses should either be eliminated or separately stated; but which of these two courses should be adopted must depend upon the probability or possibility that similarly extraordinary results may be realized in the future. If, for instance, while certain profitable contracts have terminated, other similar ones promising good results have actually been secured, it would not be fair to the vendors to exclude the profits realized from the former. And if the business is one that depends to a very large extent upon contracts, and there is no sign of any falling off in those on hand and not commenced, it would probably not be necessary even to state the results separately.

Fluctuations of Profits

A further point of considerable importance to the prospective investor is that he should know whether the profits for the period covered by the examination have remained steady, have increased or decreased steadily, or have been characterized by extreme fluctuations. For this reason the certificate should always show the results of each year separately, at any rate for the last three or five years, and on no account should the average profits only be stated, unless for some reason—which is disclosed in the certificate—the profits of separate years cannot be ascertained. Where the profits may have shown a gradual falling off, or those of the latest years are below the average, it would be most improper that the certificate should give the average without stating the actual facts year by year. From the investor's point of view a certificate in the prospectus stating merely the average profits for a certain period of years should be mistrusted, on the ground that if the business were a progressive one and there were in fact nothing to conceal, the promoters would always prefer to get the fullest possible benefit from that fact by stating the results of each year separately; if this course is not adopted it may be presumed that there is good reason for concealment from the promoter's point of view.

It frequently happens, owing to delay in completing arrangements, that a considerable time elapses between the date up to which the profits are certified and that of the accountant's certificate and the issue of the prospectus. In such cases it is certainly the accountant's duty to take all reasonable steps to satisfy himself that nothing has happened in the interim to throw any doubt upon the continuance of the results to which he has certified. For instance, if in a period of, say, six months so elapsing the books should clearly show a serious diminution of profits, or even a loss, this is a material fact which the accountant might and should ascertain if he used due diligence, and which, under any ordinary circumstances, should be disclosed in his certificate.

Results for Broken Periods

Just as it is improper to average the results of several years, so it is equally improper to average the results of a portion of a year to make up a complete year. Many businesses are essentially of a seasonal character, and the results of the first six months, for instance, may be, normally, entirely different from those of the last half of the calendar year; and even when the business is continuous through the year it is not safe to assume that the profits of, say, two unexpired months will equal the average of the previous ten. In dealing with such broken periods it is preferable, if possible, to give also the corresponding figures for the same period in the preceding year, so as to show the comparative increase or decrease.

Interest in Its Relation to Profits

A problem of considerable difficulty in determining the profits for a prospectus, is the proper treatment of interest paid on loans, borrowed money, or partners' capital. Speaking generally, it may be said that interest in whatever shape is profit; and that if the profit of carrying on a particular undertaking is to be ascertained, all interest paid out on money employed in the business should be treated as part of the profits of the undertaking, and similarly all interest received on any proportion of the capital which may from time to time be invested in outside securities should be excluded therefrom. But in certifying results for a prospectus regard must be had to the conditions under which the capital required for the purposes of the business is to be raised in future. If the amount to be provided is at least equal to the maximum borrowed in the past, then the whole of the profits before deducting interest charges will be available for dividends or interest on such capital. If, on the other hand, it is proposed to provide a portion only of

the average amount borrowed in the past, it will be necessary, in putting the results before an investor, to deduct
therefrom the interest on the borrowed money employed in
earning those profits in excess of that which the promoters
intend to provide; for the new concern would then have
to borrow the difference from bankers or others and pay
interest on the money so borrowed, before any distribution
of profits was made to those providing the capital called
for in the prospectus. It is perhaps hardly necessary to add
that interest on partners' capital in a private partnership is
essentially a part of the profits of the business—subject to
the above remarks when, as is hardly likely, a smaller
amount of capital is to be provided in future. In every case
the certificate given should state clearly how interest has
been treated.

Salaries as Affecting Profits

The treatment of salaries that have been or may have to
be allowed to the partners or chief managers of the business is another matter of importance. In a private partnership, or in a corporation in which the managers are the chief
or only stockholders, it frequently happens either that they
have drawn no salaries, or only small ones compared to the
market value of the services rendered; a reason being that
the managers may prefer to take their remuneration in the
shape of profits entirely, rather than to consider them a
charge against the business before ascertaining such profits.
If, therefore, the profits be certified without any provision for
the salaries of those responsible for the general management
in the past, it is clear that the resulting profits to the new
concern must be materially less than those certified to.
Consequently, it is always necessary either to specify that
no provision has been made for the remuneration of future
managers, or to include, as a charge against the profits

certified, whatever amounts are contemplated or contracted for in the future.

Depreciation and Renewals in Their Relation to Profits

An important factor in connection with the prospectus is the imperative necessity of stating in the certificate as to profits whether full provision for depreciation and accruing renewals has or has not been made. While it is easy to lay down this principle, it is perhaps one of the most difficult matters to determine in practice, by reason of the frequently imperfect state of the records and often of the entire absence of reliable figures of original cost, or even of any proper distinction between expenditures on improvements, additions and renewals. In a private business run on conservative lines, a large proportion of the earnings may be put back into the property in the way of improvements and betterments; and if the operations have been of a highly profitable nature large amounts are frequently charged off from time to time in reduction of capital outlays. So far as the latter items are concerned, it is easy for the accountant to separate them and adjust his statement of earnings accordingly, but where improvements and betterments have been effected as part of the ordinary operations of the plant, and charged into maintenance and repairs almost from day to day, it becomes practically impossible at a subsequent date to separate them from the proper maintenance charges. Such a practice can not be too strongly condemned, not only as concealing the true facts and making the position appear worse than it really is, but also, from the point of view of the vendor, because the impossibility of adding such expenditures back to earnings must result in his receiving a lower price for his goodwill, based on earning capacity, than he otherwise would. The mere claim by a vendor that large expenditures have been so made and charged, without a shred of supporting evidence in the books as to the cost of such improvements, or even of the fact that they have been made, cannot be accepted by the accountant; it then becomes a question whether he can satisfy himself that the expenditures so charged, which were not directly ascertainable, have been sufficiently large to take the place of depreciation; and it will readily be seen that this is a most difficult question, involving great experience and careful judgment.

Varying Requirements of Statements of Profits

It should here be noted that there may be a marked difference between a statement of profits prepared for and certified to an annual meeting of stockholders, and one that is prepared for the purpose of showing to prospective investors the earning capacity of the business. In the former case the accounts are adopted by the stockholders at each annual meeting, reserves of various kinds are made from the profits of good years to be carried forward to bad years, changes in methods of valuations of different classes of assets are made from year to year, and, generally, the accounts are drawn up more with a view of determining the amount which can safely be divided among the stockholders in dividends, than of showing the actual earning capacity of the business. In the latter case, however, it is essential that the profits certified for each separate year be those actually earned from the operations of that year—any arbitrary additions or deductions due to changes in bases of valuations or otherwise being excluded—and that they be free also from abnormal fluctuations due to unavoidable contingencies, which should be provided for proportionately over a period of years.

Adjustments

All adjustments must be made that may be necessary to insure that the accounts fairly represent the results of each separate period. It may happen that the vendor may offer to guarantee the value of certain assets, or a maximum amount for the liabilities. Such a guarantee is of value only to a purchaser taking over the physical properties at book values, and its effect is to shift the burden of any losses or omissions from the purchaser of the property and assets, on to the vendor. Such a transfer can not in any way affect the earning capacity, and it is essential that any losses or liabilities omitted on account of such guarantees should be taken into account in determining the profits.

This factor may be of even greater importance when goodwill is included in the sale at a price based on a number of years' purchase of the average profits. In such a case the error in the profits due to the omission of guaranteed assets or liabilities may be multiplied many times over in arriving at the purchase money for goodwill.

It may also be noted that a change in the basis of inventory valuations at the end of the period, as compared with the beginning, will not only result in an erroneous statement of earning capacity, but also will affect the purchase money for goodwill.

The foregoing remarks upon guarantees by the vendor are not intended to imply that such guarantees are of no value; on the contrary, a guarantee of collection of face value of book debts, as well as of the maximum amount of liabilities, should usually be required whenever the purchaser takes over all current assets and assumes payment of all liabilities.

Estimates of Anticipated Economies

It may be asked how far an accountant is justified in certifying to estimates of the extra profits that may be realized as a result of economies in operation to be effected by the proposed new corporation. Generally speaking, it may be said that any such certificate is inadvisable and may be dangerous. Promoters are always sanguine; and experience shows that such estimates are seldom realized in practice, at any rate for some years to come. Extra expenses may be entailed which more than offset any savings effected; and the loss of personal touch and interest on the part of the former owners, who now become mere salaried employees of a corporation, may result in less careful and more extravagant management. While the vendors may be still largely interested as stockholders, it may be found that they have received cash payment for a substantial part of their original investment, and that their remaining interest in the stock represents merely goodwill or similar intangible assets; with the result that as salaried officials they may relax rather than increase their efforts. Moreover, the large capital of the modern consolidation appears to call for expenditures on elaborate offices and establishments which were previously deemed entirely unnecessary, and in fact, while the increased capital represents mainly goodwill, etc., it carries with it an increased expenditure in hard cash. Having in view all these possibilities, it is certainly not a wise thing for the accountant to certify to any estimate of possible economies.

Estimates of Future Earnings

Accountants may be asked to prepare estimates of future earnings for the purpose of publication in the prospectus, and it is well to consider whether such a request should or should not in general be complied with. It may be admitted that an accountant is perhaps in many ways particularly qualified to prepare such an estimate; and if the only questions involved were the accuracy of the figures and the reasonable probability that the bases assumed would agree with future practice, no objection perhaps could be taken to compliance with the request. But, on the other hand, the experience of the past is frequently no guide to the practice of the future, and many unforeseen contingencies may arise which will render the estimates entirely valueless. To bring out the difficulties more clearly, assume two special cases:

Firstly. That of a factory which has not been operating to its full capacity, partly because the plant is a new one and partly because its selling organization is not fully developed.

Secondly. That of a new industry which has been operating in an experimental way with one or two machines, upon the experience of which it is desired to estimate the profits that would be earned in a much larger plant constructed on the same principles.

In the first case the actual operation of the plant in the past is available as a guide for the future, but in preparing estimates of results based on a much more complete operation, the following points would have to be carefully considered:

(1) Are the capacities of the different portions of the plant dealing with the various processes of manufacture so carefully balanced that those dealing with the final processes can be worked to their full capacity without overloading those engaged on the earlier operations?

(2) Can sufficient supplies of raw material be obtained at a reasonable cost to enable the final output to be largely increased at not more than the average cost which has prevailed in the past?

(3) If the output is so increased, can a ready market be found for it at the average prices obtained in the past? It may happen that, by reason of competition of distant factories better situated and with facilities which enable them

to produce at lower cost, the territory in which the products of a particular factory can be sold will be restricted and unable to absorb the increased production upon which the estimates are based. In such cases the increase could only be sold at a considerable reduction in price, which would entirely upset the estimated results.

(4) For what portion of each year can the whole plant be operated to its full capacity? And what allowance should be made for periods of idleness necessary to undertake repairs and renewals, periodical stock-taking, etc.?

(5) Where the output depends upon the speed at which the machinery is run, can a sufficient supply of suitable labor be obtained to run the whole factory at the same average speed as it has been possible to run only a portion of it in the past?

(6) What proportion would the general management and selling expenses bear to the increased output? It may happen that a large concern can not be run as economically in some departments as a small one; and it is not always safe to assume that the same percentage of management and selling expenses which prevailed in the past will be experienced in the future.

(7) On the other hand, what consideration should be given to the possible reduction in cost resulting from the larger output, mainly by reason of the fuller use made of the facilities?

It should be clear, therefore, from the above considerations that any estimate of future earnings must necessarily depend upon so many contingencies that it would hardly seem desirable that it should be put forth without calling specific attention to the assumptions involved; and an estimate with such qualifications attached would hardly be of much service to the promoter and would not be incorporated in the prospectus.

Inasmuch as the community is being educated to consider that statements emanating from a public accountant deal with facts only, it may be said in conclusion that in such a case as that supposed, the accountant's duty should end with the submission on request of a carefully prepared estimate accompanied by all the necessary qualifications, without, however, any certificate thereto, leaving his client to print such estimate in the prospectus or not as he thinks fit, but without using the name of the accountant.

The second case is even stronger than the first, for here there is no pretense that the factory has been operated commercially at all, the whole process of manufacture being in an experimental stage. The contingencies involved in assuming that the results obtained in an experimental stage by one or two machines could be reached on a much larger scale in a fully operated factory, are so many and so unforeseen that it would be difficult to enumerate them; and under these circumstances, while the accountant can for the benefit of his client check to the best of his ability any estimates that may be prepared by the manager, and may frequently be able to point out omissions therein, it is very doubtful whether he should under any circumstances whatever attach his signature to any such statement, however much he may believe in the possibilities of its realization in the future.

Certificate of Financial Condition

So far attention has been restricted to the essentials involved in certificates of profits for prospectus purposes. It remains to consider the responsibilities of the accountant in giving certificates of financial condition for the same purpose.

Statements of financial condition are usually in the following form:

Properties owned (showing basis of
valuation) $

Current Assets:
Stock in Trade
Accounts and Bills Receivable
Marketable Investments
Cash
Less:
Current Liabilities consisting of
Accounts Payable
Net Current Assets

Net Assets $

If there is any funded debt ranking in front of the securities to be issued, this also would be deducted. The fixed properties are, or should be, appraised by responsible valuers, frequently under the direction of or assisted by the accountant, and the certificate of these valuers would usually be incorporated in the prospectus, or reference made thereto. The accountant's responsibility is usually limited to the verification and certification of the current assets and liabilities; but questions may arise on stock in trade, guarantees of debts and liabilities, contracts for purchase and sale of goods, and orders in hand, which may have an important bearing on the present and future position and should not be overlooked. For the discussion of these questions reference may be made to page 186 *et seq.*

Certificate of Profits Without Certificate of Assets

It may and often does happen that a certificate of profits is required without any certificate of assets, and, provided that the investigation made discloses no features in the assets or liabilities which have an important bearing upon

the future of the business, and should therefore be disclos
to the prospective investor, there would appear to be n
reason why such a request should not be complied with. At
the same time there can be little doubt that a statement of
profits without assets is not a complete one and should be
looked upon with some suspicion.

While the accountant may be absolved from responsibility by his instructions, he is certainly bound by his professional duty to make his examination so complete as to
enable him to ascertain for himself what the financial condition is, and whether there is anything material therein which
should be disclosed. Such features may be one or more of
the following:

(1) Accounts receivable not liquid, but tied up in loans
and not readily collectible.

(2) Inventories too large for the business carried on,
and including large amounts of old or obsolete
stock, or other doubtful items.

(3) Marketable investments not really marketable.

(4) Current liabilities largely in excess of current assets,
or with an insufficient margin for working capital
after allowing for new capital to be introduced.

(5) Large construction works in progress calling for
continuous outlay.

(6) Funded debt falling due at short future dates.

(7) Insufficiency of the new money asked for in the
prospectus to provide for these various features
for at least a reasonable period in the future.

It is difficult to lay down any general principle to cover
this point, but an examination might reveal such a general
condition that a true and full disclosure to the prospective investor would not be made, unless a statement of
assets and liabilities, together with the requirements in the

229

‎ in the prospectus. If such dis-
it might be the accountant's duty
'th the prospectus in any way, or
‎atement of earnings.

‎rtifying Accountant

‎question of the personal liability of the accountant
‎a certificate which he gives to vendors or purchasers,
and which is published in a prospectus issued to the public,
is a matter of considerable importance. The accountant is
not infallible, his judgment may be at fault, and the available
information may be incomplete or misleading in such a way
that with all his special skill the real facts are not discover-
able. It does not follow, if future results are not in accordance with past experience to which the accountant has certified, that the latter is necessarily to blame; but the public, to
whom he is chiefly responsible, is entitled to assume that he
is a man skilled in commercial and financial affairs, and particularly in the accounts relating thereto; and consequently
actions or opinions on his part, which could in no way be
considered as such in the case of a man without such special
knowledge and training, may easily subject him to a charge
of negligence. He is called upon to exercise the skill and
knowledge acquired in his profession to the utmost of his
ability; if by negligence he fails in this, he has committed
a breach of trust, has deceived the public, and must be prepared to take the consequences. On the other hand, no liability should attach to him for a mere error of judgment, or
even for errors in facts the existence of which reasonable
skill and diligence on his part would not have enabled him to
ascertain. And finally the accountant should confine himself
to certifying to facts, and should not attempt to deal with
estimates in the making of which his special qualifications
are no greater than those of other business men.

(2) In Respect of Audit

The audit here referred to is the annual re... persons entirely independent of the firm or corporation, or its accounts and affairs. Unfortunately this term "Audit" has obtained currency in a much more limited sense, being applied to the internal check upon transactions involved in the passing of accounts for payment; and the corresponding term "Auditor" more often than not is applied to, or is held to describe, an individual holding the position of comptroller or chief accountant, or head bookkeeper of a corporation. It is, perhaps, worthy of consideration whether it is desirable to continue to use the term "Audit" as applied to work done and certificates given by public accountants; but in default of any better term, and in view of the legal sanction given to its use in that respect in other countries, it is very generally adopted as applying to the work performed by the independent auditor, to enable him to certify to the accuracy of periodical statements of account. Such an audit is of far-reaching importance, not only to the directors and stockholders of the corporation interested, but also to the general public, who may frequently purchase the stock of the corporation, relying on the certificate given by the public accountant.

Audit Practice in England

Some important considerations affecting audit practice are suggested by the English Companies (Consolidation) Act of 1908, which was passed after an inquiry by a Royal Commission on which accountants were represented by one of their number, and which may be said to have crystallized into law the customs of the most reputable companies, adopted as the result of the forty-five years' experience under the law of limited liability in that country. Before considering the provisions of this act it may be interesting and useful here to state shortly the history of the independent and impartial audit of the accounts of corporations in England, where the practice, starting from small beginnings, has now become universal and has at last received the indorsement of the law.

Until the passage in England of the Companies Act of 1900, there was no law compelling a company registered under the Companies Act to have an audit of its accounts, with the exception of banking companies, which were required under the Companies Act of 1879 to have an independent audit, evidenced by a certificate in a form which practically became the standard for all companies. The original Limited Liability or Joint-Stock Companies Act of 1862 contained in a schedule, known as Table "A," a set of "Articles of Association" (here known as "By-Laws"), which was not compulsory, but which could be adopted by any company so desiring and was binding upon any company which did not adopt an alternative set. This Table "A" exercised a great influence, and where not adopted in its entirety, became the model for the articles of association of the best companies. It included a clause requiring an annual audit of accounts by persons appointed by stockholders; and the elimination of this clause in any substituted articles came to be regarded with more and more disfavor, so that in time this provision became practically universal.

The first stage of this audit consisted in the appointment by the stockholders, at the annual meeting, of certain of their number to conduct it. These lay auditors had no qualifications for the position, either by training or experience; and while the fees paid them for their services were usually small, there can be little doubt that the money was, as a rule, wasted.

The next stage appears to have been the employment by the elected auditors of public accountants to assist them in their work, provision being frequently found in the articles of association permitting this, and providing that the remuneration of the individuals so employed should be paid by the company. The next step was to recognize the fact that it was better for the stockholders themselves to make the appointment of public accountants, instead of delegating it to their own auditing committee; and the articles of association in their most modern form usually provided that at least one of the auditors should be a public accountant. In this condition matters continued until the passage of the Companies Act of 1900, which, for the first time, gave parliamentary sanction to the practice which had already become established in the majority of cases by the action of corporations and their stockholders.

The various Acts from 1862 up to 1907 are now consolidated in the Companies (Consolidation) Act, 1908, and the provisions relating to audit are contained in Sections 109 to 114 of that Act.* The general effect of these provisions is that at each annual meeting of the company the shareholders are required to appoint one or more auditors, none of whom must be a director or officer of the company; that these auditors shall hold office until the next annual meeting, and that their remuneration shall be fixed by the shareholders. Provision is made for appointment by the Board of Trade (a government department) in default of any appointment by shareholders. Appointment by the directors is permitted only in the case of a newly organized company; and such appointees can hold office until the first annual meeting, with power, however, to the shareholders to remove them by a majority vote at a previous general meeting.

The auditor being appointed by the stockholders, his responsibility was entirely to the stockholders; but he was subject to election each year; and cases frequently arose in

---

*See Appendix I.

which, owing to his making a report adverse to some action which the directors had taken, the latter, controlling the majority of stock, were able to prevent his re-election. This feature of the appointment of auditors was recognized as a defect, and the form of certificate called for in Section 23 of the Act of 1900 was also not entirely satisfactory; the Act of 1908 contains provisions safeguarding the re-election of auditors and amending the form of certificate.

The present law establishes the auditor's right of access at all times to the books, accounts and vouchers of the company, and empowers him to require from the directors and officers such information and explanations as he may think necessary. It requires the auditor to make a report to the shareholders, stating whether or no he has obtained all such information and explanations, and whether or no the balance sheet is properly drawn up so as to exhibit a true and correct view of the state of the company's affairs, according to the best of his information and the explanations given to him, and as shown by the books of the company.

The auditor's report must be read at the annual meeting, and be open to the inspection of any shareholder, who is also entitled to a copy of both balance sheet and report for a specified fee.

The act also provides that no other than a retiring auditor can be elected at an annual meeting, unless previous notice has been given of the intention to nominate another person, and a copy of such notice has been given to the retiring auditor.

It will be noted that there is still no provision in the law requiring that the audit should be made by a public accountant, but it has become so universally recognized that a lay audit is worse than useless, that it is now quite the exception to find the certificate of any but a public accountant affixed to the balance sheet.

American and English Practice as to Company Audits

There is one important point of distinction between the position of the public accountant acting as auditor of a corporation in England and in this country; viz., that in England he has always been appointed by the shareholders, while in America, at present, with a few notable exceptions, he is appointed by the directors or officers, although in most cases the directors hold the control of the company, and the appointment by the stockholders would practically have the same result. The accountant's position in such a case is, however, widely different. When appointed by the directors his legal responsibility is to them, not—as it should be—to the stockholders and to the public; and while this should not affect his moral responsibility to the two latter, it places such limitation upon his powers as to seriously diminish his usefulness; for if he reports adversely upon any of the actions of the directors, they can suppress his report and publish the accounts of the company as prepared by themselves without any certificate; and the auditor has no right whatever to communicate the true facts to the stockholders. On the other hand, if he be appointed by the stockholders, it is not only his right but his duty to bring before them—preferably in his certificate affixed to the balance sheet, but certainly in some way—any material facts with which they should be acquainted. Furthermore, if the directors appoint the auditor they can limit the scope of his inquiry in any way they think fit; while appointment by the stockholders would carry with it no limitations, and the whole responsibility as to the work which he shall do or not do is thrown—and properly thrown—upon the auditor.

Canadian Audit Practice

Reference may here be made to the Canadian Bank Act of 1913, which for the first time in the experience of Canada, provides for the compulsory audit of the accounts of all Canadian banks by persons appointed by the shareholders. The clauses of the Act dealing with this audit* provide that the bank managers shall select a list of not less than forty names of persons qualified to make such an audit. This list so prepared is submitted to and approved by the Minister of Finance; and thereafter the shareholders at the annual meeting of each bank are required to appoint as auditor one of the persons included in such list. Very wide powers are given to the auditor in the Act; his duties are clearly defined and his responsibilities are undoubtedly considerable.

Accountant's Responsibility for Audit Certificates

The responsibility which the public accountant assumes in certifying to the accounts of a corporation is well defined in the form of certificate required by the English Companies Act of 1908, above quoted; viz., that he shall report whether, in his opinion, the balance sheet is properly drawn up so as to exhibit a true and correct view of the state of the company's affairs, according to the best of his information and the explanations given him, and as shown by the books of the company. The several phrases in this certificate deserve special attention.

(a) "In his opinion," [as a skilled professional man, endowed with special qualifications resulting from his training and experience.] Every balance sheet must be largely a matter of opinion; for example: the value of the debts receivable, the inventories of materials and supplies, and particularly of work in progress, and the division of expenditures between capital and revenue; the inclusion in the books of all necessary information with regard to the affairs of the company; the sufficiency of the provision made for maintenance charges and depreciation, and for reserves for possi-

*See Appendix V.

ble losses; the efficiency of the system of organization and accounting as a reasonable protection against fraud or defalcation—all of these matters require, for their decision, skill and experience.

The criticism is often made that this phrase weakens the certificate; but if the necessities of the case be considered, and if it be remembered that the opinion is one formed after an exhaustive and careful study of all the facts and evidence obtainable by a man whose whole training and experience has specially qualified him to give such an opinion, it will be seen that the words are not a mere empty phrase but an essential part of the certificate. So far from weakening the certificate, they may rather be considered as strengthening it, in that they imply that the signer has given his certificate, not with foolhardy assurance, but with a realization of the inherent impossibility of saying, absolutely, that one balance sheet is correct and any other incorrect.

(b) "Properly drawn up." This implies that the different headings in the accounts submitted are proper descriptions of the items included thereunder: that there is no concealment of material facts, the knowledge of which is essential in enabling the present or prospective stockholders to form a judgment of the value of the investment, and the omission of which would be prejudicial to their interests. In deciding whether this requirement has been met, the auditor must recognize that there are often facts as to which it would be of interest and value to stockholders to be informed, but the public disclosure of which might damage the company and its stockholders, and yet which, in the opinion of the public accountant, are perfectly proper transactions, and in the best interests of the company. The public accountant should be the best judge as to what should or should not be disclosed, and be able to satisfy his clients that his views are correct and should be adopted.

(c) "True and correct view of the state of the company's affairs." This phrase involves, not only the clerical accuracy of the figures, but their substantial business accuracy, independently of the books, subject always to the necessary qualification that the public accountant, even with his special training and experience, is, after all, human and can not discover facts of which no trace is to be found on the books or records of which he has knowledge. Such matters as the valuation of inventories, investments, book debts, etc.; the full estimate of all ascertainable liabilities and obligations, contingent or otherwise; the full and correct statement of the profits for the period covered by the examination; and the clear and separate disclosure therein of any unusual items not incident to the ordinary business of the company, are all involved in the term "true and correct view of the state of the company's affairs."

(d) "As shown by the books of the company." This phrase does not imply that the duties of the auditor are properly fulfilled if he satisfies himself that the balance sheet agrees with the books, as is sometimes supposed. The preceding phrase, "according to the best of my information and the explanations given to me," shows clearly that a much wider duty rests upon the auditor; namely, to satisfy himself that the balance sheet, as already stated, sets forth a true and correct view of the state of the company's affairs, according to all the information obtainable; and, further, that the books also set forth this same condition. It is, therefore, incumbent upon the auditor, if he certifies the accounts of a company, to see that the books are correct as well as the balance sheet, and that any changes which he may have to make in the balance sheet have been properly recorded and put through the books.

There are many other matters frequently touched upon in the certificate, in addition to the above, which may be described as the "Operative" phrases; but whatever the form may be, it is essential that the certificate should be clear, specific, and, above all, accurate, and that any qualifications which it may be necessary to insert should be set forth in unmistakable terms, so as to put those who read it upon their guard, and to suggest to them the questions which shall be put to the management of the corporation if further information is desired.

Qualified Certificates

It may be useful here to state a few general principles in connection with the form a qualification should take. Various expressions are used, such as "accepting" or "subject to" such a condition of things. The former word should imply that, while the accountant is not in a position to verify the statement to which it relates, yet he has no reason to believe that it is inaccurate in any respect; while the expression "subject to" should imply that the accountant is not satisfied with the conditions disclosed, and is prepared only to certify to the accuracy of the statement, excluding the item to which he takes exception.

It must never be forgotten that the auditor has no right or duty to dictate the policy of the company; he can not compel it to make sufficient provision for all necessary charges, such as maintenance, depreciation, bad debt reserves, etc., but he can and must call attention in his certificate to the fact of the omission or insufficiency of any such provisions, leaving it to those interested as stockholders, or in any other capacity, to take the question up directly with the officials and satisfy themselves on these doubtful points. If the public accountant is equipped by ability and training for his duties; if the work of his subordinates is properly directed and supervised; and if his examination has been as thorough as it should have been—in other words, if he has

..... nis whole duty as a public accountant—it is hardly possible, in the absence of widespread fraud, for any substantial or material errors of omission or commission to be found afterwards in a balance sheet so certified.

Accountant's Moral and Legal Responsibility

The public accountant's responsibility in respect of his certificates is largely moral, and only to a small extent legal. It is commonly supposed that his work is a mere ascertainment of facts, and yet that is the simplest and frequently the smallest and least important part of the work involved in his periodical examinations. He is rather employing his trained mind and organization to make as near an approximation to actual facts as is practicable, but he has also to consider degrees of approximation; or, in other words, it is the percentage, and not the amount of the possible error, by which he must be guided. His legal responsibility is necessarily limited to gross errors of omission or commission, and would not extend to errors of judgment; but it must be remembered that what might be merely errors of judgment on the part of an individual without his training and experience, may easily be gross errors on the part of the public accountant.

(3) IN RESPECT OF LIQUIDATION AND RECONSTRUCTION

The duties of the public accountant in respect of liquidation and reconstruction have in this country in the past been largely confined to reporting on the condition of an insolvent concern, and on the past results, in so far as these are not already known, which have contributed to the present condition. In some few cases an accountant has been appointed receiver or manager of an insolvent business; but this, while an important, is not a large part of his duties here, as it has been for many years in Great Britain. The problems involved in such duties of management hardly have relation to accounts, and their discussion has no place here except perhaps to note that a thorough knowledge of accounts and the principles upon which they should be prepared is of the utmost value in their consideration and settlement.

The forms of reports necessary do not materially differ from those already discussed, and the principles involved are the same. There is, however, this important difference that, in the case of liquidation followed by a break-up sale, the values to be placed upon the assets will be no longer going values, but forced sale values. Under these conditions finished products on hand will bring much less than normal selling price, partly finished products may be almost valueless, while raw materials may have a value fairly close to their cost. Accounts and bills receivable, which for a going concern may be doubtful of collection, will possibly be found altogether bad; while all the varied items of deferred charges and other working assets will have little or no value. The values of capital assets under such conditions will in many cases shrink to a mere fraction of their book values, and even then may be unsaleable for a long period. With all this shrinkage in asset values the liabilities remain the same, and consequently concerns which might quite properly have shown some surplus of assets over liabilities as long as the business was continuing, will show a large and, to those most interested as owners or stockholders, a surprising deficit.

Responsibility of Accountant in Case of Business Failure

In view of the serious losses thus entailed, the public accountant, who may have been in close touch with the business for a long period before its collapse, incurs a heavy responsibility. His trained eye should be able to discover the tendency to failure, and often to suggest means for averting the impending catastrophe. The most difficult matter for his judgment is to decide at what point it is his duty to creditors, stockholders and the public, to make such references in his public reports as will necessarily bring an end to the suspense. As long as there is a reasonable prospect of a rehabilitation without recourse to the drastic remedy of liquidation, with all the losses it entails, it would seem to be his duty to all concerned to refrain from any acts which would bring it about; but his judgment must be based on facts and probabilities, and not on mere hopes or possibilities such as will naturally govern the actions and decisions of the managers and partners or stockholders. A stoppage at an early stage, while it will naturally appear a hardship and will bring loss to all concerned, may easily prevent a much worse state of things, and lead to an early reorganization, which may well be much less unfavorable to all than if the business were continued unchecked to a later date. The realization of the existence of germs of insolvency at the earliest possible date is a matter of considerable difficulty.

Causes or Conditions Leading Up to Insolvency

The most usual of these may be summarized thus:

(1) Continuous losses in operations leading to a shrinkage in available current assets and loss of credit. These losses may be due either to want of a sufficient amount of business at profitable prices; to bad workmanship; to inability—owing to inferior management and high costs—to meet competition, or to extensions of plant to an amount largely in excess of the probable demand for product. Such causes, if found out in time, can mostly be remedied; but frequently the exact cause of losses is unknown, by reason of the absence of any reliable cost accounts which would disclose weak points and enable economies to be effected.

As long as working capital is ample such losses may be continued for a long time without disaster, and frequently it happens that continued hopes of improvement in general trade, to which alone such losses are frequently attributed, lead to an almost reckless continuance of business without any attempt to detect the internal evils which may be the real cause. When working capital is exhausted the same optimistic views lead to borrowing for working capital, with the only result of a worse final disaster.

(2) Excessive borrowing on temporary loans to provide for additional permanent assets or even for working capital. In times of financial stringency loans may be called in, and even a concern with a moderately good business and excellent prospects of future increase, may find itself suddenly thrown into insolvency for want of sufficient liquid assets. This is a frequent source of insolvency, owing to the fact that temporary loans can be negotiated in good times; and even in moderately bad times they can be negotiated more easily than permanent loans. Generally it may be said that loans for short terms for the purpose of permanent improvements and extensions of a business are a source of danger at any time, and should be considered as one of the most fruitful seeds of insolvency.

(3) The expenditures out of current assets of considerable sums on capital account, thus diminishing the former unduly, in the expectation of borrowing money or raising capital in other ways which, owing to general conditions in the money market, may be found impossible at the time the money is needed.

(4) Large increases in stocks on hand or accounts receivable out of proportion to the total business done, should call for careful inquiry. The reasons may be quite sound and the increase due to temporary causes, but any continuous

increase year after year in such items, accompanied as it must usually be by a corresponding increase in current liabilities, or floating debt, is ground for anxiety. It points in the case of stock either to accumulation of obsolete or unsuitable goods, or to a continuous rise in prices of material and labor costs, or to bad management, and in extreme cases to deliberate fraud in overstating either quantities or prices. In the case of accounts receivable it may be due to attempts to increase business by dealing with less solvent customers, with consequent liability to heavier losses in bad debts; to the financing of customers or others who are not strong enough for the business they are doing, or to forcing goods onto the market in times of commercial depression to an extent beyond the power of the market to absorb.

(5) The payment of dividends to stockholders, or distribution of profits to proprietors in excess of current earnings. This may amount to payment of dividends out of capital (which is illegal), when the result is an actual deficit on the Profit and Loss account. In the majority of cases, however, the dividends will be paid out of an accumulated surplus appearing on the face of the accounts. This surplus may be fictitious; i. e., it may exist solely by reason of the overvaluation of capital or current assets, or the understatement of liabilities; or it may be a real surplus which has been already used for the extension of the business and which is not therefore available in a liquid form for any purpose. This would be disclosed at any time by a careful scrutiny of the asset and liability values and their composition; but may not be at all obvious to directors or stockholders without the aid of an adviser skilled in such matters, who would be able to indicate points of weakness. In the absence of deliberate bad faith or fraud on the part of directors and managers, the indications of possible danger here stated are usually ignored, owing to excess of optimism

or unwillingness to admit failure, and it is at this point and in the early stages that the public accountant can best exercise his functions, and, by advice based on neither optimism nor pessimism, but on a fair and impartial appreciation of all the facts, suggest a halt and propose remedies before it is too late. Neglect of such precautions will frequently lead from mere optimism to a refusal to see and recognize bad factors, and even to crime in order to conceal them.

Reorganization

Bearing in mind the heavy losses which must result from liquidation and forced sale, it is most desirable that, if liquidation comes, it should be followed as speedily as possible by an honest, conservative and successful reconstruction. When this can be carried through without any stoppage of operations, the greater part of the heavy losses which must result from a forced collection of current assets and sale of capital assets, is avoided, and both creditors and stockholders largely benefit.

The consideration of a plan for the reorganization of a property which has been reduced to a condition of insolvency, requires a full and accurate knowledge of all the existing conditions with regard to the property and its past and probable future earning capacity. The elements to be investigated and determined will therefore be as follows:

(1) The sources and nature of the gross earnings, and the prospects of any increases therein without further expenditures for development.

(2) The cost of operation, with particular reference to the effect thereon of bad management or bad organization, and to the possibility of remedying these conditions; and the proportion which the cost of operation has borne and may be expected to bear to the gross earnings.

(3) A comparison of the gross and net earnings and capitalization of the property with some actual or desirable standard, so as to determine the proportion which one should bear to the other if the reorganization is to prove successful.

(4) Hence, to arrive at the total interest-bearing and dividend-paying capital which the reorganized property will stand on some fixed interest basis.

(5) The rank of the different classes of obligations, having regard to the property pledged as security therefor; the margin of security; the rate of interest; the date of maturity; the equivalent par value on the basis of the standard rate of interest adopted for all classes; and, if practicable, the extent to which the properties specifically mortgaged show sufficient earnings to meet interest on the indebtedness secured thereon. This class of information will probably require a report from an engineer or other expert on the value and the condition of the physical property.

(6) Following upon the determination of these factors, a consideration of the various separately-mortgaged divisions of the property, with a view to determining whether any should be abandoned to the bondholders, rather than be included in a reorganization; and here it is important to observe that the contribution of any specific piece of property to the general organization is not necessarily measured by its ability by itself to earn interest on the obligations secured thereon. Numerous other factors will enter into a consideration of this point, and it may easily appear that a property earning little or nothing towards payment of its obligations is sufficiently valuable to the organization, as a whole, to be retained if possible.

(7) Another important factor is the amount of new money required to be introduced for the purpose of paying off the floating debt and rehabilitating the property, and the

best method of raising such money—whether by the issue of new prior lien securities ranking in front of or on an equality with those issued in exchange for existing mortgages, or by assessments on junior classes of securities. In the latter case it is important that sufficient inducement be given to the junior classes, in the proportion of new securities issued for old, to induce them to pay these assessments; while for the assessments themselves, the securities issued should represent the par value of the cash paid in on some reasonable market valuation.

Upon the information and facts so ascertained will depend the final allocation to be made of new securities in exchange for old, as far as possible, in equitable proportions to the different classes of security holders, although at this final stage an element of bargain must necessarily be introduced by reason of the different interests involved and the necessity of the reorganization managers coming to terms, separately, with each class of holders.

After this stage has been reached there will still remain the work of vesting the properties of the old concern in the new one, with probably a reduced capitalization, and usually involving an adjustment of asset values on the basis of appraisals.

There may be many important questions arising in this connection, not least among which may be the installation of such a system of cost and general accounting as will enable errors of the past to be avoided and put the management in a position to retrieve the situation and convert a failure into success.

A company reorganized on such a basis and placed under capable management should usually be successful, provided that all the facts outlined above are ascertained by reputable and responsible accountants and engineers, and provided that regard be had, subject to the rights of creditors, solely to the interests of the company, as represented by its stock-holders, instead of to those of outside parties who may be merely seeking to obtain as much as possible for themselves out of the wreck.

In reorganizations in the past this latter condition has sometimes prevailed with the result that the reorganized property has shown little better results than its wrecked predecessor.

CONCLUSION

In concluding this review of accounting prac.
procedure, and the duties and responsibilities of the pub.
accountant in relation thereto, it may not be out of place to
call attention to the mental qualifications required by one
who essays to attack and determine accounting problems.

These are: ability, coupled with tact and honesty, to
ascertain facts without friction and with impartiality; a mind
unbiased by previous conceptions, and free to reach independent and reliable conclusions of fact; and a will strong
enough to maintain such conclusions against the arguments,
opinions, or desires of opponents interested in some opposite
or inconsistent conclusion, and yet to adapt such parts of
their arguments as may throw new light on the questions at
issue. With such qualities, and with the added technical
training and practical experience which are equally necessary, the individual is in fact an accountant qualified to deal
with the many questions herein discussed, and to add new
principles to those which it has been the endeavor to illustrate and explain in this volume.

APPENDIX I

SECTIONS OF THE ENGLISH LAW RELATING TO THE INSPECTION AND AUDIT OF ACCOUNTS [COMPANIES (CONSOLIDATION) ACT, 1908]

INSPECTION AND AUDIT

(1) The Board of Trade may appoint one or more competent inspectors to investigate the affairs of any company and to report thereon in such manner as the Board direct—

(i) In the case of a banking company having a share capital, on the application of members holding not less than one-third of the shares issued:

(ii) In the case of any other company having a share capital, on the application of members holding not less than one-tenth of the shares issued:

(iii) In the case of a company not having a share capital, on the application of not less than one-fifth in number of the persons on the company's register of members.

(2) The application shall be supported by such evidence as the Board of Trade may require for the purpose of showing that the applicants have good reason for, and are not actuated by malicious motives in requiring, the investigation; and the Board of Trade may, before appointing an inspector, require the applicants to give security for payment of the costs of the inquiry.

Section 109.

Investigation of affairs of Company by Board of Trade inspectors.

251

(3) It shall be the duty of all officers and agents of the company to produce to the inspectors all books and documents in their custody or power.

(4) An inspector may examine on oath the officers and agents of the company in relation to its business, and may administer an oath accordingly.

(5) If any officer or agent refuses to produce any book or document which under this section it is his duty to produce, or to answer any question relating to the affairs of the company, he shall be liable to a fine not exceeding five pounds in respect of each offence.

(6) On the conclusion of the investigation the inspectors shall report their opinion to the Board of Trade, and a copy of the report shall be forwarded by the Board to the registered office of the company, and a further copy shall, at the request of the applicants for the investigation, be delivered to them.

The report shall be written or printed, as the Board direct.

(7) All expenses of and incidental to the investigation shall be defrayed by the applicants, unless the Board of Trade direct the same to be paid by the company, which the Board is hereby authorized to do.

(*In re* Grosvenor Hotel Company an application to prohibit the Board of Trade and the inspector appointed by them from proceeding under this section failed.)

Section 110.

Power of company to appoint inspectors.

(1) A company may by special resolution appoint inspectors to investigate its affairs.

(2) Inspectors so appointed shall have the same powers and duties as inspectors appointed by the Board of Trade, except that, instead of reporting to the Board, they shall report in such

manner and to such persons as the company in general meeting may direct.

(3) Officers and agents of the company shall incur the like penalties in case of refusal to produce any book or document required to be produced to inspectors so appointed, or to answer any question, as they would have incurred if the inspectors had been appointed by the Board of Trade.

A copy of the report of any inspectors appointed under this Act, authenticated by the seal of the company whose affairs they have investigated, shall be admissible in any legal proceeding as evidence of the opinion of the inspectors in relation to any matter contained in the report.

Section 111.

Report of inspectors to be evidence.

(1) Every company shall at each annual general meeting appoint an auditor or auditors to hold office until the next annual general meeting.

(2) If an appointment of auditors is not made at an annual general meeting, the Board of Trade may, on the application of any member of the company, appoint an auditor of the company for the current year, and fix the remuneration to be paid to him by the company for his services.

(3) A director or officer of the company shall not be capable of being appointed auditor of the company.

(4) A person, other than a retiring auditor, shall not be capable of being appointed auditor at an annual general meeting unless notice of an intention to nominate that person to the office of auditor has been given by a shareholder to the company not less than fourteen days before the annual general meeting, and the company shall send a copy of any such notice to the retiring auditor, and shall give notice thereof to the shareholders, either by advertisement or in any other mode allowed by the articles, not less than seven days before the annual general meeting:

Section 112.

Appointment and remuneration of auditors.

Provided that if, after notice of the intention to nominate an auditor has been so given, an annual general meeting is called for a date fourteen days or less after the notice has been given, the notice, though not given within the time required by this provision, shall be deemed to have been properly given for the purposes thereof, and the notice to be sent or given by the company may, instead of being sent or given within the time required by this provision, be sent or given at the same time as the notice of the annual general meeting.

(5) The first auditors of the company may be appointed by the directors before the statutory meeting,* and if so appointed shall hold office until the first annual general meeting, unless previously removed by a resolution of the shareholders in general meeting, in which case the shareholders at that meeting may appoint auditors.

(6) The directors may fill any casual vacancy in the office of auditor, but while any such vacancy continues the surviving or continuing auditor or auditors, if any, may act.

(7) The remuneration of the auditors of a company shall be fixed by the company in general meeting, except that the remuneration of any auditors appointed before the statutory meeting,* or to fill any casual vacancy, may be fixed by the directors.

Section 113.
Powers and duties of auditors.

(1) Every auditor of a company shall have a right of access at all times to the books and accounts and vouchers of the company, and shall be entitled to require from the directors and officers of the company such information and explanation as may be necessary for the performance of the duties of the auditors.

*There is no statutory meeting except in the case of companies limited by shares.

(2) The auditors shall make a report to the shareholders on the accounts examined by them, and on every balance sheet laid before the company in general meeting during their tenure of office, and the report shall state—

(a) whether or not they have obtained all the information and explanations they have required; and,

(b) whether, in their opinion, the balance sheet referred to in the report is properly drawn up so as to exhibit a true and correct view of the state of the company's affairs according to the best of their information and the explanations given to them, and as shown by the books of the company.

(3) The balance sheet shall be signed on behalf of the board by two of the directors of the company or, if there is only one director, by that director, and the auditors' report shall be attached to the balance sheet, or there shall be inserted at the foot of the balance sheet a reference to the report, and the report shall be read before the company in general meeting, and shall be open to inspection by any shareholder.

Any shareholder shall be entitled to be furnished with a copy of the balance sheet and auditors' report at a charge not exceeding sixpence for every hundred words.

(4) If any copy of a balance sheet which has not been signed as required by this section is issued, circulated, or published, or if any copy of a balance sheet is issued, circulated, or published without either having a copy of the auditors' report attached thereto or containing such reference to that report as is required by this section, the company, and every director, manager, secretary, or other officer of the com-

pany who is knowingly a party to the default, shall on conviction be liable to a fine not exceeding fifty pounds.

(5) In the case of a banking company registered after the fifteenth day of August eighteen hundred and seventy-nine—

(a) if the company has branch banks beyond the limits of Europe, it shall be sufficient if the auditor is allowed access to such copies of and extracts from the books and accounts of any such branch as have been transmitted to the head office of the company in the United Kingdom; and,

(b) the balance sheet must be signed by the secretary or manager (if any), and where there are more than three directors of the company by at least three of those directors, and where there are not more than three directors by all the directors.

The Act by implication requires that there shall be annually an audit of the accounts resulting in a balance sheet to whose accuracy the auditors shall certify.

Regulations which compel the auditor to withhold information which is material to the true state of the company's affairs are inconsistent with the Act. The majority of the shareholders may within limits provide for secrecy as regards matters of which knowledge will come to the auditors in the course of the audit, but the limit is passed if such a secrecy is imposed as precludes the auditors from availing themselves of all the information to which under the Act they are entitled as material for the report which under the Act they are to make on the company's affairs.

(1) Holders of preference shares and debentures of a company shall have the same right to receive and inspect the balance sheets of the company and the reports of the auditors and other reports as is possessed by the holders of ordinary shares in the company.

(2) This section shall not apply to a private company, nor to a company registered before the first day of July, nineteen hundred and eight.

Section 114.

Rights of preference shareholders, etc. as to receipt and inspection of reports, etc

APPENDIX II

EXTRACTS FROM SCHEDULE I TO COMPANIES (CONSOLIDATION) ACT, 1908, KNOWN AS TABLE A

DIVIDENDS AND RESERVE

95. The company in general meeting may declare dividends, but no dividend shall exceed the amount recommended by the directors.

96. The directors may from time to time pay to the members such interim dividends as appear to the directors to be justified by the profits of the company.

97. No dividend shall be paid otherwise than out of profits.

98. Subject to the rights of persons, if any, entitled to shares with special rights as to dividends, all dividends shall be declared and paid according to the amounts paid on the shares, but if and so long as nothing is paid up on any of the shares in the company dividends may be declared and paid according to the amounts of the shares. No amount paid on a share in advance of calls shall, while carrying interest, be treated for the purposes of this article as paid on the share.

99. The directors may, before recommending any dividend, set aside out of the profits of the company such sums as they think proper as a reserve or reserves which shall, at the discretion of the directors, be applicable for meeting con-

tingencies, or for equalizing dividends, or for any other purpose to which the profits of the company may be properly applied, and pending such application may, at the like discretion, either be employed in the business of the company or be invested in such investments (other than shares of the company) as the directors may from time to time think fit.

100. If several persons are registered as joint holders of any share any one of them may give effectual receipts for any dividend payable on the share.

101. Notice of any dividend that may have been declared shall be given in manner hereinafter mentioned to the persons entitled to share therein.

102. No dividend shall bear interest against the company.

ACCOUNTS

103. The directors shall cause true accounts to be kept—

Of the sums of money received and expended by the company and the matter in respect of which such receipt and expenditure takes place, and

Of the assets and liabilities of the company.

104. The books of account shall be kept at the registered office of the company, or at such other place or places as the directors think fit, and shall always be open to the inspection of the directors.

105. The directors shall from time to time determine whether and to what extent and at what times and places and under what conditions or regulations the accounts and books of the company or any of them shall be open to the inspection of members not being directors, and no member (not being a director) shall have

any right of inspecting any account or book or document of the company except as conferred by statute or authorized by the directors or by the company in general meeting.

106. Once at least in every year the directors shall lay before the company in general meeting a profit and loss account for the period since the preceding account or (in the case of the first account) since the incorporation of the company, made up to a date not more than six months before such meeting.

107. A balance sheet shall be made out in every year and laid before the company in general meeting made up to a date not more than six months before such meeting. The balance sheet shall be accompanied by a report of the directors as to the state of the company's affairs, and the amount which they recommend to be paid by way of dividend, and the amount, if any, which they propose to carry to a reserve fund.

108. A copy of the balance sheet and report shall, seven days previously to the meeting, be sent to the persons entitled to receive notices of general meetings in the manner in which notices are to be given hereunder.

APPENDIX III

SECTIONS OF THE ENGLISH LAW RELATING TO PROSPECTUSES [COMPANIES (CONSOLIDATION) ACT, 1908]

PROSPECTUS

(1) Every prospectus issued by or on behalf of a company or in relation to any intended company shall be dated, and that date shall, unless the contrary be proved, be taken as the date of publication of the prospectus. Section 80. Filing of prospectus.

(2) A copy of every such prospectus, signed by every person who is named therein as a director or proposed director of the company, or by his agent authorized in writing, shall be filed for registration with the registrar of companies on or before the date of its publication, and no such prospectus shall be issued until a copy thereof has been so filed for registration.

(3) The registrar shall not register any prospectus unless it is dated, and the copy thereof signed, in manner required by this section.

(4) Every prospectus shall state on the face of it that a copy has been filed for registration as required by this section.

(5) If a prospectus is issued without a copy thereof being so filed, the company and every person who is knowingly a party to the issue of the prospectus, shall be liable to a fine not exceeding five pounds for every day from the date of the issue of the prospectus until a copy thereof is so filed.

Section 81.

Specific require-
ments as to
particulars
of prospec-
tus.

(1) Every prospectus issued by or on behalf of a company, or by or on behalf of any person who is or has been engaged or interested in the formation of the company, must state—

(a) the contents of the memorandum, with the names, descriptions, and addresses of the signatories, and the number of shares subscribed for by them respectively; and the number of founders or management or deferred shares, if any, and the nature and extent of the interest of the holders in the property and profits of the company; and

(b) the number of shares, if any, fixed by the articles as the qualification of a director, and any provision in the articles as to the remuneration of the directors; and

(c) the names, descriptions, and addresses of the directors or proposed directors; and

(d) the minimum subscription on which the directors may proceed to allotment, and the amount payable on application and allotment on each share; and in the case of a second or subsequent offer of shares, the amount offered for subscription on each previous allotment made within the two preceding years, and the amount actually allotted, and the amount, if any, paid on the shares so allotted; and

(e) the number and amount of shares and debentures which within the two preceding years have been issued, or agreed to be issued, as fully or partly paid up otherwise than in cash, and in the latter case the extent to which they are so paid up, and in either case the consideration for which those shares or debentures have been issued or are proposed or intended to be issued; and

(f) the names and addresses of the vendors of any property purchased or acquired by the company, or proposed so to be purchased or acquired, which is to be paid for wholly or partly out of the proceeds of the issue offered for subscription by the prospectus, or the purchase or acquisition of which has not been completed at the date of issue of the prospectus, and the amount payable in cash, shares, or debentures, to the vendor, and where there is more than one separate vendor, or the company is a subpurchaser, the amount so payable to each vendor: Provided that where the vendors or any of them are a firm the members of the firm shall not be treated as separate vendors; and

(g) the amount (if any) paid or payable as purchase-money in cash, shares, or debentures, for any such property as aforesaid, specifying the amount (if any) payable for good-will; and

(h) the amount (if any) paid within the two preceding years, or payable, as commission for subscribing or agreeing to subscribe, or procuring or agreeing to procure subscriptions, for any shares in, or debentures of, the company, or the rate of any such commission: Provided that it shall not be necessary to state the commission payable to sub-underwriters; and

(i) the amount or estimated amount of preliminary expenses; and

(j) the amount paid within the two preceding years or intended to be paid to any promoter, and the consideration for any such payment; and

(k) the dates of and parties to every material contract, and a reasonable time and place at which any material contract or a copy thereof may be inspected: Provided that this requirement shall not apply to a contract entered into in the ordinary course of the business carried on or intended to be carried on by the company, or to any contract entered into more than two years before the date of issue of the prospectus; and

(l) the names and addresses of the auditors (if any) of the company; and

(m) full particulars of the nature and extent of the interest (if any) of every director in the promotion of, or in the property proposed to be acquired by, the company, or, where the interest of such a director consists in being a partner in a firm, the nature and extent of the interest of the firm, with a statement of all sums paid or agreed to be paid to him or to the firm in cash or shares or otherwise by any person either to induce him to become, or to qualify him as, a director, or, otherwise for services rendered by him or by the firm in connection with the promotion or formation of the company; and

(n) where the company is a company having shares of more than one class, the right of voting at meetings of the company conferred by the several classes of shares respectively.

(2) For the purposes of this section every person shall be deemed to be a vendor who has entered into any contract, absolute or conditional, for the sale or purchase, or for any option of purchase, of any property to be acquired by the company, in any case where—

(a) the purchase-money is not fully paid at the date of issue of the prospectus; or

(b) the purchase-money is to be paid or satisfied wholly or in part out of the proceeds of the issue offered for subscription by the prospectus; or

(c) the contract depends for its validity or fulfilment on the result of that issue.

(3) Where any of the property to be acquired by the company is to be taken on lease, this section shall apply as if the expression "vendor"

included the lessor, and the expression "purchase-money" included the consideration for the lease, and the expression "sub-purchaser" included a sublessee.

(4) Any condition requiring or binding any applicant for shares or debentures to waive compliance with any requirement of this section, or purporting to affect him with notice of any contract, document, or matter not specifically referred to in the prospectus, shall be void.

(5) Where any such prospectus as is mentioned in this section is published as a newspaper advertisement, it shall not be necessary in the advertisement to specify the contents of the memorandum or the signatories thereto, and the number of shares subscribed for by them.

(6) In the event of non-compliance with any of the requirements of this section, a director or other person responsible for the prospectus shall not incur any liability by reason of the non-compliance, if he proves that—

(a) as regards any matter not disclosed, he was not cognizant thereof; or

(b) the non-compliance arose from an honest mistake of fact on his part:

Provided that in the event of non-compliance with the requirements contained in paragraph (m) of sub-section (1) of this section no director or other person shall incur any liability in respect of the non-compliance unless it be proved that he had knowledge of the matters not disclosed.

(7) This section shall not apply to a circular or notice inviting existing members or debenture holders of a company to subscribe either for shares or for debentures of the company, whether with or without the right to renounce

in favor of other persons, but subject as aforesaid, this section shall apply to any prospectus whether issued on or with reference to the formation of a company or subsequently.

(8) The requirements of this section as to the memorandum and the qualification, remuneration, and interest of directors, the names, descriptions and addresses of directors or proposed directors, and the amount or estimated amount of preliminary expenses, shall not apply in the case of a prospectus issued more than one year after the date at which the company is entitled to commence business.

(9) Nothing in this section shall limit or diminish any liability which any person may incur under the general law or this Act apart from this section.

Section 82.

Obligations of companies where no prospectus is issued.

(1) A company which does not issue a prospectus on or with reference to its formation, shall not allot any of its shares or debentures unless before the first allotment of either shares or debentures there has been filed with the registrar of companies a statement in lieu of prospectus signed by every person who is named therein as a director or a proposed director of the company or by his agent authorized in writing, in the form and containing the particulars set out in the Second Schedule to this Act.

Section 83.

Restriction on alteration of terms mentioned in prospectus or statement in lieu of prospectus.

(2) This section shall not apply to a private company or to a company which has allotted any shares or debentures before the first day of July, nineteen hundred and eight.

A company shall not previously to the statutory meeting vary the terms of a contract referred to in the prospectus or statement in lieu of prospectus, except subject to the approval of the statutory meeting.

(1) Where a prospectus invites persons to subscribe for shares in or debentures of a company, every person who is a director of the company at the time of the issue of the prospectus, and every person who has authorized the naming of him and is named in the prospectus as a director or as having agreed to become a director either immediately or after an interval of time, and every promoter of the company, and every person who has authorized the issue of the prospectus, shall be liable to pay compensation to all persons who subscribe for any shares or debentures on the faith of the prospectus for the loss or damage they may have sustained by reason of any untrue statement therein, or in any report or memorandum appearing on the face thereof, or by reference incorporated therein or issued therewith, unless it is proved—

(a) with respect to every untrue statement not purporting to be made on the authority of an expert, or of a public official document or statement, that he had reasonable ground to believe, and did up to the time of the allotment of the shares or debentures, as the case may be, believe, that the statement was true; and

(b) with respect to every untrue statement purporting to be a statement by or contained in what purports to be a copy of or extract from a report or valuation of an expert, that it fairly represented the statement, or was a correct and fair copy of or extract from the report or valuation. Provided that the director, person named as director, promoter, or person who authorized the issue of the prospectus, shall be liable to pay compensation as aforesaid if it is proved that he had no reasonable ground to believe that the person making the statement, report, or valuation was competent to make it; and

(c) with respect to every untrue statement purporting to be a statement made by an official person or contained in what purports to be a copy of or extract from a public official document, that it was a correct and fair representation of the statement or copy of or extract from the document:

or unless it is proved—

(i) that having consented to become a director of the company he withdrew his consent before the issue of the prospectus, and that it was issued without his authority or consent; or

(ii) that the prospectus was issued without his knowledge or consent, and that on becoming aware of its issue he forthwith gave reasonable public notice that it was issued without his knowledge or consent; or

(iii) that after the issue of the prospectus and before allotment thereunder, he, on becoming aware of any untrue statement therein, withdrew his consent thereto, and gave reasonable public notice of the withdrawal, and of the reason therefor.

(2) Where a company existing on the eighteenth day of August, one thousand eight hundred and ninety, has issued shares or debentures, and for the purpose of obtaining further capital by subscriptions for shares or debentures issues a prospectus, a director shall not be liable in respect of any statement therein, unless he has authorized the issue of the prospectus, or has adopted or ratified it.

(3) Where the prospectus contains the name of a person as a director of the company, or as having agreed to become a director thereof, and he has not consented to become a director, or has withdrawn his consent before the issue of the prospectus, and has not authorized or consented to the issue thereof, the directors of the

company, except any without whose knowledge
or consent the prospectus was issued, and any
other person who authorized the issue thereof,
shall be liable to indemnify the person named as
aforesaid against all damages, costs, and expenses to which he may be made liable by reason
of his name having been inserted in the prospectus, or in defending himself against any action or legal proceedings brought against him
in respect thereof.

(4) Every person who by reason of his being
a director, or named as a director, or as having
agreed to become a director, or of his having
authorized the issue of the prospectus, becomes
liable to make any payment under this section
may recover contribution, as in cases of contract, from any other person who, if sued separately, would have been liable to make the same
payment, unless the person who has become so
liable was, and that other person was not, guilty
of fraudulent misrepresentation.

(5) For the purposes of this section—

The expression "promoter" means a promoter
who was a party to the preparation of the
prospectus, or of the portion thereof containing the untrue statement, but does not
include any person by reason of his acting
in a professional capacity for persons engaged in procuring the formation of the
company:

The expression "expert" includes engineer,
valuer, accountant, and any other person
whose profession gives authority to a statement made by him.

APPENDIX IV

SECTIONS OF THE ENGLISH LAW RE-LATING TO PAYMENT OF INTEREST OUT OF CAPITAL [COMPANIES (CONSOLIDATION) ACT, 1908]

PAYMENT OF INTEREST OUT OF CAPITAL

Section 91.

Power of company to pay interest out of capital in certain cases.

Where any shares of a company are issued for the purpose of raising money to defray the expenses of the construction of any works or buildings or the provision of any plant which cannot be made profitable for a lengthened period, the company may pay interest on so much of that share capital as is for the time being paid up for the period and subject to the conditions and restrictions in this section mentioned, and may charge the same to capital as part of the cost of construction of the work or building, or the provision of plant:

Provided that—

(1) No such payment shall be made unless the same is authorized by the articles or by special resolution:

(2) No such payment, whether authorized by the articles or by special resolution, shall be made without the previous sanction of the Board of Trade:

(3) Before sanctioning any such payment the Board of Trade may, at the expense of the company, appoint a person to inquire and report to them as to the circumstances of the case, and may,

270

before making the appointment, require the company to give security for
the payment of the costs of the inquiry:

(4) The payment shall be made only for such
period as may be determined by the
Board of Trade; and such period shall
in no case extend beyond the close of
the half year next after the half year
during which the works or buildings
have been actually completed or the
plant provided:

(5) The rate of interest shall in no case exceed four per cent per annum or such
lower rate as may for the time being
be prescribed by Order in Council:

(6) The payment of the interest shall not
operate as a reduction of the amount
paid up on the shares in respect of
which it is paid:

(7) The accounts of the company shall show
the share capital on which, and the
rate at which, interest has been paid
out of capital during the period to
which the accounts relate:

(8) Nothing in this section shall affect any
company to which the Indian Railways Act, 1894, as amended by any
subsequent enactment, applies.

APPENDIX V

SECTIONS RELATING TO SHARE-HOLDERS' AUDIT IN THE CANADIAN BANK ACT, 1913

SHAREHOLDERS' AUDIT

Selection of persons competent to be auditors.

56. The general managers of the banks (or in the absence of a general manager of any bank the official designated by him, or in default of such designation the principal officer of the bank next in authority) shall, at a meeting duly called by the president of the Association for the purpose before the thirtieth day of September nineteen hundred and thirteen, and thereafter before the thirtieth day of June in each year, select by ballot persons deemed by them to be competent (no one of whom shall be a body corporate) not less than forty in number, any one of whom shall, subject to the provisions hereinafter contained, be eligible to be appointed an auditor under the provisions of this Act.

List to be sent to Minister.

2. A list of persons so selected, together with their post office addresses and occupations, shall forthwith be delivered or sent by registered post to the Minister, and the Minister may, in the case of the first selection, as hereinbefore provided, within ten days after the receipt of the list, and thereafter each year within sixty days after the receipt thereof, disapprove, as to eligibilty to be appointed auditor of a particular bank or banks, or wholly disapprove, of the selection of any person named in the list, and

such person shall not, to the extent of such disapproval, be qualified to be appointed an auditor under this section.

3. The Minister shall communicate his disapproval, if any, to the Association.

Disapproval, if any.

4. The Association shall, as soon as may be after the expiry of the time given to the Minister for disapproval, cause the list of persons qualified as hereinbefore provided, with their respective post office addresses and occupations, to be published in two successive issues of *The Canada Gazette,* and any limitation as to eligibility for the auditorship of a particular bank or banks of the persons named in the list shall be stated in the advertisement.

Publication in *Canada Gazette.*

5. No person shall be qualified to act as an auditor of a bank under this Act unless his name appears in the published list for the year, but this subsection shall not apply to an appointment of an auditor made by the Minister in pursuance of the provisions of this Act.

Qualification of auditors.

6. The shareholders shall, at each annual general meeting, appoint an auditor or auditors, from the last published list of persons qualified, to hold office until the next annual general meeting.

Appointment of auditors.

7. After the appointment of an auditor or auditors under the next preceding subsection of this section, shareholders, the aggregate of whose paid-up capital stock is equal to at least one-third of the paid-up capital stock of the bank, who in writing under their respective hands allege that they are dissatisfied with the appointment so made, may in and by the same writing, make application to the Minister to have the person or persons so appointed superseded, and the Minister may, after such inquiry as he may deem necessary, select an auditor or

Supersession of auditors.

auditors instead of the auditor or auditors appointed at the annual general meeting, and the auditors so appointed shall thereupon cease to be the auditors of the bank and the auditors so selected shall be the auditors of the bank until the next annual general meeting.

Appointment by Minister on application of shareholder.

8. If an appointment of auditors is not made at an annual general meeting, the Minister shall, on the written application of a shareholder, appoint an auditor or auditors of the bank to hold office until the next annual general meeting, and the Governor in Council shall fix the remuneration to be paid by the bank for the services of the auditor or auditors so appointed.

Officers disqualified.

9. A director or officer of the bank shall not be capable of being appointed auditor of the bank.

Notice required of intention to nominate auditor.

10. A person, other than a retiring auditor, shall not be capable of being appointed auditor at an annual general meeting unless written notice of an intention to nominate that person to the office of auditor has been given by a shareholder to the bank at its chief office, not less than twenty-one days before the annual general meeting, and the bank shall deliver a copy of any such notice to the retiring auditor,

Retiring auditor notified.

if any, and shall give notice of the names of the persons eligible for nomination at the said meeting, and by whom such persons are respectively intended to be nominated, to every

Notice to shareholders.

shareholder of the bank, by mailing the notice in the post office, post paid, to the last known post office address of the shareholder as shown by the records of the bank, at least fourteen days prior to the annual general meeting.

Vacancies.

11. If any casual vacancy occurs in the office of auditor the surviving or continuing auditor or auditors, if any, may act, but if there is no

surviving or continuing auditor, and such vacancy has occurred more than three months before the annual general meeting, the directors shall, as hereafter in this section provided, call a special general meeting of the shareholders for the purpose of filling the vacancy.

Special meeting.

12. Before calling such special general meeting the directors shall, as soon as may be after the vacancy occurs, give public notice by advertisement in six consecutive issues of one or more daily newspapers published in the place where the chief office of the bank is situate, and if no daily newspaper is published at that place, then by advertisement in two consecutive issues of a newspaper published weekly in that place, of the vacancy in the office of auditor, and that the vacancy will be filled in the manner provided by this Act.

Public notice by advertisement.

13. A person shall not be capable of being appointed auditor to fill such vacancy unless notice of an intention to nominate that person to the office of auditor has been given by a shareholder to the bank at its chief office within ten days after the last publication of the notice called for by the next preceding subsection.

Notice of nomination to fill vacancy.

14. The directors shall, as soon as may be after the expiry of the ten days mentioned in the next preceding subsection, call a special general meeting of the shareholders for the purpose of filling the vacancy, and notice of such meeting, specifying the object, and stating the names of the persons eligible for nomination, and by whom such persons are respectively intended to be nominated, shall be given to every shareholder of the bank by mailing the notice in the post office, post paid, to the last known post office address of the shareholder as shown by the records of the bank, at least fourteen days prior to the date fixed for the meeting.

Special general meeting.

Notice to shareholders.

Appointment of auditor by Minister in case of vacancy.

15. If the vacancy contemplated by subsection 11 of this section is not filled in the manner provided, or if a casual vacancy occurs in the office of auditor less than three months before the annual general meeting, the Minister in the former case shall, and in the latter case may, on the written application of a shareholder, appoint an auditor or auditors to hold office until the next annual general meeting, and the Governor in Council shall fix the remuneration to be paid by the bank for the services of the auditor or auditors so appointed.

Remuneration.

16. The remuneration of auditors appointed by the shareholders shall be fixed by the shareholders at the time of their appointment, and in the event of such appointees being superseded and other auditors selected, as provided by subsection 7 of this section, the remuneration so fixed shall be divided between them according to the length of time they respectively are auditors of the bank.

Powers and rights of auditors.

17. Every auditor of a bank shall have a right of access to the books and accounts, cash, securities, documents and vouchers of the bank, and shall be entitled to require from the directors and officers of the bank such information and explanation as may be necessary for the performance of the duties of the auditors.

Audit of branches or agencies.

18. If the bank has branches or agencies it shall be sufficient for all the purposes of this section if the auditors are allowed access to the returns, reports and statements and to such copies of extracts from the books and accounts of any such branch or agency as have been transmitted to the chief office, but the auditors may in their discretion visit any branch or agency for the purpose of examining the books and accounts, cash, securities, documents and vouchers at the branch or agency.

19. It shall be the duty of the auditors once at least during their term of office, in addition to such checking and verification as may be necessary for their report upon the statement submitted to the shareholders under section 54 of this Act, and at a different time, to check the cash and verify the securities of the bank at the chief office of the bank against the entries in regard thereto in the books of the bank, and, should they deem it advisable, to check and verify in the same manner the cash and securities at any branch or agency.

Duty of auditors to check cash and verify securities.

20. The auditors shall make a report to the shareholders—

Report of auditors to shareholders.

(a) on the accounts examined by them;

(b) on the checking of cash and verification of securities referred to in the next preceding subsection; and,

(c) on the statement of the affairs of the bank submitted by the directors to the shareholders under section 54 of this Act during their tenure of office;

and the report shall state—

(a) whether or not they have obtained all the information and explanation they have required;

Particulars.

(b) whether, in their opinion, the transactions of the bank which have come under their notice have been within the powers of the bank;

(c) whether their checking of cash and verification of securities required by subsection 19 of this section agreed with the entries in the books of the bank with regard thereto; and,

(d) whether, in their opinion, the statement referred to in the report is properly drawn up so as to exhibit a true and correct view of the state of the bank's affairs according to the best of their information and the explanations given to them, and as shown by the books of the bank.

Attached to annual statement and read.

21. The auditors' report shall be attached to the statement submitted by the directors to the shareholders under section 54 of this Act, and the report shall be read before the shareholders in the annual general meeting.

Audit and report on further statements.

22. Any further statement of the affairs of the bank submitted by the directors to the shareholders under section 55 of this Act shall be subject to audit and report, and the report of the auditors thereon shall state—

Particulars.

(a) whether or not they have obtained the information and explanation they have required;

(b) whether, in their opinion, such further statement is properly drawn up so as to exhibit a true and correct view of the affairs of the bank, in so far as the by-law requires a statement thereof, according to the best of their information and the explanations given to them, and as shown by the books of the bank.

Attached to statement and read.

23. The report shall be attached to the further statement referred to in the next preceding subsection, and shall be read before the shareholders at the meeting to which such further statement is submitted, and a copy of the statement and report shall be sent by the directors at and after the meeting to any shareholder applying therefor.

Copies.

AUDITORS' REPORT TO MINISTER

Examination by auditor appointed by Minister.

56A. The Minister may direct and require any auditor appointed under the next preceding section of this Act, or any other auditor whom he may select, to examine and inquire specially into any of the affairs or business of the bank, and the auditor so appointed or selected, as the case may be, shall, at the conclusion of his examination and inquiry, report fully to the Minister the results thereof.

2. For the purposes of this section the auditor appointed or selected as aforesaid shall have all the rights and powers given to an auditor under the next preceding section.

Powers of auditor.

3. For the performance of the duties imposed by this section the auditor shall be paid as remuneration, out of the Consolidated Revenue Fund, such sum as the Governor in Council may direct.

Remuneration.

4. The person selected by the Minister under this section shall, for the purposes of section 153 of this Act, be deemed to be an auditor of the bank.

To be deemed auditor of bank.

APPENDIX VI

(1) FORM OF GENERAL BALANCE SHEET STATEMENT AS PRESCRIBED BY THE INTERSTATE COMMERCE COMMISSION FOR STEAM ROADS

ASSETS

Property Investment:
  Road and Equipment:
    Investment to June 30, 1907
    Investment since June 30, 1907
    Reserve for Accrued Depreciation—Cr.
  Securities:
    Securities of Proprietary, Affiliated, and
      Controlled Companies—Pledged
    Securities Issued or Assumed—Pledged
    Securities of Proprietary, Affiliated, and
      Controlled Companies—Unpledged
  Other Investments:
    Advances to Proprietary, Affiliated, and
      Controlled Companies for Construction,
      Equipment, and Betterments
  Miscellaneous Investments:
    Physical Property
    Securities Pledged
    Securities Unpledged

Working Assets:
  Cash
  Securities Issued or Assumed—Held in
    Treasury
  Marketable Securities
  Loans and Bills Receivable

Traffic and Car-Service Balances Due from Other Companies

Net Balance Due from Agents and Conductors

Miscellaneous Accounts Receivable

Materials and Supplies

Other Working Assets

Accrued Income Not Due:

Unmatured Interest, Dividends, and Rents Receivable

Deferred Debit Items:

Advances:

Temporary Advances to Proprietary, Affiliated, and Controlled Companies
Working Funds
Other Advances

Rents and Insurance Paid in Advance

Taxes Paid in Advance

Unextinguished Discount on Securities:
On Capital Stock
On Funded Debt

Property Abandoned, Chargeable to Operating Expenses

Special Deposits

Cash and Securities in Sinking and Redemption Funds

Cash and Securities in Insurance and Other Reserve Funds

Cash and Securities in Provident Funds

Other Deferred Debit Items

Profit and Loss:

Balance (if a debit)

LIABILITIES

Stock:
    Capital Stock:
        Common—
            Held by Company
            Not Held by Company.
        Preferred—
            Held by Company
            Not Held by Company
        Debenture—
            Held by Company
            Not Held by Company
        Receipts Outstanding for Instalments Paid
        Stock Liability for Conversion of Outstanding Securities of Constituent Companies
        Premiums Realized on Capital Stock

Mortgage, Bonded and Secured Debt:
    Funded Debt:
        Mortgage Bonds—
            Held by Company
            Not Held by Company
        Collateral Trust Bonds—
            Held by Company
            Not Held by Company
        Plain Bonds, Debentures, and Notes—
            Held by Company
            Not Held by Company
        Income Bonds—
            Held by Company
            Not Held by Company
        Equipment Trust Obligations—
            Held by Company
            Not Held by Company
        Miscellaneous Funded Obligations—
            Held by Company
            Not Held by Company
        Receipts Outstanding for Funded Debt.

Receivers' Certificates
Obligations for Advances Received for Construction, Equipment, and Betterments

Working Liabilities:
Loans and Bills Payable
Traffic and Car-Service Balances Due to Other Companies
Audited Vouchers and Wages Unpaid
Miscellaneous Accounts Payable
Matured Interest, Dividends and Rents Unpaid
Matured Mortgage, Bonded, and Secured Debt Unpaid
Working Advances Due to Other Companies
Other Working Liabilities

Accrued Liabilities Not Due:
Unmatured Interest, Dividends, and Rents Payable
Taxes Accrued

Deferred Credit Items:
Unextinguished Premiums on Outstanding Funded Debt
Operating Reserves
Liability on Account of Provident Funds.
Other Deferred Credit Items

Appropriated Surplus:
Additions to Property through Income
Reserves from Income or Surplus:
Invested in Sinking and Redemption Funds
Invested in Other Reserve Funds
Not Specifically Invested

Profit and Loss:
Balance (if a credit)

(2) FORM OF GENERAL BALANCE SHEET STATEMENT FOR CARRIERS BY WATER AS PRESCRIBED BY THE INTERSTATE COMMERCE COMMISSION

ASSETS

Permanent and Long Term Investments:
Real Property and Equipment:
    Investment:
        Floating Equipment $
        Terminal Property
        General Expenditures   ———
    Less—Reserves for Accrued $
        Depreciation
            ———
            $

    Trust Deposits for Mort-
      gaged Property Released ———
               $

Transportation Securities:
    Securities of Transportation
    System Corporations
        Pledged
        Unpledged
            ———
               $

Long-Term Advances to:
    Transportation System
    Corporations

Other Investments:
    Miscellaneous:
        Physical Property
        Securities Pledged
        Securities Unpledged
        Other Miscellaneous Investments
    Intangible Assets

Working Assets:
    Cash
    Marketable Securities
    Loans and Bills Receivable
    Traffic Balances Owed by Other Companies
    Net Balance Due from Agents, Pursers, and
        Stewards
    Insurance Claims against Underwriters
    Miscellaneous Accounts Receivable
    Materials and Supplies
    Other Working Assets

Accrued Income Not Due:
    Unmatured Dividends and Interest Receivable
    Unmatured Rents Receivable

Deferred Debit Items:
    Temporary Advances to System Corporations
    Working Funds
    Other Advances
    Rents Paid in Advance
    Insurance Premiums Paid in Advance
    Taxes Paid in Advance
    Unextinguished Discount on Capital Stock
    Unamortized Debt Discount and Expense
    Abandoned Property Chargeable to Operating Expenses
    Special Deposits
    Sinking Fund Assets
    Insurance and Other Reserve Fund Assets
    Provident Fund Assets
    Open Voyage Expenses
    Other Deferred Debit Items

Profit and Loss:
    Balance (if a debit)

LIABILITIES

Stock:
>Capital Stock—Common
>" " —Preferred
>Receipts Outstanding for Instalments Paid
>Stock Liability for Conversion of Securities
>Premiums on Capital Stock

Long-Term Debt:
>Funded Debt:
>>Mortgage Bonds
>>Collateral Trust Bonds
>>Plain Bonds, Debentures and Notes
>>Equipment Trust Obligations
>>Miscellaneous Funded Obligations
>>Receipts Outstanding for Funded Debt
>>Receivers' Certificates
>Obligations for Long-Term Advances Received

Working Liabilities:
>Loans and Bills Payable
>Audited Vouchers and Wages Unpaid
>Traffic Balances Owed to Other Companies
>Miscellaneous Accounts Payable
>Matured Dividends and Interest Unpaid
>Matured Rents Unpaid
>Matured Long-Term Debt Unpaid
>Working Advances Owed to Other Companies
>Other Working Liabilities

Accrued Liabilities Not Due:
>Unmatured Dividends, Interest, and Rents Payable
>Taxes Accrued

Deferred Credit Items:
    Unextinguished Premium on Debt
    Operating Reserves
    Liability on Account of Provident Funds
    Open Voyage Revenues
    Other Deferred Credit Items

Appropriated Surplus:
    Surplus Invested in Property
    Reserves from Income or Surplus:
        Invested in Sinking Funds
        Invested in Other Reserve Funds
        Not Specifically Invested

Profit and Loss:
    Balance (if a credit)

APPENDIX

FORM OF STATEMENT FOR NATIONAL BANKS AS PRESCRIBED
(Use the blank lines if necessary, but do not

Enter Charter Number
of Bank here.

No.....................

REPORT of the condition of "The............
At........................, in the State of......................., at the
Dr.

Resources.	Dollars.	Cts	
1. Loans and Discounts (see schedule)........	...	...	...	1
2. Overdrafts, secured, $........; unsecured, $........(see schedule)..	...	...	...	2
3. U. S. Bonds to secure Circulation (par value),........ per cents, ...per cents............................	...	...	...	3
4. U. S. Bonds to secure U. S. Deposits (par value), $........; to secure Postal Savings, $...............	...	...	...	4
5. Other Bonds to secure U. S. Deposits, $........; to secure Postal Savings, $.............................	...	...	...	5
6. U. S. Bonds on hand (par value), ...per cents....	...	...	...	6
7. Premium on Bonds for Circulation, $........; Premium on other U. S. Bonds, $.............................	...	...	...	7
8. Bonds, Securities, etc., including premium on same (see schedule)	...	...	...	8
9. Banking House, $........; Furniture and Fixtures, $........;	...	...	...	9
10. Other Real Estate owned (see schedule)...............	...	...	...	10
11. Due from National Banks (not approved Reserve Agents)	...	...	...	11
12. Due from State and Private Banks and Bankers, Trust Companies, and Savings Banks....................	...	...	...	12
13. Due from approved Reserve Agents (see schedule)....	...	...	...	13
14. Checks and other Cash Items (see schedule)..........	...	...	...	14
15. Exchanges for Clearing House.........................	...	...	...	15
16. Notes of other National Banks........................	...	...	...	16
17. Fractional Paper Currency, Nickels, and Cents........	...	...	...	17
18. **Lawful Money Reserve in Bank.**				

Specie, viz:

	$					
Gold Coin.............................		...	...	...	...	
Gold Certificates......................		...	...	...	...	
Gold Certificates payable to order....		...	...	...	...	
Clearing-House Certificates (Sec. 5192)		...	...	...	...	
Silver Dollars........................		...	...	...	...	
Silver Certificates.....................		...	...	...	...	
Fractional Silver Coin................		...	...	...	...	
Total Coin and Certificates......		...	...	...	...	
Legal-Tender Notes.................		...	...	...	...	18

	Dollars	Cts	
19. Redemption Fund with U. S. Treasurer (not more than 5 per cent on Circulation)............................	...	...	...	19
20. Due from U. S. Treasurer..............................	...	...	...	20
Total (to avoid discrepancies the total should be footed)	...	...	...

Place for official
seal to be affixed by
officer before whom
acknowledged. See
Act Feb. 26, 1881.
Notary must not
be an officer or di-
rector of the bank.

State of...

County of..................................

Sworn to and subscribed before me this........

day of...........................191 ; and I
hereby certify that I am not an officer or a director
of this bank.

....
Notary Public.

NOTE.—This report must be sworn to by the **President or Cashier, NOT**
to the Comptroller of the Currency with the least possible delay, as it is
has been issued.

VII.

BY THE COMPTROLLER OF THE CURRENCY.

erase or change any of the printed items.)

Treasury Department,
Office of the Comptroller of the Currency.
Form 2130.—Reports.—Ed. 50,000—F. C., July 9-13.

...."

close of business on the....................day of ...., 191

Cr.

Liabilities.			Dollars.	Cts.	
1. Capital Stock paid in.............................	...	...	...		1
2. Surplus fund...................................	...	...	...		2
3. Undivided Profits (including amounts, if any, set aside for special purposes, except Item 22)......................... $	...	...	...			
Less Current Expenses, Interest, and Taxes paid............................	...	...	...	...	...	...	3
4. Circulating Notes secured by U. S. Bonds $..	...	...				
Less amount on hand and in Treasury for redemption or in transit..........	...	...	...	...	...	...	4
5. State Bank Circulation outstanding....................	...	...	...		5
6. Due to National Banks (not approved Reserve Agents)	...	...	...		6
7. Due to State and Private Banks and Bankers..........	...	...	...		7
8. Due to Trust Companies and Savings Banks..........	...	...	...		8
9. Due to approved Reserve Agents (see schedule).......	...	...	...		9
10. Dividends Unpaid.................................	...	...	...		10
11. Individual Deposits subject to Check $	...	...	...	...		
12. Demand Certificates of Deposit....	...	...	...	...		
13. Time Certificates of Deposit........	...	...	...	...		
Enter amount of Savings Deposits included in Items 11, 12, and 13 in Schedule Y on back of Report.						
14. Certified Checks..................	...	...	...	...		
15. Cashier's Checks outstanding......	...	...	...	...	...	...	15
16. United States Deposits..........................	...	...	...		16
17. Postal Savings Deposits........................	...	...	...		17
18. Deposits of U. S. Disbursing Officers......................	...	...	...		18
19. Bonds Borrowed	...	...	...		19
20. Notes and Bills rediscounted.....................	...	...	...		20
21. Bills payable, including obligations representing money borrowed (see schedule)...........................	...	...	...		21
22. Reserved for Taxes......................	...	...	...		22
23. Liabilities other than those above stated..............	...	...	...		23
....	...	...	..		
....	...	...	..		
....	...	...	..		
....	...	...	..		
....	...	...	..		
Total (to avoid discrepancies the total should be footed)	...	...	...		

I, ..., of the above-named
(Cashier or President.)
bank, do solemnly swear that the above statement is true, and that the
SCHEDULES on back of the report fully and correctly represent the true
state of the several matters therein contained, to the best of my knowledge
and belief.

Correct.—Attest:

To be attested by three ....
Directors other than the Cashier.
officer verifying the re- ....
port. ....

Directors.

by any other officer; attested by not less than three Directors, and forwarded
desired to complete the summary of reports as soon as possible after a call

APPENDIX VIII

FORM OF ANNUAL STATEMENT OF LIFE INSURANCE COMPANY AS PRESCRIBED BY THE SUPERINTENDENT OF INSURANCE, STATE OF NEW YORK

I—CAPITAL STOCK.

1. Amount of capital paid up in cash......... $.. ....
2. Amount of ledger assets (as per balance) December 31 of previous year $.. ...
3. ——crease of capital during the year.................................... ... ...

4. Extended at $.. ...

II—INCOME.

5. First year's premiums on original policies, without deduction for commissions or other expenses, less $.... for first year's reinsurance.... $.. ...
6. Surrender values applied to pay first year's premiums........ ... ...

7. Total first year's premiums on original policies............ $.. ...
8. Dividends applied to purchase paid-up additions and annuities ... ...
9. Surrender values applied to purchase paid-up insurance and annuities ....
10. Consideration for original annuities involving life contingencies ... ...
11. Consideration for supplementary contracts involving life contingencies ....

12. Total new premiums.... $.. ...
13. Renewal premiums (in addition to items 14, 16 and 17), without deduction for commissions or other expenses, less $.... for reinsurance on renewals.... $.. ...
14. Dividends applied to pay renewal premiums.... ... ...
15. Dividends applied to shorten the endowment or premium paying period ... ...
16. Surrender values applied to pay renewal premiums.............. ... ...
17. Renewal premiums for deferred annuities..................... ... ...

18. Total renewal premiums............................... $.. ...

19. Total premium income................................. $.. ...
20. (A) Consideration for supplementary contracts not involving life contingencies ....
21. Dividends left with the company to accumulate at interest....... ... ...
22. Ledger assets, other than premiums, received from other companies for assuming their risks.... ... ...
23. Gross interest on mortgage loans, per Schedule B, less $.... accrued interest on mortgages acquired during 1912........ $.. ...
24. Gross interest on collateral loans, per Schedule C............ ... ...
25. Gross interest on bonds and dividends on stocks, less $.... accrued interest on bonds acquired during 1912, per Schedule D ... ...
26. Gross interest on premium notes, policy loans or liens........ ... ...
27. Gross interest on deposits in trust companies and banks, per Schedule E.... ... ...
28. Gross interest on other debts due the company (give items and amounts): ... ...
29. ....
30. ....
31. Gross discount on claims paid in advance........................ ... ...
32. Gross rent from company's property, including $.... for company's occupancy of its own building, per Schedule A...... ... ...

33. Total gross interest and rents............................ ... ...
34. From other sources (give items and amounts):
35. .... $.. ...
36. ....
37. ....
38. ....
39. ....

40. From agents' balances previously charged off.................. ... ...
41. Gross profit on sale or maturity of ledger assets, viz.:
    (a) Real estate, per Schedule A............................. $.. ...
    (b) Bonds, per Schedule D.................................... ... ...
    (c) Stocks, per Schedule D................................... ... ...

42. Gross increase, by adjustment, in book value of ledger assets, viz.:
    (a) Real estate, per Schedule A............................. $.. ...
    (b) Bonds, per Schedule D (including $.... for accrual of discount) ... ...
    (c) Stocks, per Schedule D................................... ... ...

43. Total Income .... $.. ...
44. Amount carried forward $.. ...

(A) Including commuted value of instalments or other benefits not payable at the time of death or maturity of endowments, such commuted value being entered also under Nos. 1 or 2 of Disbursements.

| | | | Amount brought forward | | | $.. | ... |

III—DISBURSEMENTS

1. **(A)** For death claims (less $.... reinsurance), $....; additions, $....; .... $... ...
2. **(A)** For matured endowments (less $.... reinsurance), $....; additions, $....; ....
3. Net amount paid for losses and matured endowments........... $.. ...
4. For annuities involving life contingencies........................ ... ...
5. Premium notes and liens voided by lapse, less $.... restorations........ ... ...
6. Surrender values paid in cash, or applied in liquidation of loans or notes ... ...
7. Surrender values applied to pay new premiums (see Income No. 6), $....; to pay renewal premiums (see Income No. 9), $....; ....
8. Surrender values applied to purchase paid-up insurance and annuities (see Income No.).................................. ... ...
9. Dividends paid to policyholders in cash, or applied in liquidation of loans or notes................................. ... ...
10. Dividends applied to pay renewal premiums (see Income No. 14)...... ... ...
11. Dividends applied to shorten the endowment or premium paying period (see Income No. 15).... ....
12. Dividends applied to purchase paid-up additions and annuities (see Income No. 8)................................. ... ...
13. Dividends left with the company to accumulate at interest (see Income No. 21)................................. ... ...
14. (Total paid policyholders, $....)
15. Expense of investigation and settlement of policy claims including $.... for legal expense........................... ... ...
16. Paid for claims on supplementary contracts not involving life contingencies ....
17. Dividends and interest thereon held on deposit surrendered during the year ... ...
18. Paid stockholders for interest or dividends....................... ... ...
19. Commissions to agents (less commission on reinsurance): first year's premiums, $....; renewal premiums, $....; annuities (original), $....; (renewal), $....; ....
20. Commuted renewal commissions......................... ... ...
21. Compensation of managers and agents not paid by commission for services in obtaining new insurance................ ... ...
22. Agency supervision and traveling expenses of supervisors (except compensation for home office supervision)............. ... ...
23. Branch office expenses, including salaries of managers and clerks not included in item 21........................ ... ...
24. Medical examiners' fees, $....; inspection of risks, $....; ....
25. Salaries and all other compensation of officers, directors, trustees and home office employees........................ ... ...
26. Rent, including $.... for company's occupancy of its own buildings, less $.... received under sublease................... ... ...
27. Advertising, $....; printing and stationery, $....; postage, telegraph, telephone and express, $....; exchange, $....; ....
28. Legal expense not included in item 15..................... ... ...
29. Furniture, fixtures and safes........................ ... ...
30. Repairs and expenses (other than taxes) on real estate............ ... ...
31. Taxes on real estate............................. ... ...
32. State taxes on premiums............................. ... ...
33. Insurance department licenses and fees..................... ... ...
34. All other licenses, fees and taxes (give items and amounts):
35. Federal corporation tax......................... $.. ...
36. ....
37. ....
38. Other disbursements (give items and amounts):
39. .... $.. ...
40. ....
41. ....
42. ....
43. ....
44. ....
45. Agents' balances charged off..................... ... ...
46. Gross loss on sale or maturity of ledger assets, viz.:
    (a) Real estate, per Schedule A...................... $.. ...
    (b) Bonds, per Schedule D...................... ... ..
    (c) Stocks, per Schedule D...................... ... .
47. Gross decrease, by adjustment, in book value of ledger assets, viz.:
    (a) Real estate, per Schedule A...................... $.. ...
    (b) Bonds, per Schedule D (including $.... for amortization of premiums)...................... ... ..
    (c) Stocks, per Schedule D...................... ... .
48. **Total Disbursements** | $.. ...
49. Balance | $.. ...

(A) Including commuted value of supplementary contracts—see No. 20 of Income.

IV—LEDGER ASSETS

1. Book value of real estate, per Schedule A......................... $.. ...
2. Mortgage loans on real estate, per Schedule B, first liens, $....; other than first liens, $....; ....
3. Loans secured by pledge of bonds, stocks or other collateral, per Schedule C... ... ...
4. Loans made to policyholders on this company's policies assigned as collateral ....
5. Premium notes on policies in force, of which $.... is for first year's premiums ....
6. Book value of bonds, $....; and stocks, $....; per Schedule D.......... ... ...
7. Cash in company's office....................................... $.. ...
8. Deposits in trust companies and banks, **not** on interest, per Schedule E.. ... ...
9. Deposits in trust companies and banks, on interest, per Schedule E.. ... ...
10. Bills receivable, $....; agents' balances (debit, $....; credit, $....); net, $....; ....
11. ....

12.   **Total Ledger Assets, as per "balance" on page 3** $.. ...

NON-LEDGER ASSETS

13. Interest due, $....; and accrued, $.... on mortgages, per Schedule B.. $.. ...
14. Interest due, $.... and accrued, $.... on bonds, per Schedule D, Part 1 ... ...
15. Interest due, $.... and accrued, $.... on collateral loans, per Schedule C, Part 1.. ... ...
16. Interest due, $...., and accrued, $.... on premium notes, policy loans or liens ....
17. Interest due, $.... and accrued, $.... on other assets (give items and amounts): ... ...
18. ....
19. ....
20. Rents due, $.... and accrued, $.... on company's property or lease.... ... ...

21.   Total interest and rents due and accrued ... ...
22. Market value of real estate **over book value**, per Schedule A.......... ... ...
23. Market value (**not including interest** in Item 14), of bonds and stocks **over book value**, per Schedule D... ... ...
24. Due from other companies for losses or claims on policies of this company, re-insured ....

	(1) New Business	(2) Renewals		
25. Gross premiums due and unreported on policies in force December 31, 1912 (less reinsurance premiums).....................	$.......	$.......		
26. Gross deferred premiums on policies in force December 31, 1912 (less reinsurance premiums)...........................	....	....		
27. Totals	$.......	$.......		
28. Deduct loading...	....	....		
29. Net amount of uncollected and deferred premiums............	$.......	$.......	...	...

30. All other assets (give items and amounts): ....
31. ....
32. ....
33. ....
34. ....

35.   **Gross Assets..............** $.. ...

DEDUCT ASSETS NOT ADMITTED

36. Company's stock owned $....; loans on $....; .... $.. ...
37. Supplies, stationery, printed matter, $....; furniture, fixtures and safes, $....; ....
38. Commuted commissions, $....; agents' debit balances, gross, $....; ....
39. Cash advanced to or in the hands of officers or agents.............. ... ...
40. Loans on personal security, endorsed or not, $....; bills receivable, $.... ... ...
41. Premium notes and loans on policies and net premiums in Item 29 in excess of net value of their policies............................... ... ...
42. Overdue and accrued interest on bonds in default.................... ... ...
43. Book value of Ledger Assets over market value, viz.: ....
44. ....
45. ....

46.   **Admitted Assets..............** $.. ...

V—LIABILITIES, SURPLUS AND OTHER FUNDS

Net present value of all the outstanding policies in force on the 31st day of December, 1912, as computed by the.....................
on the following tables of mortality and rates of interest, viz.:

1. Actuaries' table at....per cent. on*.... ....
....
.... Same for reversionary additions................... $.. ... $.. ...

2. American Experience table at.... per cent. on*...............
....
.... Same for reversionary additions................... $.. ...

3. American Experience table at....per cent. on*.................
....
.... Same for reversionary additions................... $.. ... ...

4. Other tables and rates, viz.:*
.... $.. ...
....
....
....
....
.... Same for reversionary additions................... ... ...

5. Net present value of annuities (including those in reduction of premiums). Give tables and rates of interest, viz.:
.... $.. ...
....
....
....

Total .... $.. ...
6. Deduct net value of risks of this company reinsured in other solvent companies ....

7. Reserve to provide for health and accident benefits contained in life policies $.. ...

8. Net Reserve **(Paid-for basis)**.................................... $.. ...
9. Present value of amounts not yet due on supplementary contracts **not** involving life contingencies, computed by the...................... ... ...
10. Liability on policies cancelled and not included in "net reserve" upon which a surrender value may be demanded............................. ... ...
11. Claims for death losses due and unpaid............................. $.. ...
12. Claims for death losses in process of adjustment, or adjusted and not due ... ...
13. Claims for death losses incurred for which no proofs have been received ... ...
14. Claims for matured endowments due and unpaid..................... ... ...
15. Claims for death losses and other policy claims resisted by the company ... ...
16. Due and unpaid on annuity claims involving life contingencies........ ... ...

17. Total Policy Claims..................................... ... ...

18. Due and unpaid on supplementary contracts **not** involving life contingencies........ ... ...
19. Dividends left with the company to accumulate at interest, and accrued interest thereon ....
20. Premiums paid in advance, including surrender values so applied................. ... ...
21. Unearned interest and rent paid in advance........................... ... ...
22. Commissions due to agents on premium notes when paid................. ... ...
23. Commissions to agents, due or accrued............................. ... ...
24. "Cost of collection" on uncollected and deferred premiums, in excess of the loading thereon.. ... ...
25. Salaries, rents, office expenses, bills and accounts due or accrued.................. ... ...
26. Medical examiners' fees $....and legal fees $....due or accrued.............. ... ...
27. Estimated amount hereafter payable for federal, state, and other taxes based upon the business of the year of this statement................................ ... ...
28. Advances by officers or others on account of expenses of organization or otherwise ... ...
29. Borrowed money $.... and interest thereon $....; ....
30. Unpaid dividends to stockholders.................................... ... ...
31. Dividends or other profits due policyholders, including those contingent on payment of outstanding and deferred premiums.................................. ... ...
32. Dividends declared on or apportioned to **annual dividend** policies payable to policyholders during 1913, whether contingent upon the payment of renewal premiums or otherwise... ... ...
33. Dividends declared on or apportioned to **deferred dividend** policies payable to policyholders during 1913... ... ...
34. Amounts set apart, apportioned, provisionally ascertained, calculated, declared or held awaiting apportionment upon deferred dividend policies, not included in Item 33 ....
35. Reserve, special or surplus funds not included above (give items and amounts separately, and state for what purpose each of said funds is held):
36. ....
37. ....
38. ....
39. All other liabilities (give items and amounts): ....
40. ....
41. ....
42. ....

43. ....
44. Capital stock.. $.. ...
45. Unassigned funds (surplus).. ... ...

46. Total.. $.. ...

*State definitely the dates of issue and class of policies covered by each basis of valuation.

INDEX

Invoice, 23
Invoice card, 26
Issued stock or bonds held in treasury, 117, 130

J

Journal entries, 29
Journal voucher, 23, 29

L

Land, improvements on, 76 (See also "Improvements")
Leaseholds, amortization of, 173
Ledger,
  expense, 28
  general, accounts in, 29
  loose-leaf or card, 22, 23
  subsidiary, 18, 29
Legal responsibility of accountant as to audit certificates, 240
Liabilities,
  and credits, inventory of, 112
  guarantee of, 223
Liabilities, balance sheet, 41-47, 127-152
  analysis of, 41-47
  appropriations, 149
  available capital resources, 143
  bonded debt, 133-143
    annual income charges, 134-141
      varying conditions affecting, 135
    discount on bond issues, 142
    effective interest rate on bonds, 134
    methods of determining annual charge to income, 137-141
  capital stock, 41, 127-133
    discounts and premiums on, 127
    railway companies, requirements for, 130
    redemption of, 129
    steamship companies, requirements for, 130
    treasury stock, 130
      English rule, 133
    without par value, 128
  contingent liabilities, 145
    bills discounted, 146
    contracts,
      liability under for labor or goods, 146
      of purchase, 147
    guarantees on loans, 146
    shares not fully paid, 146